HIGHWAY
TO
SWADES

'Entrepreneurship is a very critical element of democracy and inclusive development. By being able to exercise their economic choices, entrepreneurs reinforce political and personal freedoms and are an important force in establishing and maintaining an open democracy. From our very first interaction when I was the planning secretary for the Government of Meghalaya, I noticed that Bhairavi managed to grasp the idea of using entrepreneurship as a tool for socio-economic transformation. Later, as the development commissioner in the ministry of MSME, Government of India, I again observed her unwavering commitment to unleashing of India's power of enterprise. And when I was serving as the secretary for the ministry of women and child development, Government of India, I saw her bring data and ingenuity to the issues of gender equality and development in the country. For over an entire decade I have witnessed Bhairavi and her work. She always gave her time, knowledge and energy pro-bono for the nation. This, I know, came from the deep passion and care she has in her heart for Indians from every walk of life and from every corner of the country. This book is a love letter because it emanates from the love and reverence Bhairavi has for India and Indians. A must-read for anyone having interest in India and her people.'

—**Ram Mohan Mishra**, executive chairman, State Investment
Promotion Board, Government of Meghalaya

'When I was growing up, I would hear many Indians complain about everything in India and blame others without taking any responsibility. I felt young Indians were different and they need to think about how they can give back to their country and take on the responsibility of creating an India of their dreams. This thought led to the birth of Young Indians (Yi). Over the past twenty years Yi has become a national organization with a presence across India and while a lot has been done, it is just at the cusp of an incredible journey into the future. Bhairavi was the youngest member of the Yi founding team and I can't think of a better person who truly reflects the ideals of what Yi stands for. This book is a great way for young Indians to know our India more intimately and be inspired to engage in nation-building.'

—**G.V. Sanjay Reddy**, founding chairman,
CII's Young Indians, and vice chairman, GVK

'Bhairavi writes like the Ganga—powerful, forceful, sparkling and engaging. Back in 2014, Bhairavi sent me such a write-up on the possible vision of India that inspired both of us to explore its realization in our own ways; I started from the outside by examining the math to get there and Bhairavi from the inside by going on a road trip around the nation to speak to the people on the ground. Seven years later those insights crystallized into this book with a conclusion that both of us furiously agreed on—India needs to shake off its colonial mindset of control-conformance and instead enable its core superpowers. Read this book to understand India's roadmap to unlock its latent greatness.'

—**Gitanjali M. Swamy**, senior legislative and policy advisor,
Massachusetts State Senate, USA

'I have known Bhairavi Jani for close to two decades. Our association began when we started the Young Indians initiative together back in the early 2000s. And over the years she has grown to be one of my good friends and a confidant. A fourth-generation entrepreneur, Bhairavi Jani's passion for sustainable livelihoods is reflected in her projects and this book is an extension of that. Aptly titled *Highway to Swades: Rediscovering India's Superpowers*, this book provides a fresh perspective on how our great nation has managed to maintain a close bond between past and future, as she has experienced it during her travels spanning across two decades.'

—**Jayadev Galla**, member of Parliament, Lok Sabha, and chairman, Amara Raja Group

'Bhairavi Jani is an adopted honorary Naga and a sister to so many of us here in Nagaland. Honest and true, Jani has many friends across all sections of society here in Nagaland. This is testimony to her long-standing work for the development of our people that stems from deep concern for our people. Quietly, she has undertaken several initiatives that have positively impacted our society. She is a mentor to young entrepreneurs, a resource person for the government's various youth-oriented programmes and a constant support for Nagaland. Over the years she has connected us with captains of industry, intellectuals, scholars and world-renowned leaders. Her association with this part of the country is not just with Nagaland but with the entire northeastern region. She has been a supporter and partner of the North East Leaders Connect (erstwhile Young Leaders Connect) which is a fellowship and a think-tank of leaders belonging to different arenas from all the northeastern states. Her inputs and advice have always been priceless and highly meaningful.

Bhairavi Jani is a true nation builder—with heart and soul. This book captures so many stories of people and places from the north-east of the country and gives our people a rightful place in the narrative of India's growth story. A must-read.'

—**Abu Metha**, adviser to the chief minister,
Government of Nagaland

'To call Bhairavi Jani just a "Supply Chain Maven" is definitely an understatement—she is much more than that. A multifaceted entrepreneur with a deep empathy for national and global youth issues and unwaveringly committed to the well-being of our planet, she is one of those personalities with a rare talent of coming up with innovative solutions to global problems, probably stemming from her many years of working and interacting with both the corporate and government sector. This book captures her many learnings over a period of almost two decades engaging in nation-building with an enterprising spirit. A definitive read for anyone who cares for India's future.'

—**Baphin Kerlang Sohliya**, executive adviser, Meghalaya Farmers'
(Empowerment) Commission

'I have for years experienced first-hand Bhairavi's commitment to nature and her intelligence to see beyond and analyse what opportunities we have for our today and tomorrow. The outcome is this insightful book. It succinctly shines the light on realistic and effective ways for Indians to solve the many issues we face: including climate change. The book is an important read for one and all.'

—**Karuna Singh**, regional director, Asia, Earth Day Network

'Many years ago, I entered the principal's office at our school—Delhi Public School Srinagar—and found a young lady sitting there. She introduced herself as Bhairavi. She was discussing how to introduce our children to music. She helped us bring two faculty members, musicians themselves and graduates of the K.M. Conservatory founded by musician A.R. Rahman, to Kashmir for several weeks to teach music to our students. This eventually led to a rekindled interest for music in the youth of the Valley and we did a music competition (SHIRIN) where 186 schools participated and the finale was attended by 9,000 people. Bhairavi also brought to the school experts on career counselling. Those interactions changed the mindset of the youth. They had not thought of anything beyond becoming a doctor, lawyer or government servant. After these interactions, children suddenly jumped into other professions related to information technology, artificial intelligence, art, music, journalism, tourism, entrepreneurship and innovations. It is a delight to see how some of the students supported by Bhairavi have spread out all over the world and are doing well in different spheres. Bhairavi brought her logistics knowledge to use for the flood relief work in Kashmir in 2014. She brought her expertise and voluntarily helped the state get back on its feet and get over the deluge. Bhairavi is an exemplary human being and with the help of her better half Alok, she has a Kashmiri heart of gold. Over the years, through her selfless and tireless efforts, Bhairavi has woven herself into the story of Kashmir and thus into our hearts and our families. This book has wonderful examples of our Kashmiri youth striving despite our difficult conditions and they come from Bhairavi's deep bonds with our land and people. A must-read.'

—**Vijay Kumar Dhar**, educationalist and founder,
Delhi Public School, Srinagar

'Bhairavi's book is based on her years of travel within and outside India and her deep observational skills combined with a solution-driven mindset. Her deep compassion is a legacy from her maternal family of medical doctors and her pragmatic solution-driven mindset is a gift from her paternal lineage of entrepreneurs. This book is bound to affect you with its narrative which has an honest and emotional appeal coupled with meticulous journalling of facts and data.'

—**Shikha Nehru Sharma**, founder, One Health

'Bhairavi and I have been privileged to be associated with LEAP along with other committed individuals who share the importance of Srinivasan's work in building a future generation of culturally committed citizens. LEAP is an extraordinary NGO which works to foster a love of music through singing in children of all talents. In the chapter "Power of Heritage", the descriptions of each area are a plea to the citizens of India to understand the power of the individual and communities in the preservation of our heritage. As the chapter shows, only the involvement of citizens can protect this wonderful heritage of ours. The chapter is well worth reading and reflecting on.'

—**Deborah Thiagarajan**, founder and director,
Dakshin Chitra Museum

'It's undoubtedly a moment of great joy and privilege for me to write few words for the author of this thought-stimulating and research-oriented book. Bhairavi, over last so many years, has travelled to every nook and corner of the Kashmir Valley and has interacted with countless people. Her helping hand, international exposure, passionate and enthusiastic interest for youth development in the valley is greatly appreciated. It makes this masterpiece authored by her an exceptional read.'

—**Waseem Trumboo**, director, Trumboo Industries, and former chairman, CII J&K State Council

'In *Highway to Swades*, Bhairavi Jani has truly spoken from her heart. I have known Bhairavi and her husband, Alok, for a few years now and have first-hand witnessed their commitment for our country's farmers. Bhairavi inspired me and others in our industry to explore affordable and environmentally sustainable options for establishing a cold-chain network for millions of Indian farmers. She reminded us that all of us who are educated and are privileged in life have the opportunity to help and connect India's small farmers to markets across the world with our prowess in engineering and technology. This book is inspiring at many levels and Bhairavi's passion for our country shines through it. Read it to learn how you can help India unleash its superpowers.'

—**Pankaj Dharkar**, presidential member, Indian Society of Heating, Refrigerating and Air-conditioning Engineers, and founder, Pankaj Dharkar and Associates

'*Highway to Swades* is many things: a road trip, a discovery and a coming-of-age story. In a day and age when returning to our roots is a journey we don't have a map for, Bhairavi Jani has shown us a way home. At its heart, *Highway to Swades* is a narrative of hope: of finding answers to questions we didn't know how to ask and of retelling the story of India and her people. Jani's writing is at once personal and provocative, pushing the reader to think of new ways to see India as it used to be, and swades as it could be. Written with simplicity and charm, *Highway to Swades* is a vital conversation-starter, giving every Indian the chance to participate in constructing the present from the building blocks of the past.'

—**Narayani Basu**, author of *V.P Menon: The Unsung Architect of Modern India*

'I am and have always been a huge fan of Bhairavi Jani. Her energy and outlook towards life has always been inspirational! Bhairavi Jani was instrumental in introducing me to the music maestro A.R. Rahman and sowed the seed for the Sunshine Orchestra, Nagaland Chapter, which is under the A.R. Rahman Foundation and has around twenty children from the Kohima Destitute and Orphanage Home learning the violin, and I am always grateful to her for this kindness. Creativity in any field is divinely inspired. In some way, creative people are an extension of divinity's continued engagements with humanity. Creative ideas and actions have the power to influence and impact society. In my youth, I saw music and the arts as a positive and ameliorative way for my generation to navigate the many traumas faced by the people of Nagaland and the North-east at large. As a pioneering musician, songwriter and performer among my people, I saw first-hand that creativity enabled cooperation, understanding through cultural exchange, healing and ultimately, peace and love. Clichéd as it sounds, I understood that to create, one must hope, one must dream. After over three decades of building a creative culture, my naïve faith in the power of creativity has proved itself over and over again. By cultivating creativity, we have been able to reach out to our fellow Indians and people from around the world and foster a sense of oneness and belonging. Such is the power of creativity. I was thrilled to read how India can unleash its power of creativity in this book, something I suggest every parent reads so that they can nurture the creator in their child.'

—**Theja Meru**, adviser, Task Force for Music and Arts, Government of Nagaland

HIGHWAY TO SWADES

REDISCOVERING INDIA'S SUPERPOWERS

BHAIRAVI JANI

HarperCollins *Publishers* India

First published in India by HarperCollins *Publishers* 2022
4th Floor, Tower A, Building No 10, DLF Cyber City,
DLF Phase II, Gurugram, Haryana – 122002
www.harpercollins.co.in

2 4 6 8 10 9 7 5 3 1

Copyright © Bhairavi Jani 2022

P-ISBN: 978-93-5629-194-2
E-ISBN: 978-93-5629-209-3

Typeset in 11/15.2 Adobe Caslon Pro at
Manipal Technologies Limited, Manipal

Printed and bound at
Thomson Press (India) Ltd.

To India

To Indians

To my parents Anjani and Tushar, who taught me to dream

To my husband Alok, who gave me the confidence to write

To my friend Ejji, who always wanted me to write

Contents

Contents

Foreword

If there was something common that ancient chroniclers like Faxian (fourth century CE), Hiuan Tsang (seventh century CE), Ibn Batuta (fourteenth century CE) and Duart Barbosa (sixteenth century CE) took away from India—it was capturing the magnificence of this country in a single canvas with two distinct end points: the start date and the end date of their journey. Their canvases were some of the most precious gifts that our generation has inherited because they were end-to-end documentation of India's vast ethnographic profile with vivid descriptions of its geography and social order in a specific time period.

Inspired by these chroniclers, Bhairavi, Ejji, Venkat and I started our Highway to Swades journey on 16 March 2014 at St. Thomas Mount, Chennai—the very spot where Lt Col. William Lambton started the first trigonometrical survey of India in the year 1802. We ended our journey on 5 May 2014 in Mahabalipuram to mark our respect to the ancient chroniclers of India. While our overall idea was to capture India in the summer of 2014 in a single canvas, little did we expect our people and our culture to mimic the same characteristics as they have for eons.

After meeting and interviewing hundreds of diverse groups of people from Kashmir to Kanyakumari and from Kohima to Kutch, we learnt a few simple facts about Indians. We learnt that, in India, everyone strives to make life better and yet are content at the same time. We were amazed that no one asked us who we are, where do we come from, what caste or religion we belong to or why we were interviewing them. Everyone was happy meeting us—we did not see any social or religious tensions. India was in complete peace and harmony, despite it being the general election time.

While all of us were passionately soaking in India during the fifty-one-day, 18,181-km journey, Bhairavi was not just soaking it in but was also experiencing it all with empathy. Ejji and I were for the most part engaged in figuring out what is India, who are our people, where did all this come from. But Bhairavi was a keen listener who was taking it all in like a blotting paper. At times we would see a huge smile on her face and another moment inexplicable tears. We never understood for a long time what she was processing so silently.

We eventually realized that her mind was always working on the 'why' questions. She would break her silence at breakfast and begin narrating: why is India behaving the way we said it was behaving; why are none of the interviewees asking us who we are; why are people welcoming us with open arms; why are people so happy despite being so poor; why do people strive to grow and are content at the same time; why do people across the country have the same wish list for a better future? By mid-point in the journey it was clear that she had a greater purpose in doing this journey and a deeper call for action. I believe that this book is just the beginning.

Mahesh Sriram,
founder, I-India

In Gratitude

It was late April and a warm breeze was brushing my face. From the window of my hotel room I could see a sandstorm brewing on the not so distant dunes of the Thar Desert. The sun was setting on the horizon. I had never felt so much in touch with myself as I did that evening. As the rays of the setting sun lit up the fort of Jaisalmer in a deep yellow-golden hue, I found myself ablaze with the elemental flame of my soul and the idea of a book took shape.

Indeed, it had been on the banks of the Ganga at Rishikesh, a year or so ago, that I had first felt like sharing my ideas with the world. But I never had in mind a book. I was thinking in terms of blogs or articles then.

In the months that followed my Jaisalmer moment of epiphany I remained hesitant, fighting my own doubts about whether I really had something useful to say, and whether I would be able to write. Then, later that year, in the peak of winter, I visited Kashmir. While caught in a snowstorm on the rolling meadows of Gulmarg, I finally let go of my inhibitions and penned down some thoughts.

I had started writing, but there was still a want of courage. I felt scared initially to put my ideas out there in the world. A magical Kathakali performance in the backwaters of Kerala helped me conquer this fear. I think it was the conviction in the eyes of the artiste who was performing a story from the Hindu epic of Ramayana, that gave me the courage to believe in the story I wanted to tell—the story of the many highways I took to Swades[1] and what I learnt from those travels about India and Indians. Eventually, on a spring day, inside a sacred forest in Meghalaya, on the forest floor covered with rhododendrons, I sat down and wrote the first chapter of this book in a small diary while my friends took a guided tour of the forest.

In a manner of speaking, the journey of this book from an idea to its present shape was inspired and aided by the people and landscapes of India. Therefore, my foremost and deepest gratitude for the book is to India and Indians.

I am an entrepreneur by profession and had never dabbled in writing. I shared my dream of writing a book with my parents, Anjani and Tushar. As always, they encouraged me to pursue it. I am thankful to God that I am born to parents who believe in dreaming big and chasing your dreams. They are the wind beneath my wings always. I wasn't sure how to begin but Rinku Paul, who had written a chapter about me in her book *Daughters of Legacy*, came to the rescue and introduced me to Kanishka Gupta from Writer's Side.

I still remember the day I went to meet Kanishka, whom I fondly call Kan. I was scared. What does a literary agent look like? What will he ask? How will this play out? I was extremely nervous and asked my husband, Alok, to accompany me to the meeting. Sipping coffee at the Starbucks at Cyber Hub in Gurugram, Kan, my husband and I discussed this book. From that day, and through the three years it took to bring this book to its final shape, my husband Alok has walked the road with me. I would often discuss my ideas for a chapter with him and he would challenge my hypothesis and at times also proofread a section. I always wanted to marry someone who would walk the road with me, and I thank my stars that Alok is just that person.

From writing a proposal to choosing the publishing house, Kan's vast experience has guided my nascent journey as a writer. Without him I would not be here! We signed the contract with HarperCollins in the early weeks of the pandemic in 2020. Since I was in our home in Munsyari in the Himalaya[2] and there was a nationwide lockdown for several weeks, I had to vastly rely on my notes, journals, videos and the internet for research. Through those initial months of the pandemic, while managing my work remotely, addressing the challenges of broken supply chains for our customers and worrying endlessly about the safety of our employees, I kept writing. My beloved dog Sheeba fell ill during this period, and for several months I worked during the day and researched for the book while staying up nights with Sheeba. If there were any romantic notions I had about writing a book in a secluded village staring out of my window at the Himalaya, they were shattered almost every night. Sheeba kept it real for me!

When I was finally ready with the first draft of the manuscript, the prolific Narayani Basu—author of the book *V.P. Menon: The Unsung Architect of Modern India*—was kind enough to help test many of the ideas in the book. With her background in history and foreign affairs, Narayani was the perfect person to provide insights on the book. My heartfelt thanks to her for making the time to be my guide and friend on this journey.

In 2021, I came down with Covid and for a few months could not work on the book. I was too weak post Covid to even sit on a chair for an hour, leave alone write. Kan, Narayani and HarperCollins were very understanding of my situation. This book is here today largely because of their patience and constant support.

My profoundest gratitude in this venture is to my dearly departed friend Ejji K. Umamahesh, who was the first person to suggest that I should write. He is not here today, but I am glad I could share with him that I had finally embarked on the mission.

My closest friends Radhika Shapoorjee, Sudha Iyer, Gitanjali Swamy, Sheyna Baig and Shalaka Joshi were my circle of trust and strength all through the process of writing this book. Whenever I felt unable to move forward, they gave me a patient hearing, a gentle nudge and much strength.

I have heard that the fruits of patience are sweet, but I can say from the experience of writing this book that the fruits of perseverance are even sweeter. After months of hard work and all kinds of challenges, this book has finally been written. In its final edit phase my younger dog Mishti took ill and I almost thought the book would not see the light of the day. But Mishti's fighting spirit nudged me to fight my own shadows and as she recovered, the book too found a new lease of life.

I have always known that what seems like an easy process from the outside—of getting an idea into action—is often a road filled with many obstacles and learnings. But writing this book was not about some personal vanity of getting published. It was for me to share with my fellow Indians that we have the opportunity to become second to none in the community of nations and that we should not squander it. Therefore, the purpose of this book is to really speak my heart and mind out about our India.

Last but not least, I am indebted to you, the reader, who is about to devote their precious time to read this book. I sincerely hope you will find it a worthwhile endeavour.

Bhairavi Jani
15 August 2022

1

The River of Dreams

Civilization and Nation

'What do you mean by resurrecting the Idea of India?'
      'Is it dead?'

The passenger seated behind us was clearly eavesdropping on our conversation. My friend Sudha and I looked at each other and decided to let his questions be. The train was slowly pulling into the station at Haridwar. Our group had boarded it a few hours earlier at New Delhi. Our final destination was a camp on the banks of the river Ganga, upstream from Rishikesh.

The members of our motley group came from different parts of the country. We had recently become part of a youth organization called Young Indians (Yi), initially set up as a youth business forum within the Confederation of Indian Industry (CII). But it was soon clear to those of us who had been part of its genesis that Yi needed to be a platform for young people from every walk of life and not just

1

from business. We were hopeful that the organization would provide an opportunity for young Indians to contribute to India's promising future. A lofty ideal, yes; but it was September of 2004 and all of us were young. I was barely twenty-five myself.

Since the inception of Yi in December 2002, we had spent several months discussing and reflecting on the role that young Indians could play in the country's developmental journey. Therefore, the goal during this retreat on the Ganga was to dive deeper into what Yi could do to attract more young people to contribute their time and energy to the cause of the nation.

The Bharatiya Janata Party (BJP)-led National Democratic Alliance (NDA) had just been defeated in the general elections a few months ago and a new government, a coalition led by the Indian National Congress (INC), called the United Progressive Alliance (UPA), had been sworn in. A group of varied parties with distinct ideologies had come together to form this government, and I was trying to comprehend how the ideology of the Marxist left was part of a government led by India's chief pro-market reformer till date: the prime minister and economist, Manmohan Singh. As a young woman deeply in love with her country, I was witnessing at that point in time far too many contradictions within my country—social, political, economic and cultural.

The bus that picked us up from Haridwar was now passing by the Lakshman Jhula bridge at Rishikesh. I had only seen the Ganga at Varanasi before. There she flows calmly, the doorway to salvation. But at Rishikesh, closer to her origins in the Himalaya, she flows like a bundle of energy, transforming everything she touches. In the late monsoon, her ethereal beauty matches her formidable gusto. Her waters overflow with fresh rains and melting glacial streams and give her an aquamarine hue. The bus came to a halt near the Aquaterra camp site, and we picked up our bags and walked down the forested trail to reach the white sand beach. We were all thrilled to be finally getting closer to the river, and my friend Sudha—Sudha Iyer from Hyderabad, a PhD in health education—literally leaped towards the river in excitement.

We had planned an easy afternoon, with some play and rest. As evening approached, Sudha and I walked along the beach, barefoot, the soft sand beneath our feet. We were soaking in the beauty of the serene river gorge surrounded by the densely wooded Himalayan mountains. The evening sky was splashed with vermilion clouds. Mahesh Sriram, an innovation and travel expert from Chennai, caught up with us. We found a few large boulders and decided to perch on them, our feet dipped in the flowing waters of the river. No one said anything for some time. The silence was magical!

Then Mahesh broke the silence and asked, 'So, what do you think it will take to attract more and more young people to do their bit for India?'

'It is a difficult ask, Mahesh.' I instinctively replied.

'Why do you say that, Bhairavi?' Sudha probed further.

'I don't have the exact answer but I feel India is too complex, too vast and to a large extent misunderstood by her own. It is hard to ask people to contribute to something in a sustained manner when they don't understand it too well.'

Mahesh intervened, 'Why do you think India is misunderstood?'

'Well, I think most Indians don't know their country that much. I am not talking about the history, geography or civics taught in schools. I am talking about the on-ground experience of knowing one's country, seeing its eclectic civilization at play with one's own eyes, grasping its grandeur and its imperfections and coming to terms with what is possible to change whilst being optimistic about the future,' I replied.

The camp coordinator was now calling us for a briefing about the rafting trip the next day, so we paused our discussion and joined the rest of the group.

A beautiful fire had been lit. We sat around it in a circle. Once in a while the flames crackled, breaking the constant song of the gushing Ganga. The coordinator was instructing us about the 'what and how' of the rafting expedition. He clearly emphasized that although he knew that many of us could swim, rafting on the Ganga and navigating her rapids was more about being fully present in the moment and about working as a team. Awareness and agility would give us the presence of mind to respond quickly in case the raft capsized or if one of us inadvertently fell overboard.

Although Sudha, Mahesh and I were listening to the instructor, our minds were still preoccupied with the discussion we had been having earlier. Sudha whispered to Mahesh and me, 'You guys think India is aware and agile?' I smiled and looked at Mahesh.

He spoke with the passion of someone who loves Indology, 'If she was not aware and agile, would her civilization have lasted for thousands of years?'

By now the instruction session had ended but most of us continued to sit by the fire, engrossed in our own conversations. I looked at Mahesh and pointed out:

'But we are not talking about the civilization, Mahesh, we are talking about the nation—a democratic republic.'

He jumped up and asked, 'So you are saying they are different? India, the civilization, and India, the nation?'

I tried to explain what I meant: 'I don't know, Mahesh. I travelled a lot across the country with my parents when I was young, wherever my father (Tushar Jani) was opening his courier offices. People would queue up outside Blue Dart offices in towns like Tirupur and Guwahati to book shipments for textiles or tea samples to be exported to destinations abroad. As a child, I loved the stories shared by people from different parts of India who worked with my father. I have seen a lot of India, and have understood her through those travels and stories.'

Sudha interjected, 'But I think it was also your school, Bhairavi, with its unique method of interspersing travel with learning that has also given you a different perspective, right?'

I nodded, 'Yes, our school, B.A.K. Swadhyaya Bhavan, was an experiment in learning by doing. Apart from teaching us about the history and geography of the country through well-curated trips, the school also held elections, convened its own parliament and had a student government that took decisions on almost everything, from sports day to school rules. India was not some distant, intangible, formless idea for us in school. India was a persona—fully present, tangible and proximate. In my experience, back then, India's civilizational values and national characteristics were intertwined. That's why when I was a child, I didn't see India's civilization as apart from its identity as a nation.'

'So, did things change when you grew up?' Mahesh was curious.

'Yes, by the time I finished college and began my first job, confusion had started clouding my understanding. The more I observed the making of politics and political choices based on caste, religion, region, language, the more lost I felt. Somehow, the ideas of civilization and nation had taken divergent paths in my head. For some years now, I have remained immensely proud of India's civilizational heritage but in deep doubt about its political outlook. Often, I feel they don't have much in common anymore. I also think constantly about civilizational values and national identity. If they are truly diverging, then how can we stay united?'

Sudha admitted, 'I agree, these are important questions and they play on my mind too.'

Night had fallen and stars were sparkling in the clear sky. I lay awake inside our tent for some time, thinking about our discussions through the day. My mind was racing in several directions, questions crisscrossing it like shooting stars in the Milky Way. I was unable to focus on any common point in the myriad subjects we had covered—

unity, identity, polity, civilization, nation and youth. I felt my own relationship with India was in a state of turbulence. My identity as an Indian was getting mixed-up. And I found myself asking a question I had never imagined I would: *What does it mean to be an Indian?*

During my travels, I had met Indians from different backgrounds, all of whom were visibly distinct from each other. There was not much in common between a Gujarati from Kathiawar and a Naga from Kohima. In terms of identity, a Gujarati might be at ease with her Indian identity, but a Naga may not. Despite this, there was something—unidentified and nameless, a bond that connected them. *What was it?*

Morning arrived with the promise of adventure. With our life jackets fastened across our chests, we were ready for a day on the Ganga. Rafting on the river near Rishikesh involves several grades of difficulty. Today we were going to definitely encounter grade 2, grade 3, and maybe even grade 4 rapids that would make us experience the ferocity of the river. We took our positions on our rafts and the oars were handed to us. One of the camp staff gently pushed the raft into the river. We felt the sudden rush of the waters and, instinctively, we dropped our oars into the river. Once we were in the river, we didn't have a choice. We had to row fast and in sync. It took some time for all of us to adjust to the rhythm of this. Eventually we got our act together and the raft started moving downstream. As we manoeuvred through the rapids, the spray of the river waters drenched us thoroughly. But the warm sun helped, as did the fact that there was no time or space to think of anything else but to move forward.

Each raft had an expert from the camp guiding us through it all, but the responsibility of keeping the raft afloat, making sure it moved forward and ensuring that everyone stayed aboard, was collectively ours. As we improved on our team work, we began to enjoy the ride. The guides slowly started steering us towards the more difficult grades of the rapids. Some members of the team began yelling, terrified of moving out of their current comfort zone. But the guides insisted that without going through the more difficult rapids, there was no way we could reach our destination camp downstream. We braced ourselves for more splashes, turns, obstacles and adventure.

At one point where the river took a sharp turn, one of our group mates on another raft fell into the water. For a while, commotion prevailed as he was pulled out of the water and back onto his raft. As the day progressed, what had initially been challenging and frightening now became enjoyable and gratifying. Maybe we had learnt something about being mindful of our own vulnerabilities as humans. Maybe we had accepted the unpredictability of the river. Maybe we had summoned courage from within the very depths of our being. Ernest Hemingway famously wrote that courage was grace under pressure. Maybe we had learnt to be grateful and graceful to each other under pressure. It was just a rafting adventure, but it had changed something in each one of us. For me, becoming proximate with the Ganga and her waters had lifted certain inhibitions and fears. For Sudha, it had created a feeling of spiritual oneness. And for all of us, the morning's adventure had deepened our bonds with each other.

As the new campsite appeared within sight, on yet another white sand beach, there was a sense of jubilation on board the rafts. It was as if we had won an Olympic gold. We hadn't realized that the simplicity of being alive and well at the end of an adventure could bring feelings of such elation. Working with each other to keep our rafts afloat had somehow diminished the separateness between us and bonded us in a shared purpose. Through our collective experiences of fear, courage, doubt, love, empathy and trust, we had somehow crossed over to a sense of unity, the kind that we hadn't experienced as a group before. The Ganga had done her magic.

After drying ourselves and eating some delicious camp food, we spent the rest of the day relaxing on the beach. My mind wandered to the dialogue of the day before. At that moment I had an epiphany of sorts. I felt that *the Ganga was the civilization of India*, flowing forcefully and eternally across time, merging separate strands of the Alaknanda and the Bhagirathi tributaries into her mighty waters, before emptying into the Bay of Bengal. One could not know the Ganga from a distance. One had to take a dip in her waters, raft on them, and swim in them to fully understand her. And, perhaps, *the Republic of India was the raft* pushed into the ebb and flow of this river of civilization, tossing and turning through the churnings of the past decades.

Weren't the rafts initially like our politics, directionless and discordant, because we, the people steering them, were full of fear and dissonance? Was it not our collective responsibility to ensure that the raft of the republic moved forward, stayed afloat and that everyone remained on board? The analogies were quite a few. Initially, our rafts had struggled to move forward, but as we began to pull together as a team, the divisions subsided and we found a way to make sure that they reached their final destination in one piece. Of course, along the way there had been some accidents—people had fallen off and had needed to be rescued, and some rafts had capsized—but in the end we had been able to restore them all to safety. Wasn't this how we needed to act when it came to the nation as well? But, when we all spoke different languages, ate different foods, dressed differently and worshipped different gods, how could we work together as ONE?

The River of Dreams

The next morning, Sudha woke up early. She asked me to join her in the Ganesh pooja she wanted to do. It was Ganesh Chaturthi.

Across many parts of India, especially in Sudha's home town of
Hyderabad and mine in Mumbai, people were gearing up for the
ten-day Ganesh festival. In 1893, to counter the restrictions placed
by the British government on public gatherings, freedom movement
leader Bal Gangadhar Tilak transformed a devout Hindu festival
into a sarvajanik one—a public and social phenomenon. In 1996,
when I was an undergraduate student in the United States at Miami
University of Ohio, I was summoned to a class of religious studies
to explain the 'miracle' of statues of Ganesh drinking milk, which
had taken India by storm a year ago. I was questioned on the blind
faith of my people. In answer, I tried to explain the popularity of
Lord Ganesh and how he was worshipped quite universally across
the country by the Hindus and how the festival of Ganesh Chaturthi
was now a social event, with those of other faiths participating in the
festivities too.

A student in the class asked me, 'So you're telling me that Lord
Ganesh is worshipped by everyone in India in a public festival
because a freedom fighter used the festival to bring people together
and organize public gatherings as they were banned otherwise?' I
nodded. He continued, 'And you're saying that this festival continues
in many parts of India, even though it is almost five decades since
India got its Independence, and the purpose of such a gathering is
now redundant?' My answer was still a resounding yes, but I think
that student never managed to wrap his head around what I had
said. As an Indian, however, this was completely normal for me.
Ideas introduced into the mosaic of our civilization have consistently
become part of its larger picture. This was something India did all
the time, and with the craft and panache of a maestro.

The bus was ready to take us to Haridwar for our train back
to the national capital. We boarded it almost reluctantly. As it
drove down the road that ran alongside the Ganga, I looked out
at her with deep gratitude. She had opened a window for me,

allowing me to see the connections between India, the civilization, and India, the nation. She had kindled the flame of exploration in me, nudging me to seek and rediscover the values, forces and powers that bind us Indians as a people. She had made me ask pertinent questions of myself that needed further probing. She had brought back memories from my childhood and reignited the idea that diversity is the blood in India's veins but as a country, India breathes a common set of values. I surmised that our unity needed expression and celebration that went beyond the national flag, the national anthem and cricket.

I confessed to Sudha that the Idea of India was like the eternal Ganga herself. It could never die and therefore needed no resurrection. On the contrary, it was my own understanding of my country that needed a practised resurrection. I was grateful to my friends from Yi who had made me think of ways in which I could give back to my country and maybe encourage others to do so too. But before I did that, I would have to travel, unlearn and learn, explore and connect with India, and Indians. I wanted to understand the subtle connections that tied a Naga to a Gujarati and I wanted to comprehend the massive policy failures that kept India away from its rightful place in the world as a developed and thriving democratic republic. There was much to imbibe, internalize and share. I made a promise to myself that I would commit to learn about India and its ways whenever the opportunity presented itself, not just because it would help me contribute better to my country but also because it was the calling of my heart to do so.

I looked out one last time at the Ganga. A mystical mist was gliding above her waters, once in a while giving a glimpse of her aquamarine hues. She flowed with a sense of purpose and a dream-like fluidity. Earphones firmly in my ears, I listened to Billy Joel's *The River of Dreams* on my iPod. Its words seemed apt for the Ganga:

In the middle of the night, I go walking in my sleep
Through the desert of truth, To the river so deep
We all end in the ocean, We all start in the streams
We're all carried along, By the river of dreams[1]

Unseen Bonds

In the years that followed, I willingly got carried along by the Ganga, our river of dreams, and in earnest began my rendezvous with India. It has been fifteen years since the retreat at Rishikesh, and through these years I have had the pleasure and privilege of travelling extensively across the country. In fact, a lot of my travel also happened because we were expanding Yi as an organization and opening up city chapters across different states.

On one such occasion, I travelled to Nagaland, a state in India's far north-east, on the invitation of Hekani Jakhalu, the founder of Nagaland's own youth association, Youth Net. She wanted to explore the possibility of starting a Yi chapter in the state capital, Kohima. Atul Chaturvedi, my Yi colleague from Kolkata, had already made a presentation to a small group there and I was going over to interact with the prospective members. As I boarded the BG Express train from Guwahati station in Assam, I was advised, 'Please don't talk to anyone on the train and don't tell them why you are going there.' Strange, I thought to myself, but there was not much time for questions. I presumed the cautionary nudge was in context of the ongoing insurgency by armed groups in Nagaland.

The train ride was quite pleasant. I initially tried to keep to myself, but my co-passengers from Dimapur, our destination in Nagaland, were so warm and friendly that I couldn't remain aloof for long. They were a family of four, a couple and their two daughters, originally from Mokokchung district in Nagaland. They now lived in Guwahati and were going to Dimapur for a family wedding. As soon as the mother learnt that I was a vegetarian, she asked her husband to get some vegetarian snacks for me at the next station. She felt terrible about not being able to share their food with me as the home-cooked food they were carrying with them was non-vegetarian. Their two young daughters were studying in college, and I thought it was a great opportunity to ask them if a Yi Nagaland made sense. 'I like the idea of a youth platform but please don't call it Young Indians, no one will then join it in our state,' the younger of them said. I must have looked bewildered. So her sister, two years older, explained, 'See, the thing is, we don't feel Indian.'

I looked at their parents, who were now paying close attention to our discussion. The father expanded on what his daughters had just told me. 'Since the very beginning, when the lands of the Naga tribes were included in the Union of India and then later divided amongst several north-east states, we Nagas have felt that we need to unify our ancestral lands and live together as one people with autonomy.'

While trying to comprehend what they were saying, I asked, 'Don't you guys have special status through several schedules of the Constitution and Articles where you do enjoy special privileges of certain autonomy under the Union?'

He replied, 'Yes, all those provisions are there, but people don't feel they have much in common with the rest of India and we feel that our way of life is completely different. It is this mission to unite all the Naga people and their lands that has led a large number of Naga youth to take up arms and fight an insurgency.'

I shook my head, 'But does that justify violence?' He thought for a moment and then replied, 'How else can we express our desperation? Over the years, peace efforts have failed and people have been disheartened. Corrupt politicians have made a lot of money, while a large number of people in the state have remained very poor. Through the years, conflict just took root in our society.'

It was already dark when the train pulled into Dimapur station, but this wonderful family of four insisted on waiting there till my receiving party arrived. They said, 'If for some reason they don't turn up, you are coming to our family home with us tonight. Then tomorrow, we can contact your friends.' I looked at them in deep gratitude. Hekani had sent a vehicle with the staff of Youth Net to pick me up from the station and drive to Kohima. I bid goodbye to my fellow passengers and thanked them for their generosity. On the way to Kohima, I spotted a board that read, 'Welcome to Nagaland. Nagas are not Indian.' For a moment, I thought maybe it was not such a good idea to come here to start a Young Indians chapter. *I mean*, I thought, *they don't even feel they are Indian!*

But then my thoughts went to the warmth, openness and care shown by my co-travellers on the BG Express. They reminded me of another family I had met on a train from Mumbai to Bengaluru. A south Indian family of four—a couple, their young son and the husband's aged mother. They lived in Mumbai but were originally from Karnataka in south India. I recollected how they had shared their 'tiffin' with me, some delicious south Indian savouries. The old lady was not conversant in Hindi or English and the young grandson kept translating her Kannada into English for me. They had asked me what was taking me to their hometown, and when I mentioned work, the boy's father offered a slew of advice. When we reached Bengaluru, they gave me their address and insisted that I visit them for a meal. The grandmother even put her hand on my head and blessed me.

I pondered on the fact that both these families were very different from each other. The Naga family were Baptist Christians, non-vegetarian, spoke English and even good Hindi. The Kannadiga family, on the other hand, were strict vegetarians, Hindu by faith, and spoke very little Hindi. And yet, both families had been open and warm towards me, a complete stranger. They had both been generous with their advice and care. I thought of the times I had travelled by train in Europe. I remembered how everyone kept their distance from you, and how the locals didn't chat with you with much interest or welcome you to their homes. I recollected one train journey in Austria in the early 1990s with my parents, when another couple from our first-class compartment got up and left because they didn't want to sit next to Indians. I faced no such treatment in Nagaland, even though some people there were struggling with their identity as Indians.

The Naga family and the Kannadiga family may have had very little in common in terms of faith, language, race and food, but they shared a common set of values. They had both been warm to a fellow traveller, happy to share their meals and make accommodations— culinary and linguistic—for a stranger clearly not from their part of the country. They had been willing to invite me into their homes, unafraid and were completely uninhibited when it came to learning about and interacting with people who might be different from them. This commonality between them was subtly articulated but fully pronounced in the way they conducted themselves as people. To my mind, this ability to be both at ease with the unknown and to welcome it with open arms was ubiquitous across India. I am told it is also prevalent in the other South Asian nations of Bangladesh and Pakistan. But, as an Indian, I can only speak for India.

Eventually, we launched the Yi Nagaland chapter. It was Yi's first chapter in the north-east of India. Over the past two decades, I have had many more opportunities to travel across the state and get to know its people and their traditions, their aspirations and challenges. I have made friends for a lifetime and some of my Naga friends even read out Naga blessings at my wedding. Over the years, the residual issues around their Indian identity have remained for some of the Naga people, but beyond that we have had much in common, and we have built on that.

Working in the logistics sector and starting my own ventures also immersed me neck-deep in the rich tapestry that is India. On warehouse floors in my company, I have seen a Hindu operation executive from the north Indian state of Uttar Pradesh collaborate with a Muslim machine operator from the south Indian state of Andhra Pradesh. Their team was led by a half Sikh-half Zoroastrian manager from Mumbai. During the Muslim holy month of Ramzan, the Hindu team members would clean the prayer room daily for their Muslim colleagues. During the Ganesh Chaturthi festival, the Muslim team members would clean and decorate the mandal enclosure for the idol of Ganesh to be welcomed. It was evident that people from diverse races, regions and faiths *could* work together towards shared goals and that they had a common set of values that bound them. Designing and operating supply chains for large multinationals took me to several parts of India. I found that this ability to work together for a company despite identity and cultural differences was prevalent everywhere in the country. Even at Yi, as the organization expanded, people from diverse backgrounds joined the mission and we were able to achieve a convergence of minds through discussions and follow a shared purpose. One of our biggest challenges came when we wanted to start a Yi chapter in Srinagar in Jammu and Kashmir, in India's far north.

I had visited Kashmir frequently throughout my childhood, but once the conflict there got out of hand in the 1990s, we stopped travelling to the Valley. During those terrible years of violence, this beautiful 'paradise on earth' had transformed into a wretched hell of blood and sorrow. In 2002, a professor from a college in Srinagar met me at a conference in Mumbai. He requested me to visit their campus for a guest lecture on supply chain management. I promised him that I would certainly do so. I took a flight from Delhi to Srinagar later that year. As the aircraft approached the runway of Srinagar airport, I saw bunkers and fighter aircraft from the air. Momentarily, I was unnerved—until I looked up at the horizon, where the beautiful Zabarwan Mountains basked in the sun. Something in their quiet strength made me believe that there was hope.

From the airport, I was escorted by an armoured vehicle to my hotel. The next day, I had a very engaging session with the students, and many of them requested that I visit again. Their curriculum had suffered from years of neglect and they had no connect with the world of business outside the Valley. I was more than willing to do their bidding. In earnest I began my work with the Kashmiri youth, and thus was born the deep bond I share with the land and its people. Initially, I visited once a quarter, but soon that was not enough and the visits became monthly. Like in Nagaland, I became friends with many Kashmiris, who are practically family today. I ended up marrying a man who is half Kashmiri Pandit and half Gujarati by blood, and my Kashmiri friends recited blessings and escorted me to my wedding mandapa.

My work with the youth in the Kashmir Valley made me understand the issues around the conflict there—beyond the geopolitics, and through a humane lens. Some places I went, I was greeted with warmth, but I was asked, '*Aap India se aaye ho?*' (Have you come from India?) The question clearly implied that some Kashmiris didn't consider their land or themselves as Indian. Apart from that, however, there was much in common between us. We shared the values of respecting guests, honouring teachers, celebrating heritage, appreciating beauty and creativity, and welcoming strangers, just to name a few. I felt the same warmth among Kashmiri families that I had experienced among my fellow travellers on the BG Express to Nagaland. The openness of the Kannadiga family was matched by the generous Kashmiri hospitality. Here again, the food, language and faith were different, but there was a common set of values that tied us all together.

Hidden Superpowers

Eventually, in 2009, when I took over as the national co-chairperson of Yi, we were able to launch the Yi Srinagar chapter. There were some initial difficulties, but as in the case of Nagaland, we were able to build on what we shared despite our differences. It was also during this time that I had the opportunity to interact closely with the late Professor C.K. Prahalad on his vision for India for year 2022–India@75. CK, as we called him, was regarded as one of the most celebrated strategic thinkers in the world. He had authored the book (amongst many others) *Fortune at the Bottom of the Pyramid*. It is a book that continues to inspire development enthusiasts and business leaders who wish to advance grassroots development by using markets and entrepreneurial tools. He made us think of audacious societal goals we could aspire to achieve by the time India celebrated seventy-five years of Independence.

CK passed away in 2010 and the Confederation of Indian Industry decided to set up a foundation to carry forward the work of the India@75 mission. In order to do my bit for the mission, I sold two of my ventures and took a leave of absence from my family business so that I could devote time to build this foundation for India's future. My work with India@75 gave me the unique advantage of being able to think and work for the country on a scale I had never done before. It exposed me to policy formulation and to the working of development programmes, civil society and stakeholder consultations, mass volunteer movements, governments, Parliament, politics, media and much more. But while I saw many of these programmes and movements succeed, I also witnessed quite a few policies and programmes failing, simply because of a lack of connection between the leaders in the government and the people. Often, during consultations, people would say that they wished their governments understood them better.

Upon stepping down from my full-time role at India@75, I searched for answers to the questions that kept coming up during the initial years of the mission. What was that 'connect' that people were seeking with their government? It was not about elections and votes or rights and citizen services. They craved something deeper and more profound. Why were governments, with all their experience, unable to communicate their policies effectively to the people? This propelled me to speak to Mahesh, who was by now one of my closest friends from Yi. We decided to take a road trip across India during the general elections in 2014. Ejji K. Umamahesh, the curator of major transcontinental car rallies and the erstwhile deputy secretary for the Formula-1 India Grand Prix, and Venkatesan Nagarajan, a cinematographer and digital media professional, were the other two friends who joined in our crazy journey.

We drove 18,181 km across the country for fifty-one days, during which time we met thousands of Indians from all walks of life and visited all the states except Jharkhand, Sikkim and Chhattisgarh (where we had to abruptly change our travel plans because of Naxal threats). We could not visit a few Union Territories because of adverse weather conditions and paucity of time. We called the adventure 'Highway to Swades'—a road trip to better understand our country. Our extensive and intense time on the road made me connect with India even more deeply.

What we saw and experienced through our travels across India and our interactions with a wide cross-section of Indians was that there is something much more powerful than simply the idea of a polity that keeps 1.38 billion people in this country together. With the use of multiple lenses of business, policy, markets, economics, race, religion, caste and even history, I felt I could finally understand and appreciate India's story. It was a narrative that was alive, constantly evolving into something new even as it held on to the flavours of India's ancient civilizational heritage. I concluded, that there is an inner core—the very being of India, nourished by inherent unseen powers—common to Indians from all corners of the country. These powers have ensured a continuous civilization for thousands of years. These are India's *Superpowers*. Each superpower is a shared idea, a shared value system and a shared aspiration. If applied judiciously to policy frameworks and implementation, these superpowers have the immense potential to transform the future course of the country. But for some reason, those in charge of formulating our national policies have paid scant attention to these powers and largely continue to ignore them even now. I have identified twelve of these superpowers that are currently relevant to our path ahead as a country, but I am sure there are even more. These twelve superpowers contain the tools to bring Indians across the length and breadth of the country together, towards a shared ambition for our nation.

In the general elections of 2019, more than 900 million Indians were eligible to vote—that is, almost a seventh of humanity. In April and May 2019, braving scorching heat and intense summer temperatures, 67 per cent of Indians voted, the highest percentile to vote in the electoral history of the country. What are these people voting for? What do they want? How can a people so diverse in religion, language, caste and race decide collectively on what they want for their today and their tomorrow? How does India decide its priorities for development and progress? How can the individual aspirations of a billion-plus people converge for the collective good of the nation?

Today, India is at an important crossroads. There is much to be optimistic about, and yet there is a fear we are transforming the mosaic of our society and polity into a melting pot. As citizens, we are allowing our individual identities to be subsumed by a few dominant personas. A mosaic allows for each individual piece to have its own presence whilst being part of a larger picture, whereas a melting pot mixes everything together and the individualities are subsumed.

The times we live in, the challenges we face and the opportunities we have as a country … all call on us to strike a healthy balance between our diversity and unity, between our individual dreams and our shared destiny as a collective. I would like to think that some of the answers to these challenges lie in our inherent superpowers, which are common to all Indians, even to those who don't feel quite Indian yet.

Over the years, I have journaled interviews and experiences and observed how these superpowers operate on a civilizational scale. A holistic understanding of these twelve superpowers, their manifestations in policy, and their application in the daily lives of citizens can create path-breaking opportunities for all Indians. It will also create avenues for Indians, young and old, to involve themselves in the task of nation-building. It is 'we' who have to keep the raft of the republic afloat and move it forward in the flow of civilization. And, whilst doing that, we must ensure that everyone stays safely onboard and that our raft does not capsize. The truth is that we can outsource many services and tasks, but we cannot outsource nation-building.

I continue to take my inspiration from the eternal Ganga. She connects people, places and possibilities in a uniquely Indian way. As the eternal river of dreams who carries everyone along, she nudges me to share my experiences from different corners of the country about Indians who live these unique superpowers to the fullest. She encourages me to ask questions and probe for answers about what ails our progress as a nation. She is forever present, both as a guide and as a talisman, as I embark on this journey of sharing India's Superpowers with the world at large.

2

Power of Enterprise

Rewaj of Turuk

When I first met Rewaj Chettri in 2016 in Itanagar, Arunachal Pradesh, I could not have guessed how exceptional his life story was. I was a jury member for an entrepreneurship contest organized by Young Leaders Connect, and he was a finalist. My friend Hekani of Youth Net (Nagaland) and other like-minded young leaders from north-east India had collaborated to create Young Leaders Connect, a platform for young people in the region. As one of its initiatives, an annual conference and competition was organized across the north-east to inspire the youth of the region to choose entrepreneurship as a career. During the pitch round, where finalists presented their ventures to the jury, we were struck by the clarity of purpose Rewaj had about his venture. His business model was sharp and he displayed deep knowledge about the sector in which he operated. Therefore, despite being the youngest contestant,

Rewaj won the competition and with it the prize money of Rs 5 lakh. This is his story.[1]

Rewaj was born in Turuk to a farming family in 1994. With its expansive mountain vistas, lush green farmlands and dense forests, Turuk is an idyllic village in the south of Sikkim, in India's north-east. Tucked away in the Himalaya, it is the kind of little hamlet one reads about in story books, where the pace of life is gentle. Soon after his birth, Rewaj and his mother moved to Gangtok, Sikkim's capital, while his father continued with his farming in Turuk. His mother sold vegetables to make a living. When Rewaj was about five years old, she started a small restaurant. Every morning, while his mother finished the household chores, young Rewaj would head to the restaurant-shop to open it for business. In 2004, his mother moved back to Turuk to support his father, who was making a foray into politics. Rewaj and his brother were sent to a boarding school in Kalimpong, approximately 75 km from Gangtok.

Life took an unfortunate turn a year later, when Rewaj's father passed away in December 2005. His mother somehow managed to put both her sons through school, right up to class ten at the boarding school in Kalimpong. Describing his student life to me, Rewaj pointed out that he was academically average and in no way considered extraordinary. Like most students, he expected to finish school and then move on to college and, subsequently, to a job either in the private or public sector. Entrepreneurship was not on his mind at all. The possibility that he, a village boy from Turuk, would go on to start thirty-eight enterprises by the time he was twenty-seven years old was unthinkable.

Rewaj sat for his class twelve examinations in Turuk, while attending a nearby senior secondary school. By then he had been given some timely advice from an uncle—that scoring well at this level would get him into a good college, giving him some decent career prospects. He fared well in the exams. Medicine and dentistry were his first choices. But his family did not have the finances required to put him through these programmes. So Rewaj decided to opt for forestry. In 2012, he arrived at the North East Regional Institute of Science and Technology in Nirjuli, in the state of Arunachal Pradesh. Rewaj vividly remembers the sense of freedom he felt at being so far away from home with other young people from almost every tribe and corner of north-east India. For the first time, his mind opened up to new possibilities that life had to offer. He made friends and learnt about places he had never been and people he had never met. This exchange of ideas and new-found freedom catalysed a fresh thought process in Rewaj's mind. And so, it was that while he was still in his first year as a student, he decided to start his first entrepreneurial venture, RZ Printers.

As the name implied, RZ Printers was a printing business. Rewaj charged his batchmates for printing their documents, assignments etc. The venture became hugely popular in the small town where printing options on campus were scarce. His fellow students started calling Rewaj by his company's brand name—RZ! Rewaj believes that this was his first lesson in branding. Since his business was small, every rupee mattered. The business taught the young entrepreneur the value of money. Today, Rewaj calls it 'chillar wisdom'—chillar, being the colloquial word used for small change in Hindi. With RZ Printers, Rewaj learnt to spot a market opportunity, explore it, take risks and find innovative ways to explore it. Reminiscing about those days, Rewaj laughs. He says, 'Recently, I was invited to speak at a TEDx event at my college. After all these years, I went back to my hostel and right there, on the door of my room, the poster for RZ Printers was still pasted.'

Rewaj tasted success with his first venture and he never looked back. His second venture was a Facebook community page for his college. He tried his hand at different things whilst pursuing his degree in forestry. But, as he confessed to me, even though he was running a few ventures, he had not found anything that fired his imagination and ignited his passion for a deep dive into the world of entrepreneurship. As a fellow entrepreneur, I understood what he was saying. A passion for one's idea and venture is imperative for an entrepreneur. For most of us, it is the rush of blood we feel about our venture that keeps us going despite the many odds we face. For Rewaj, his heart's calling finally came when he set out on a trip to the Land of the Lamas—Tawang.

At an altitude of approximately 3,000 m, Tawang is a sought-after destination for those visiting Arunachal Pradesh. Rewaj, who had been studying in the state, had always wanted to visit this enchanting hill station he had heard so much about. But by the time Rewaj reached Bomdila, 176 km from Tawang, he had run out of most of his money. So, he decided to end his journey there. Bomdila is a small town and sees much tourist footfall. Before starting for Tawang, Rewaj searched the internet for good accommodation and transport options. He did not find many options online. But to his surprise, when he reached Bomdila and walked around the little town, there were quite a few good hotels. He ended up staying at a place called Hotel Elysiam. While staying there, Rewaj struck a deal with the owner.

As per the deal, Rewaj would make a website for the hotel, free of cost, but he would take a 30 per cent share from all online bookings. Upon his return to the campus, Rewaj began executing his deal. He created a website for the hotel and listed it on all the major travel portals. As luck would have it, during the next tourist season there was a robust response to the website. The hotel started receiving quite a few bookings and Rewaj made a commission of a hefty Rs 3 lakh. In the process, however, he realized that tourists were not just looking for hotels but also for reliable transportation to hire. Here was a market opportunity to serve, and to meet it, he launched a tourism venture, NE Taxi. Rewaj had finally found his dream to chase.

Like all start-ups, NE Taxi had humble beginnings. To start with, Rewaj booked an online domain for Rs 300. He was clear that he wanted his venture to focus initially on giving tourists assured and curated travel options in all the eight north-eastern states. He reached out to a junior on campus and asked for a reliable driver in Shillong, Meghalaya. Mukesh, who had a Swift Dzire car, was the first driver Rewaj on-boarded. Since its inception in 2014, NE Taxi has now on-boarded more than 400 drivers across north-east India. Today, it is recognized as the Uber of the north-east. Rewaj is proud that Mukesh continues to be part of the NE Taxi community to this day, even though Mukesh himself owns and runs four vehicles as part of the NE Taxi network.

The journey from on-boarding his first driver to the 400-plus that are now part of the NE Taxi network has not been easy. Studying on a campus open to people from every corner of north-east India was an undoubted advantage. Using this campus network, Rewaj was able to reach out to reliable drivers everywhere. After graduating in 2016, Rewaj moved back to Gangtok. He admits that even at that time he was still unsure about the future of NE Taxi. That was why he launched a music app venture, Cisum, even as NE Taxi continued to run. He made mistakes and continued to learn from them. He realized, for instance, why he needed to work directly with drivers, train them and partner with them. He identified the specific needs of different types of tourists and created options for different price preferences. When it came to managing the business online, Rewaj learnt a thing or two about search engine optimization and working with internet tools to drive his business. He met Geet Gera, a young lad from Rajasthan who was looking for a job in Gangtok, and hired him as his first employee. They took a two-room house in Gangtok, where out of one room they ran the NE Taxi operations and in the other Geet took up residence.

NE Taxi continued to grow, and in 2018 Rewaj rented a fifty-seater office space, even though the company had only three employees. He was now fully committed to making NE Taxi a success. As a responsible business, NE Taxi also did its bit for society. Drivers were trained with the help of the Meghalaya-based Impulse NGO to identify human trafficking, and samples of regional handicraft products were kept in the cars for tourists to order. The more I listened to Rewaj talking about his venture, the clearer it became to me that NE Taxi was not just a tourism venture but it was also a platform for creating livelihoods for hundreds of drivers. To me, NE Taxi was an enterprise that flawlessly married profit with purpose. For Rewaj, entrepreneurship was no longer a career choice but a way of life. Every day was an opportunity for innovation. He continued to start other ventures—from laundry services to food delivery. In recognition of his entrepreneurial zeal, Rewaj was selected in the Forbes Asia 30 under 30 list in 2018.

Today, Rewaj is committed to building successful ventures in Sikkim and north-east India because he wants to tell the world that both his home state and the region are capable of producing successful entrepreneurs. But the irony is that Rewaj could not register NE Taxi as a company in Sikkim initially because the Indian Companies Act 2012 was not applicable in the state. As a result, NE Taxi had to be registered in Rajasthan. He also laments that there is a lot of joblessness in Sikkim but that young people only want government jobs. So he has taken it upon himself to promote and nurture entrepreneurship in Sikkim. Rewaj has convened a community of entrepreneurs, and together they have started Start-up Harbour, through which they organize learning sessions on entrepreneurship for the state's youth and for themselves. They conduct masterclasses for enterprise skills and work with the government to develop a dynamic start-up policy for Sikkim. Rewaj has been awarded by the state government for his efforts. Currently, as Rewaj focuses on his latest venture NE Origins, which sells produce from across the region online, he is proud of the fact that Gangtok has more than fifty food and delivery app companies.

I am aware, from my own personal experience, that entrepreneurship calls for fearless exploration of the unknown and constant adaptation to circumstances. It demands an unwavering commitment to self-reliance. As an entrepreneur, I can attest to Rewaj being an exception in his relentless pursuit of market opportunities and in providing entrepreneurial solutions. But I also believe that unique as Rewaj is as an entrepreneur, he has company from people across India. I have observed the ingenuity of entrepreneurial purpose in Indians from all walks of life. And their enterprising drive is on full display even in some of the most remote corners of the country.

Bhumia, Paroja and Gond

During our pan-India travel in 2014, Mahesh insisted that we drive through the Eastern Ghats and engage with the tribes that dwell in their dense forests. The Eastern Ghats of India run parallel to India's eastern coast from Odisha to Tamil Nadu in a series of discontinuous mountain ranges. The four major rivers of Krishna, Godavari, Kaveri and Mahanadi cut through these mountains and make their way through broad valleys, rice fields and plains to meet the waters of the Bay of Bengal. These Ghats are home to thick jungles, gushing waterfalls and deep ancient caves. For eons, tribes of different types have lived here, depending largely on forest produce for their livelihood.

As we drove from Araku Valley in Andhra Pradesh to Koraput in Odisha, a single-lane road took us through forests and valleys. We crossed water bodies of varied sizes and shapes, and flat meadows stretched for miles under the sunny skies. Our drive gave us a glimpse into the life and livelihood of tribes such as the Bhumia, the Paroja and the Gond. These tribes have been living in these forests for generations and have been disconnected from most parts of the country for decades.

A very unique feature of tribal societies is their market day, and we were fortunate to witness one such day. As our car turned down a curved road and entered an open meadow, we saw vehicles of all types—from a small three-wheeler to a large bus—all packed with men and women from the Bhumia, Paroja and Gond tribes. The air was filled with excitement and our eyes were treated to some colourful revelry. The women disembarked from the vehicles with baskets full of produce, while the men were selling the products they had brought from the nearby towns. Under canopies of bright blue, pink, orange and yellow tarpaulins, the market day commenced. Fresh vegetables and fruits, handicrafts, hand tools, spices, sweets, snacks, exotic forest produce, bidis (hand-rolled cigarettes), coffee, chickens and eggs were being sold alongside farm equipment, seeds, mobile phones, cookware, jewellery and clothes. The place was buzzing with activity.

In our interactions with the tribal women, we learnt that these markets were their only means by which they could sell the forest produce they harvested. When we asked them about what they thought of entrepreneurship, they shook their heads and many even laughed. It was an alien concept; they had never heard of it. They had no hope of getting jobs. Employment opportunities were far away from their traditional community dwellings and they relied on producing and selling forest products for a living. As they went about their work amidst the hustle and bustle of the market, we saw that these women were fine entrepreneurs; perhaps not by training, but by sheer instinct. They knew, for instance, how to display their products; they knew how to convince a buyer, and they knew how to seize the opportunity for more sales. To us, these women were a reminder that entrepreneurship is not just about start-ups and unicorns, but also about individual initiative and enterprise. Being able to grow and harvest produce, or handicraft products and sell them at a profit was their version of entrepreneurship. I felt it was no different from what new-age ventures do in Silicon Valley. They too build products and sell them in a market. It is just that their tools, resources and market conditions are starkly different.

As the sun rose in the sky towards noon, the market wound up. The women and men boarded their vehicles to return to their homes deep inside the forest. Market days have been an integral part of the Bhumia, Paroja and Gond way of life for a long time, though the products they vend have changed with time in some aspects. Even though they live in the forest, cut off from the world of technology and formal market forces, these tribal people have managed to establish the basic tenets of self-reliance and individual enterprise. Such tribal markets are the mainstays of local economies across the length and breadth of India. They are a means to livelihood for many tribal communities and an outstanding example of enterprise displayed by the 700-plus tribes that constitute 8.6 per cent of India's 1.38 billion citizens—approximately 118 million people. I could appreciate why Mahesh wanted us to come this way and meet these women. I had boxed entrepreneurship in my head as something that is rooted in urban India. But observing the Bhumia, Paroja and Gond women, it occurred to me that entrepreneurship was a vast landscape and the power of enterprise was not limited to a privileged few in India. In fact, it was a universal force, present in great abundance across the country.

Enterprising India

Whether among its tribal folk or in its young start-up visionaries like Rewaj, I have found that India is endowed with the enterprise of its people. Nano-entrepreneurship is widespread across the country, especially visible in the millions of street vendors who hawk their wares on a daily basis. During an interaction with women members of the National Association of Street Vendors of India (NASVI) almost a decade ago, I witnessed the ambitious and go-getter attitude possessed by India's street vendors. I can only compare it with that of the best and the brightest of start-up founders I have met. After my interactions with the Bhumia, Paroja and Gond women, I would not hesitate to call the street vendors entrepreneurs in their own right. In fact, in India's unincorporated sector, which consists of a large number of street vendors, contractors and small traders, we see the universal power of enterprise.

In 2018, while volunteering with Shri Ram Mohan Mishra, the development commissioner of the ministry of micro, small and medium enterprises (MSME) of the government of India, I met MSME business owners from across the country. We were collecting feedback from the MSMEs on ease of doing business and the entrepreneurship ecosystem they operated in. We were also taking their views for the Udhyam Sangam programme of the ministry, which was to be launched by the President of India. During these discussions, the determination of the MSMEs to succeed and their sharpness of business acumen filled my heart with pure joy. I feel it is their enterprising power that makes India's economy rise and resurge, despite the many domestic and global challenges that we face as a country.

A few years ago, Mahesh invited me to speak to a group of senior management representatives from an American healthcare company who were visiting Mumbai. Through his company I-India, Mahesh was curating experiences, workshops and learning immersions for global executives to understand India's grassroots conditions. He was collaborating with renowned global universities to pursue the idea that India's market conditions provided opportunities for unique product and service innovations which can be offered at affordable price points. During the workshop, I introduced the term 'jugaad' to the visitors. Jugaad is a colloquial term for the on-the-ground, frugal innovations one finds across India. Whether it is the use of a tractor to run a small production unit, or a bicycle wheel to pump water, or clay to make affordable water filters, the examples of jugaad are far and wide. Its prevalence is so wide that the Oxford English Dictionary has officially accepted the word 'jugaad' as a noun which means a flexible approach to solving a problem.

I believe that entrepreneurship is about solving a problem. An entrepreneur like Rewaj, for instance, identifies a gap in the market and creates products or services that meet that gap. The ability of Indians from different socio-economic backgrounds to engage in jugaad is a fair indication of their problem-solving aptitude and innovative mindset. In fact, India's ability to take global products and create home-grown and affordable versions of them is both recognized and applauded across the world today.

Looking at the street vendors, young entrepreneurs like Rewaj, India's MSMEs, the Bhumia, Paroja and the Gond women and our informal, unincorporated sector, I am convinced that the one superpower that is found in abundance in our country is the *Power of Enterprise*. The question therefore arises as to how India can unleash the full potential of this power of enterprise for both the individual prosperity of its citizens and the collective development of its society.

Pahale India

In 2012, while still working at the India@75 foundation, I was introduced to the technique of 'generative scenario thinking'. Arun Maira, member of the Planning Commission and former chairman of Boston Consulting Group (BCG) India, had invited experts from civil society, business, government, media and youth organizations to collaborate with the Planning Commission to solicit feedback on the draft of the Twelfth Five-Year Plan. The group was to use generative scenario thinking to ideate future scenarios for the nation. Mr Maira asked me to look at an earlier scenario report published in 2005 by the World Economic Forum (WEF) and the Confederation of Indian Industry (CII) as a reference. As the co-director and leader of that earlier exercise, he felt there were many learnings from it that we could use. The WEF report identified three different scenarios for India's future role as a global player by 2025.[2] The three scenarios were named: 'Atakta Bharat', 'Bollyworld' and 'Pahale India'. Interestingly, the earlier exercise done by CII and BCG had used animal imagery from India's Panchatantra tales to convey the scenarios to the people at large.[3]

The first scenario, 'Atakta Bharat', literally means 'India getting stuck'. A picture of buffalos wallowing in a pond was assigned to it. Herds of buffaloes bathing in local water bodies are a common sight across rural India. This particular image was used to convey a possible future where people in leadership positions from different walks of life behaved like buffaloes in a pond, unable to move because they were a hindrance to each other. The scenario looked at a future where leaders in Indian society would be unable to converge and collaborate and in opposing each other they would deter the advancement of the nation, while the general population could only helplessly look on. Hence 'Atakta Bharat'.

The second scenario, titled 'Bollyworld', was an inspiration from the dramatic movies produced by the Hindi film industry. This had two different images associated with it. One was of a scene where a woman is feeding sparrows. Pigeons arrive to drive away the sparrows, followed by a peacock, which drives away the pigeons. The peacock then struts about, eating, while the sparrows wait endlessly for their turn, which never comes. Here, the possible outcome being conveyed was that a handful of the wealthy and powerful receive the benefits of growth, while the less privileged or the poor are pushed out and left out. The second image depicted a growling tiger and preying wolves. Here due to the injustice suffered in the first scene, people resort to giving power to strong-man politics, electing leaders who keep the people in fear, while the wolves, representing those closer to the centre of power, prey on the vulnerable in the country.

The third scenario, titled 'Pahale India', means 'India First'. Here, the imagery used was of a village landscape at dusk, with fireflies rising by the thousands into the early night sky and lighting it up with their individual lights. The message here was that a possible outcome awaits India, where systemic changes deepen democracy and collective action fuelled by individual enterprise would create an equitable future for one and all. A possible outcome where leaders from all walks of life manage to put the 'nation first' and commit themselves to the overall development of the country.

The idea behind scenario thinking is to give people a peek into the future. The truth is that all three scenarios are possible and can coalesce concurrently. How India acts on its systemic challenges can determine which of the three scenarios will be more dominant. It has been almost fifteen years since these scenarios were first shared. Many may have even forgotten about them. But they give us a vivid picture of possible future realities that await the Indian nation. In fact, many of the outcomes highlighted in each of the scenarios have transpired over the years. The debates on Goods and Services Tax

(GST) implementation that went on for years are an example of 'Atakta Bharat'. The rising income inequality in the country is a stark reminder of the 'Bollyworld' scenario. And Indian businesses bringing their enterprise to work for the manufacturing of PPEs during the Covid-19 pandemic and establishing India as the second largest manufacturer of PPEs in the world within a few months, is a more recent example of the 'Pahale India' scenario.

The twenty-first century has ushered in significant changes in the way human society interacts and how markets respond to human needs. For one, there is a shift in the global economic power base. Today, developed and emerging economies enjoy a greater balance in terms of how they influence global trade. Secondly, climate change is upon us, demanding that we drastically shift our way of doing business if we want to avoid catastrophic outcomes for our planet and our species. The amelioration of digital platforms and digital interconnectedness, powered by social platforms and cheap mobile data, has opened up new avenues for collaboration and co-creation like never before. Lastly, demographic aspects are deciding the ability of nations to remain productive and competitive. Given these factors that are shaping the global order, what must we in India do with our power of enterprise? What kind of entrepreneurship we should encourage that will allow us to realize the Pahale India scenario on a large scale?

If we aspire to have the Pahale India scenario as the most dominant one, then we will need to nurture and enhance the native spirit of enterprise in our people, amongst other things. This should be done not just for the sake of economic progress but also for overall societal development. I have always wanted to explore how India can use its power of enterprise to address its developmental challenges. Can we innovate products and services to create affordable access to education, healthcare and housing? How can India nurture the power of enterprise among its youth in order to meet its unemployment crisis? Can we use our power of enterprise as our strongest weapon against poverty, climate change and inequalities of gender, income and access? Can India's entrepreneurs marry profit with purpose? If we go by what Rewaj has done with NE Taxi and NE Origin, then the answer is *Yes!* But for India to have millions of young entrepreneurs like Rewaj pursuing their dreams, we will need to co-create a vibrant entrepreneurship ecosystem that encourages and rewards ventures that synergize profit with purpose.

The cornerstone of identifying, recognizing and augmenting purpose-driven entrepreneurship is to encourage children at school to explore ideas of entrepreneurship and develop it as a life skill. Through the Atal Tinkering Labs in schools and Entrepreneurship Cells in colleges, we have made a start. But it is just not enough. We need entrepreneurship skills to be taught at the same scale as we teach computers. After my graduation from Miami University in 1999, I joined the Public Service Consulting practice of KPMG in Washington DC. It was the time of the Y2K transition, and there was a lot of concern about transitioning the world's IT systems smoothly into the new millennium. One day, one of our clients asked me in a meeting, 'So, do they teach Oracle enterprise system to class six students in India? All of you seem to be so good at it.' It was a recognition of the venerable IT skills that India was providing to the world. The truth is, we would not have reached this milestone as a nation had it not been for organizations like NIIT and APTECH who worked with IT companies to skill young Indians in marketable and time-relevant computer programming skills on a scale never done before. We need to do the same for entrepreneurship. If we teach entrepreneurship as a life skill for problem-solving, then we will train our youth to be enterprising about social needs as much as about market demands. Teenagers can be challenged to solve problems using innovative ideas that result in new products and services. We have, therefore, an opportunity to create one of the largest cadres of social entrepreneurs in the world. It may seem like a tall order, but India has had stupendous success in building social enterprises. A case in point is Amul.

A cooperative brand, Amul was started to mitigate the unfair trade practices of the dairy industry. Today, it is owned by 3.6 million farmers in rural Gujarat and has a revenue of USD 5.14 billion. Its social impact has been in the areas of women empowerment, nutrition, agriculture, education, livelihoods and the environment. It continues to remain true to its purpose, which is the welfare of dairy farmers, while exploring product innovations in cheese, buttermilk, ice cream and even chocolate. Amul is now recognized by Rabo Bank (one of the thirty largest financial institutions in the world) as one of the top twenty dairy companies in the world;[4] and it is a social enterprise that has brought profit and purpose together.

Amul has company in Lijjat, a cooperative of women which has over 45,000 members and sells fast-moving consumer goods (FMCG). It was started with a seed capital of USD 1.50 by seven women from Mumbai, and today it boasts of annual revenue of over USD 200 million. These examples should motivate us to think of creating a larger ecosystem of social entrepreneurship in India. We can boost impact investment capital, link venture philanthropy to grassroots organizations and create standards to measure and reward social impact through enterprise. We may not need all such enterprises to operate on a large scale. Many of them can serve local needs and become hyper-local components of a larger network. That choice we may leave to the entrepreneurs themselves. The government's obligation is limited to creating a systemic shift that allows for such enterprises to flourish in the country and make way for Pahale India to be realized. Imagine if the Bhumia, Paroja and Gond women could have their own social enterprise for forest produce, and if we were able to connect their produce using e-commerce to buyers beyond those who come for their tribal market days. Imagine if the proceeds from such an enterprise go into building schools and health centres in their communities. There are remarkable civil society organizations who try to do this today, but we need to make it a more sustainable model, where community development is not dependent on grants and corporate social responsibility (CSR) funds but is linked to the enterprise of the local people themselves. Imagine the societal transformation they would experience if their power of enterprise were put to action to solve their developmental problems as a people. Just imagine!

In fact, in intentionally co-creating conditions for Pahale India and choosing entrepreneurship as a means to achieve societal goals, India may offer a new model of capitalism to the world. It will advance the idea of stakeholder capitalism to a scale never seen before. In his book *Stakeholder Capitalism: A Global Economy that Works for Progress, People and Planet*, Klaus Schwab,[5] founder and executive chairman of the World Economic Forum, notes that at its core, stakeholder capitalism is a form of capitalism in which companies are not solely focused on optimizing short-term profits for shareholders, but also seek long-term value creation by taking into account the needs of all their stakeholders and of society at large.

By harnessing the individual and collective power of enterprise of its people and giving them the necessary tools and conducive conditions to innovate products and services that address climate change, healthcare, education, safety, et al., India has the opportunity to deepen stakeholder capitalism on a national and global scale. In order to achieve a truly path-breaking transformation, in addition to applying their power of enterprise, Indians will also need to reimagine and reengineer Jugaad to create a virtuous cycle of innovation, enterprise and stakeholder value creation.

Jugaad for India

As robust as the Silicon Valley ecosystem is, it still ushered in an era of huge income inequalities in the United States. While high-skilled workers found jobs in the tech sector, millions were left jobless in other parts of the country. Therefore, we have some learning to do in order to not repeat the mistakes of that ecosystem. The foremost mistake made by policymakers, investors and market pundits is to focus on innovative tech products only through the lens of their profit and discount impact.

Technology has now made inroads into all segments of industry and, therefore, instead of only focusing on building a tech-led enterprise model, we may need to think of making technology and digital data flows part of the larger entrepreneurial landscape. More importantly, we can nudge entrepreneurs with technical know-how to think of products and services that use technology to solve issues in banking, logistics, healthcare, education, agriculture, etc. for Indians from all walks of life, even those who live in remote rural areas. There is also the challenge of making enterprise tools available for businesses at a nano and micro scale.

The idea that tech ventures with a focus on impact don't generate enough valuation is flawed. A good example is edX, the massive open online course provider started by the scientists and academics at Massachusetts Institute of Technology (MIT) and Harvard University in 2012. When Sanjay Sarma, the Fred Fort Flowers (1941) and Daniel Fort Flowers (1941) professor of mechanical engineering and vice president for open learning at MIT, who was part of the team that launched edX, asked me to try out the course provider in 2012, I wasn't sure. He insisted that I look at this platform and compared it with the advent of the printing press in fifteenth-century Europe. He said that online platforms like edX would change the way we learn and how education is imparted in the same way that the printing press revolutionized the process of disseminating knowledge. The first course I took on edX was a class on Justice offered by Harvard University. It was an incredible experience to take a course offered by a renowned university, free of cost, sitting in a different country. Today taking an online class seems like the most normal thing to do, but back then it felt like a huge privilege.

From its early days, edX was clear about its purpose. It wanted to create and promulgate an open-source platform for the distribution of free online education worldwide and study how students used online platforms to learn. In 2021, when the educational tech company 2U bought edX, it had 150 universities offering courses and 33 million students taking 3,000 courses on its platform. Post the acquisition, edX will be converted into a public-benefit entity that is fully owned and operated by 2U. 2U will use its resources to grow the online learning platform with the speed and to the scale that learners need today. The USD 800 million 2U paid for edX to the not-for-profit company led by Harvard and MIT will be used to focus on closing the learning and opportunity gap and inequities in education. This is how profit has followed purpose, even for a not-for-company.[6]

We also know now that as the Covid-19 pandemic raged across the world, it was online courses that allowed many students in higher education to continue their studies even though physical classes had been cancelled. The impact of online courseware, for at least those who can access it, has been monumental, and its role in the continuity of education during the pandemic has been massive. An educational set-up that encouraged innovation to address societal and market needs helped edX to take birth. How do we create these conditions in India? Does limiting such ecosystems to IITs and IIMs do justice to the widely prevalent ability of Indians to innovate? Can we incentivize jugaad on a mass scale through an open-source platform? How about a public–private platform for open innovation and collaboration to encourage tech start-ups to build tools that meet societal needs? Why must jugaad be limited to on-the-ground and in-the-field contexts? We can institutionally fire up jugaad in our tech sector. A project called 'Jugaad for India' can be institutionalized in the form of a collaborative tech platform. This platform could pose challenges that technology and digital solutions can solve. We can accelerate this work by addressing problem statements that need affordable technology solutions for developmental sectors such as education, health, agriculture, etc. A recent example was the government's challenge to create an Indian alternative to Zoom video conferencing.[7] It was followed by Prime Minister Modi himself launching an app innovation challenge to build the Atmanirbhar app ecosystem in the country.[8] But why must this be a one-off? If supported by vibrant funding and a capacity-building mechanism, a platform like Jugaad for India can catalyse innovation at mass scale.

In 2010, when I was serving as the national chairperson of Yi, we received an invitation from Canada to participate in the formation of the G20 Young Entrepreneurship Alliance. The world was just coming out of the 2008 financial crisis and the G20 country leaders had indicated that for a full global economic recovery we would need to pay attention to entrepreneurship as an alternative to jobs. The alliance was being formed to address the issues that young entrepreneurs faced in G20 countries. As the president of the Indian delegation, I had the privilege of signing the first communiqué of the alliance on behalf of India. My friend Rahul Mirchandani, who had just stepped down from Yi chairmanship and is himself a successful entrepreneur in the agriculture sector, led the negotiations as India's Sherpa. Through our discussions with other young entrepreneur organizations, we learnt how countries were using innovative ways to augment entrepreneurship. One example that struck us immediately was the INOVAR programme of Brazil.

The INOVAR programme has brought together several agencies in Brazil to establish a single institutional framework for developing and nurturing a venture capital investment culture in the country. A key funding component of the INOVAR programme is the INOVAR Fund and Incubator. The Brazil Innovation Forum, Brazil Venture Capital Investment website, INOVAR Business Prospecting and Development Framework, and the development of capacity-building and training programmes for venture capital agencies, are all integral parts of the programme and together have contributed significantly towards the development of a venture capital ecosystem in Brazil. We can take a leaf out of this and apply it to creating a jugaad ecosystem which would have different types of funding sources—government, multilateral, venture capital, banking, angel investors, impact investors and even venture philanthropists. It could also include academia, mentors and capacity-building organizations. If the track record of our offline jugaad is anything to go by, then we are bound to see some path-breaking innovations that can be applied globally, in the long run. This is the kind of tech and digital entrepreneurship that will amplify the conditions for a Pahale India scenario.

As per the Global Innovation Index 2021 published by the World Intellectual Property Organization,[9] Switzerland is the most innovative economy in the world. The ranking is done for 132 countries across eighty-one parameters. India has now managed to enter the top-fifty club at the forty-sixth position. This is a significant achievement, but we have much work to do. We can further deepen our industry–academia linkages to improve our capacity for research and development, with direct market application and adaptation. Such endeavours will need government leadership and the private sector's active participation. We have to enhance our innovation financing channels and create larger government support for domestic and international intellectual patent processes too. Only then can we imagine a flourishing Indian version of a Google, Tesla or IBM.

Gig Entrepreneurship

In fact, the accelerated pace of digital interconnectedness has brought up new models of doing business that can be fantastic allies to India's power of enterprise. The growth propelled by the *shared economy* business models, such as Airbnb or Uber, have brought new avenues of income for many. Online platforms also connect skilled workers such as carpenters, plumbers, gardeners, etc., to urban households. In urban as well as tourist-frequented areas in the hinterland, the homestay market has grown sharply because of companies like Airbnb. The shared economy landscape offers much opportunity for Indians from all walks of life. It allows for individuals to become part of a larger system with benefits of scale thrown in. Aggregator companies like Rewaj's NE Taxi not only create livelihoods but also nurture self-reliance and entrepreneurship. The growth experienced by his first driver Mukesh is a fine example of that.

Many people who work in the shared economy are not simply skilled workers but do their work with a sense of enterprise. They use their skills to meet market demands but without being employed in the traditional sense; they are called *gig entrepreneurs*. Gig entrepreneurship is simply about individuals with skills accessing the market and providing their skills to organizations, as a musician would for many different gigs. They often work with multiple companies and customers at the same time; many of them don't even have an office and work from home or out of co-working places or even cafes. In fact, gig entrepreneurship opens up new possibilities for embracing entrepreneurship, especially for India's women. Large numbers of skilled women in India choose not to take up formal employment due to commitments on the family front. Gig entrepreneurship can provide them with an avenue to use their skills and earn a livelihood in unique ways. Gig entrepreneurship can also be a great avenue for India's retired and senior citizens who may have exited from the formal workforce but have skills and loads of experience. Success as a gig entrepreneur needs clarity on what you have to offer and the ability to see what a customer will pay for it. Once you have established that, you can focus on forging and sustaining relationships with your market, just like you would in any other business.

The Washington DC-based Global Entrepreneurship and Development Institute in its 2019 index rated India at the seventy-eighth position in a group of 137 nations.[10] This calls for concern and concrete action at all levels of the government. India adds approximately 13 million people to the job market annually, and by 2030 will have 1 billion people of working age. It is amply clear that we will not be able to create so many jobs without intensifying the growth of home-grown entrepreneurship. The government of the day, therefore, has the responsibility to examine why, despite the high entrepreneurial spirit of its people, India continues to be relatively unfavourable for entrepreneurs and entrepreneurship. Even with recent strides having been made in ease of doing business, a complex web of laws on matters ranging from corporate affairs to taxes, and other permissions to run a business, lead to loss of time and hamper competitiveness. This was also what MSME owners from across the country had voiced when I had met them in 2018. A case in point is Rewaj's own predicament where he had to register his company out of his home state. This, then, is India's Achilles' heel.

A robust entrepreneurial ecosystem is at the heart of harnessing India's power of enterprise. An ecosystem that encourages, supports and advances entrepreneurs and those with entrepreneurial aspirations, irrespective of where they come from, is imperative. Entrepreneurial ecosystems have several distinct pillars: access to finance, access to digital and tech tools, access to education and skills, access to markets, access to government and regulatory support, access to networking and mentoring, and access to innovation and research and development. We need to continue to improve on each of these pillars to build a strong foundation for Pahale India.

If you ask a first-generation serial entrepreneur like Rewaj, about the ideal conditions in which an entrepreneur can operate, he quips, 'There can never be any ideal condition for entrepreneurs, we will always be dissatisfied and therefore continue to find better ways.' Entrepreneurial ecosystems need all their aspects to function and operate at full steam, but, most importantly, they need clarity of purpose from the entrepreneur. It becomes vital for the enterprise owner to understand her or his own values and create a shared value system—a concept that is often assumed to be meant for large corporations. An enterprise seeded with purpose and built on shared values is designed to proliferate stakeholder capitalism. Pahale India is therefore a dream that can be only realized if millions unleash their power of enterprise for the larger good of the nation.

Tabish Habib

Autumn is my favourite season to visit Kashmir Valley. In late October, Srinagar is ablaze with the deep red leaves of the chinar swooshing in the light breeze that comes from the surrounding Zabarwan Mountains. As November starts, a blanket of red, maroon and brown envelopes the majestic Mughal-era gardens and the vast grounds of the Kashmir University campus. From the expansive blue skies, the rays of the sun beam through the naked chinars and light up the carpets of fallen leaves. On one such afternoon, the autumn chill accompanied me on a stroll through the campus grounds. The chinar leaves, half dead, half alive, crackled beneath my feet. I was thinking about Tabish Habib, a young Kashmiri woman in her late twenties, whom I had met earlier that day. I thought of the year she was born—1989. A time of conflict and pain, a time when the chinars were not the only ones turning red and the streets of Kashmir were drenched in blood.

Two years earlier, the state elections of 1987, widely suspected to have been rigged, had lit a fire of angst and disillusionment amongst the people. They took to the streets and many took up arms. This was the moment when armed insurgency, fuelled by the Pakistani army and intelligence services, took root in the vale of Kashmir. Killings, shootings and kidnappings became the norm of the day. Kashmiri Hindus were killed in the name of religion and many fled, leading to their mass exodus in the years that followed. Even Muslims who supported the government or worked with state actors were butchered. Young men crossed over high mountain passes and were trained by Pakistani forces to fight with guns and bombs. Groups of armed young men would move around from house to house and demand money, cars and food. Those who wanted peace became the silent majority. The Indian Army deepened its presence and was called to hunt out those with arms. A storm of violence engulfed Kashmir and young men started dying and disappearing by the hundreds. The sight of the coffins of Indian Army personnel wrapped in the tricolour and Kashmiri women beating their chests to mourn the death of their young sons who had taken up arms, became a common one. Conflict became the new normal and Kashmiri society was ripped and ravaged by it. In such precarious circumstances, when humanity in the valley of Kashmir was drowned in the sounds of gunfire, during the period of chillai kalan—the forty harshest days of Kashmiri winter—Tabish Habib was born in Srinagar, the capital of the state of Jammu and Kashmir.

Tabish had a childhood one can hardly call normal. Every day heralded a new conflict, and an atmosphere of fear prevailed throughout her growing-up years. To be a child in the Kashmir

of the 1990s was akin to a cursed existence—no play, no regular
school and no way of knowing who would live and who would die.
The nursery rhymes were replaced by aazaadi (freedom) slogans;
school grounds became army camps; cinema halls were converted
into interrogation centres; streets and markets were stunned into
silence and curfews prevailed. Tabish lost her father at the young
age of eight, and the lack of a continuous education at an all-girls
missionary school hardly provided her any solace. She yearned to
break free from the cycle of violence and conflict she was born into.
She wanted to breathe freely and her heart ached for a 'normal' life.
Therefore, it was hardly surprising that as a child she dreamt of
leaving Srinagar and finding a job elsewhere, so as to live a decent,
dignified human existence.[11]

In 2012, Tabish joined the National Institute of Electronics
and Information Technology (NIELIT), a small college located in
Rangreth, a few kilometres from downtown Srinagar. She remembers
a class dominated by men. Only 10 per cent of the class consisted of
women, pursuing an education in computer science. Tabish recollects
the days when some semblance of peace had started returning to the
Kashmir Valley and says that despite that, she was still focused on
getting a job outside the state. But she also saw seniors and friends
take up jobs in the mega metros of India and in other parts of the
world return home after some years. Seeing them return, she would
wonder, 'Why are they coming back?' Most returned because they
simply missed home, and others returned because the jobs had not
met their expectations.

Tabish got her first job while still in college in Srinagar. Someone
known to the family and based in the United States wanted to start
a back-office operation in Srinagar. She joined a four-member team
and led the operations from the front. The business grew to a decent
size. While running the operations, a thought occurred to Tabish—
that she could do this on her own too. But being an entrepreneur

was a far-off reality as she came from a patriarchal family to whom a woman running a business was not easily palatable. In many ways, this millennial young woman was more constrained in following her vocation than the fearless Bhumia, Paroja and Gond women, who could travel to markets and sell their produce to earn their livelihood. As a woman entrepreneur myself, I could empathize with Tabish's story. When I started my first venture in 2001, customers, bankers and even employees had a difficult time taking me seriously. My youth and my gender became my bane. Clients would refuse to give me contracts as they felt a woman could not manage logistics. But supply chain and logistics were my passion and I decided to follow my heart, no matter what. It was my belief in my own dreams that ensured I didn't give up.

Tabish's passions since childhood lay in photography and painting. She indulged in them, with the breathtaking natural splendour of Kashmir serving as her muse. She would upload her pictures on Facebook and other social media platforms. They caught the eye of Omer Tramboo of the TCI Group, one of Kashmir's leading business conglomerates. He asked her if he could buy her photographs for their corporate calendar. She responded saying that she would rather design the layout and print the calendars herself. He was happy with that. She got the contract, was paid well for the work and even made a 12 per cent profit. Thus, Tabish Habib, a young Kashmiri woman, a child born in a time of intense conflict, began her journey as an entrepreneur.

Prism Creationz was started as a sole proprietorship, with Tabish owning 100 per cent of the shares. After the first success with the TCI Group, Tabish approached other potential customers and generated business. Initially, she didn't have her own printing equipment and there was no financial support from the family. She did have some emotional support from her aunt and cousin who encouraged her, but also warned her, saying, '*Izzat sambhalana*'— 'uphold your (family) respect'. Prism went on to record a 100 per cent growth in turnover just within a year and today has a staff of twelve located in Srinagar, Jammu and New Delhi. The company designs and prints all kinds of marketing collaterals and packaging material.

In 2016, acutely aware of how difficult it was for young people to take the entrepreneurial route in Kashmir, Tabish decided to start ThinkPod. She knew her own struggle all too well. Tabish had encountered a whole lot of challenges during her first two years as an entrepreneur—she did not know how to register a business or obtain tax registration or bank facilities, or how to develop a marketing and sales plan or generate a statement of accounts, or to even rent an office space. Now she wanted to do something that would make the path easier for others who might want to follow in her footsteps.

ThinkPod was set up as Kashmir's first co-working space with the objective of eventually becoming a full-fledged incubation centre. Tabish chose a location close to the famous Amar Singh College of Srinagar because she wanted to make it easier for young college students to explore entrepreneurship. When it started operations in March 2016, she received eighty-six applications. This encouraged her to stay committed to the initiative despite the months of violence, curfews and conflict that ensued later that year. ThinkPod has thirty-six work stations, a private meeting room and even an event area where Tabish has organized a few events and learning sessions for entrepreneurs, some of them in partnership with my own IEF Entrepreneurship Foundation.

In 2017, when I was conducting an IEF masterclass at ThinkPod, someone came in and announced that stone pelting had begun in the neighbouring campus of Amar Singh College. The students were pelting stones from inside the campus on security forces stationed outside the college gates. I asked Tabish and other entrepreneurs in the class whether we should continue or pause. They all wanted to continue. The class was full of entrepreneurs from different parts of

Kashmir and from different sectors. From furniture manufacturers, e-tailers, web designers, social entrepreneurs, IT service providers and hoteliers ... they all sat through the class while the sounds of stones crashing into windows and car shields continued outside. One of the entrepreneurs had to bear the brunt of violence himself when he discovered that his car was badly damaged by the stone pelting. Such was their commitment to their enterprises.

The power of enterprise is deeply embedded in the Kashmiri people. Kashmir was a trading post on the Silk Route and other Central Asian trade routes. Kashmiri entrepreneurs can be found in cities across the world, selling carpets, handicrafts and the famous Kashmiri pashmina shawls. Kashmiris are blessed with an uncanny ability to trade and conduct business. This power of enterprise may have been dampened by three decades of conflict, but if entrepreneurs like Tabish and others I met during the masterclass are anything to go by, then we can say the fire is still alive and needs to be stoked by a vibrant ecosystem.

Tabish Habib was awarded the International Visitor Leadership Program Fellowship by the US State Department. During the three weeks of the programme, the participants were taken across the US to meet women entrepreneurs and policymakers, and visit institutions, in order to witness the impact women-owned businesses had on US society. Tabish gained perspective on what women entrepreneurs could do for the overall development of the communities they belonged to. It renewed her faith in her chosen path of entrepreneurship. Today, she continues to remain committed to fostering an entrepreneurship ecosystem in Jammu and Kashmir.

India is rich with stories of entrepreneurs like Rewaj and Tabish, or of the tribal women and men who trade in forest produce. India's streets are abuzz with ambitious nano entrepreneurs; 94 per cent of all Indian businesses are MSMEs. The power of enterprise has been abundantly seeded in Indian society and its manifestation finds expression in grassroots jugaad and in the tech giants of Bengaluru in equal measure. What India needs is an entrepreneurship ecosystem which is rooted in our constitutional values of liberty, equality and fraternity, and which is designed to harness the power of enterprise of Indians from all strata of society without prejudice. It must be a system that is curated to help entrepreneurs like Tabish Habib and Rewaj Chettri to not only chase their own entrepreneurial dreams but also support others in making their dreams come alive.

As the saying goes, 'It takes a village to raise a start-up.' The best way for entrepreneurs to invite others on their journey is to have authenticity of purpose, commitment to shared value creation, and ability to build and sustain trust. A purposeful, sustainable and financially growing venture can give wings to the entrepreneur, give scalability to the local economy, create livelihoods, impact society and create a virtuous ecosystem of trust and equity. Such an ecosystem would enhance the native power of enterprise of the Indian people and advance the nation socially and economically, making Pahale India a reality. It has the promise to end poverty in the world's largest democracy.

When I think of such a possibility, the image of an early night sky lit up with a billion fireflies rising on the horizon comes to mind. It takes me to an aspirational landscape where a billion-plus people are energized by enterprise and innovation and the atmosphere is steeped in the promise of a brighter tomorrow. A tomorrow where jugaad for India and purpose-driven entrepreneurship have deepened stakeholder capitalism and where enterprise is the way of life for every Indian—a la Pahale India.

3

Power of Nature

Davos

In January 2019, I had the privilege to speak at the annual meeting of the World Economic Forum (WEF) in Davos, Switzerland. As a Young Global Leader of the Forum, it was an opportunity for me to connect with and learn from leaders from business, government, society and the arts who had gathered at Davos from across the world.

The WEF organizes its annual meeting in the middle of the peak alpine winter, more suited to skiing and ice skating than walking on icy roads with stilettoes in formal business attire. But, despite the winter chill, it was exciting to be part of the eclectic gathering of some of the finest minds from across the globe—world leaders and influencers who shape the future of our world. My husband Alok and I learnt a lot from the people we met and the sessions we attended.

51

Our 'fan moment' came when Sir David Attenborough went up on the stage to accept the Crystal Award conferred on him for his commitment towards and passion for the natural world of our planet. Upon receiving the award, Sir David spoke from his heart. He spoke of the opportunity we had to save the planet and its natural world from irreversible damage. He reminded us that it was climate stability and the resources of the natural world that had enabled human beings to accelerate progress to a point where we were now in a position to steer the future of our planet. He pleaded to the hall full of leaders to engage people on a large scale and make them aware of the precipice on the edge of which our planet was teetering. He insisted that if we reached out to our customers, shareholders, voters and citizens, and made them aware of the risks our planet was facing, people would be willing to change their way of life with decisive action. Both Alok and I felt that his words resonated with everyone in the hall, irrespective of their background.

The next day, the opening plenary of the annual meeting began with a conversation on 'nature' between His Royal Highness Prince William, the Duke of Cambridge, and Sir David Attenborough. Sir David spoke of his early days in filming and narrating wildlife films. He compared those days with today's new-age technologies which allow us to have a glimpse of our natural world from a proximity unthinkable before. He spoke of the power of platforms like Netflix, with whom he was collaborating for his series *Our Planet*. As he spoke with the earnest passion of a man who has dedicated his entire life to nature, we thought of our own actions or inaction that had contributed to the precarious state of nature on our planet. What role should we play in mitigating the colossal loss in our natural world?

As the session came to a close, Sir David reminded the audience that as human beings we were not different from the natural world but were an integral part of it. And yet our actions were setting off life-threatening chain reactions across a wide stratum of species on a scale never seen before. He elaborated with insightful examples on the interconnectedness and interdependencies in the natural world and how they impacted humanity. As his parting message, he urged the world leaders in the hall to treat nature with respect and reverence. His words took me back in time, to a road trip I had taken with a few friends, and when for the first time in my life I had seen how human beings could live in harmonious interdependence with their natural world and how respect and reverence for the power of nature can create possibilities for life and livelihoods.

Hemis

Darcha is a village at an altitude of 11,020 ft (3360 m) above sea level in the Lahaul and Spiti district of Himachal Pradesh, in India's far north. A few years ago, I decided to go on a drive from Manali in Himachal Pradesh to Leh in Ladakh with some friends. Darcha was our tea-stop en route. It was mid-September already, and the air was getting cooler. As we drove up the rough road from Darcha to Sarchu, the scenery changed dramatically. The riverine valleys lined with conifer and alpine forests gave way to landscapes of alpine meadows and views of the Himalayan edifice covered in stone and rock. As we drove ahead the valleys became broader and the altitude higher.

At Sarchu, we crossed into Ladakh and stopped for the night. The next morning, we took the twenty-one-hairpin-bend road, known as the Gata Loops, to climb to even higher altitudes. Ladakh literally means 'land of high (mountain) passes', and it lies between the Greater Himalaya and the Karakoram mountains. As we drove further through the More Plains, a cold empty vastness enveloped us, and the sand, the rocks and the ice seemed to be taking us into their fold. Above us, the azure sky stretched endlessly in the bright sun. An occasional sighting of a herd of yak was the only rare glimpse of life that these high altitudes afforded. Of human life, there was even less, with Tibetan prayer flags fluttering against the skies, adding some much-needed colour to the sandy backdrop. As we approached Tanglang La (at an altitude of 5328 m or 17480 ft), it became crystal clear to me why the Himalaya are called the roof of the world. Driving on the narrow road that wound along the sides of these snowy and barren mountains, I felt as though I was moving along the curvature of the earth itself. A marginal descent from one of the highest mountain passes in the world led us to a valley full of barley fields and the gushing waters of the river Indus. Driving along its banks, we finally reached Leh, the capital of Ladakh.

Ladakh is a cold, high-altitude desert, and Leh is its oasis. An old stopover on the trade routes between Tibet in the east and Kashmir in the west, Leh was also an erstwhile trading post between India, China and Central Asia. The Indus runs along the south-west periphery of the town and the mountains of the Ladakh range adorn its horizon. After a day spent acclimatizing to the altitude, we were told by our hosts that they could take us to Hemis National Park, where we could spot the Himalayan brown bear, the Asiatic ibex, and even try our luck at spotting the elusive and endangered snow leopard. It was an offer we couldn't refuse.

The next day, we drove from Leh for approximately 50 km in order to reach Hemis National Park. Named after the Hemis Monastery which is located within its boundaries, the Park is known for the highest density of endangered snow leopards in any protected area in the world. The only national park of India to the north of the Himalaya, the 4,400 sq. km-Hemis is the largest national park in South Asia.

Over a cup of gur-gur chai—the local salty butter tea made from yak milk, our hosts shared with us the unique geographical and natural attributes of the park. The altitudes in the park area range between 12,000 ft and 20,000 ft and the park falls within the Palearctic realm, one of the eight bio-geographic realms of the Earth. These are divisions of the earth's land surface based on the distribution patterns of terrestrial organisms. The Palearctic is the largest of all, covering most of north Africa, Eurasia and the territory of India north of the Himalayan foothills. The rest of India falls in the Indomalaya realm.

Hemis is home to several endangered species, in addition to the famous snow leopard. Species of the blue sheep, Asiatic ibex, the Tibetan wolf, the Himalayan brown bear and the Himalayan marmot also call the Park their home. When it was first declared as a National Park in 1981, the handful of local residents who lived within the park were in constant conflict with the wildlife, particularly the snow leopard, which has a tendency to kill a large number of livestock, irrespective of its appetite. Not surprisingly, this led to a situation where, in order to protect their livestock (also their chief source of income), villagers killed or poached the snow leopard. Things changed when Hemis was demarcated as a protected area. Forest conservation officers suggested that the only way to reduce the man–animal conflict was to lower the number of households with livestock within the parameters of the park. But this meant a dramatic change in livelihood for the families living in the park area.

In 2001, the Snow Leopard Conservancy India Trust (SLC-IT) brought their expertise and resources to help these families. In addition to skilling the locals in protective herding techniques and building predator-proof corrals for livestock, the Trust conducted a survey among trekkers and tourists who visited the park.[1] In the survey they asked the trekkers whether they would be willing to stay with the locals in a homestay instead of in the tents they normally carried along, and what would they be willing to pay for it. The results were positive, and a process began in training the villagers in running homestays where they would host tourists and also be nature guides helping them spot wildlife and flora in the park. We stayed in one such homestay and had the opportunity to interact with the local people and understand first-hand how this new way of life had benefited them and their natural environment.

Our homestay hosts informed us that more than 1,000 homestays operated within the park and the local forest department had formed a committee in every part of the park, with one person representing every village. The villagers were asked to decide on a name for their committee, register it and draft their own rules and regulations. The role of the committees is to ensure objectives such as protection of livestock, compensation and insurance for loss of animals and other goals for mitigating man–animal conflicts are met in a timely and fair manner. Our hosts told us with exuberance that they made more money with this new model of interdependent life with their natural habitat than they did through rearing livestock and poaching.

Today, the Hemis National Park is a community where humans and nature co-exist through a model of ecotourism that has incentivized the protection of the endangered species in the area. From being trapped in a helpless conflict with their natural world and risking the loss of species in their habitat, the residents of Hemis National Park have now become the guardians of these very species. Tourists and trekkers who come to spot these endangered species have become the means of livelihood for the locals. In their willingness to change their means of livelihood, the villagers have created a model of partnership between humans and nature. Now their life and livelihood are interdependent and in sync with their natural habitat.

Sir David Attenborough is right in pointing out that when we understand the full scope and impact of our interdependence with our natural world, we become fully aware of the implications of our actions. Hemis is a fine example of how even the most remote and poor communities can create a way of life in partnership with nature, when they are communicated with clearly, and supported through expertise and knowledge.

Back in Leh, our hosts noticed that I couldn't get my mind off the wonder the Hemis residents had created. It was the first time that I had witnessed man and nature acting in cooperation, and it fascinated me. Growing up in Mumbai, my proximity to nature was either the seashore or Sanjay Gandhi National Park on the outskirts of the city. But I never felt any interdependence with either of those. Maybe I was not aware of this kind of interdependence as a child and no one had spoken of it either. On the other hand, our hosts pointed out to me that traditionally, the Ladakhi way of life was always interdependent with nature. As children they grew up in full knowledge of the sway nature had over their lives. They explained that for the Ladakhi people, the power of nature was God-like. Their ancestors had lived not just in partnership with nature but had complete reverence for it as a divine force. This was an intriguing idea, and I wanted to further explore it. Our hosts suggested that to understand it more deeply, I must travel back to Ladakh in the winter and experience the winter migration of the Changpa.

The Changpa

The only way to reach Ladakh in winter is by air. My flight from New Delhi landed in Leh in early December later that year. At 9 a.m., the temperature stood at -15 degrees centigrade. For a moment I wondered what had I gotten myself into. It took me two days to acclimatize and prepare for our journey ahead. On the third day of my arrival, my hosts and I drove 125 km south-east of Leh to reach the Changthang Plateau.

The Changthang Cold Desert Wild Life Sanctuary is located in the Ladakhi adjunct of the Changthang Plateau and is spread across 4,000 sq. km. Changthang is a high-altitude Tibetan Plateau that extends into south-east Ladakh. It is the home of the Changpa, a semi-nomadic people who live a migratory life and move from one grassland to another with their livestock, whose milk, meat and pashmina wool are their only source of income. They speak a variant of the Tibetan language known as Changskhat and practise Tibetan Buddhism. They are classified as a scheduled tribe of India.

Our plan was to spend three or four days with a Changpa family my hosts from Leh knew well. We had carried sleeping bags with us and tents, but the Changpa family we were visiting insisted that we stay in their tent where a small fire fed with sun-dried yak dung kept everyone warm. At night the temperature plummeted to -25 degrees centigrade and we were glad to have the warmth of the fire and some warm food with butter tea. The life of the Changpa is tumultuous, to say the least. They live in extreme conditions and with very little resources. Their way of life is completely dictated by and dependent on nature and its benevolence. In the summer, the temperatures in the Changthang can reach up to 25 degrees centigrade, but in winters they can drop as low as -30 degrees centigrade, which, at an altitude of average 14,000 ft, is inhospitable for most humans.

The next morning, we woke up at 5.30. The day starts very early for the Changpa. The animals need to be taken out of their pens for grazing on the pastures. After a quick breakfast we stepped out of the tent. A cold, icy wind brushed our faces, and our Changpa host commented that there might be a snowstorm later in the day. As he looked up at the skies, he said a little prayer. My co-travellers from Leh later explained to me that it was a request to their masters that the snowfall happens later in the day so that the sheep and the yak can graze enough to last them a day or more.

The Changpa believe in the powers of their spiritual masters, whom they summon frequently to please Mother Nature. Sometimes the masters are called upon for rains in the summer and at other times to moderate the snow in the harsh winters. The Changpa approach nature with immense reverence, something I had never seen before. Their pastoral life is a gargantuan challenge in the Ladakhi winter. Every time there is heavy snowfall and the patches of grass and shrub on which their livestock feed wither away, the Changpa move their tents and their lives to yet another piece of land. On that freezing winter day, as clouds started appearing in the sky, a snowstorm seemed imminent. Once it passed, this settlement of the Changpa would need to migrate to another meadow where there might still be grass for their livestock. My fellow travellers from Leh, looked at me with a smile and said, 'It seems you are destined to experience the winter migration of the Changpa.'

Later that day, the Changpa came back earlier than usual from their grazing as the snow had started falling in large quantities. The animals huddled close to each other in their pens to weather out the storm and the humans got inside their tent and sat around the slow-lit fire with warm yak milk tea. The discussion soon veered towards the migration to the next meadow. I was trying to follow the animated conversation via the translation my hosts were providing. The elderly matriarch of the family said something about listening to the nature gods, which prompted me to ask, 'When most of the world has started using modern tools to mitigate natural elements, why do the Changpa continue to submit to the forces of nature?'

The wise old woman smiled with knowing eyes at me. She went out in the middle of the snowstorm and got some fresh snow in her fist. Putting the snow and her prayer beads in my hand, she said a prayer and then began to explain something. According to the interpretation given to me, she was saying, 'the human mind is highly evolved and capable and believes that it can subjugate nature. But nature is all powerful. It was here before the first man and the first woman and it will be here later. Nature is divine and when we live life ordained by the divine then we seldom go wrong.' I looked at her and nodded. I must have looked completely lost because she then burst into roars of laughter and patted me on the head, as one might an ignorant child who has just discovered something new. The next morning, the young Changpa men loaded their pick-up vehicles with the goods and tools they needed to set up the next settlement site. Today, pick-up vehicles have replaced the ordinary yak for transporting their goods. Generally, the Changpa pre-identify the pastures they will next move to, but it is a tedious process. Most of that day was spent by the Changpa in preparing for their migration the next morning.

On the morning of the move, the Changpa herded their animals out of their pens, guiding them towards the open plains, covered in sheets of ice and snow. One at a time, each family took out their herd of livestock. The entire community moved in a staggered manner, their herds maintaining a few metres' distance from each other in order to avoid their getting mixed up. In numbers as large as 10,000, the animals moved in a straight line across the whitewashed desert along with their human owners. It would take them an entire day to reach their next settlement. But I didn't notice any anxiety or fear. The Changpa way of life was in complete harmony with the harsh forces of nature that dominated their habitat. The equanimity with which the Changpa have accepted their role in the vast theatre of nature was apparent to me. There were no distinctions between man and animal in the Changthang— both were at the mercy of the forces of nature.

Fast forward to 2019, and as I sat in an audience of 2,000-plus, listening to Sir David Attenborough talk about humanity's interdependence with nature and to his pleas to his audience to revere and respect nature, the memories of my time with the dwellers of Hemis National Park and the Changpa came alive. Despite the advent of modernity, they continued to respect the power of nature as divine. Nature continued to be an integral, interwoven and interdependent part of their existence. Their ability to recognize and accept this in totality was at the core of their way of life.

Alok and I decided to head back early to the hotel that evening. Something in Sir David's words was so profound that we wanted it to stay with us a little longer. We wanted to mull over his words a bit more. While waiting for our shuttle in the icy cold, I told Alok about the Changpa and he was quick to point out that maybe the Changpa didn't have a choice but to live with reverence for nature and perhaps they were unique in their way of life. But I shook my head. I reminded him of the time when he came with me to Meghalaya, at the other end of the Himalaya in India's north-east and how communities there too continued to revere nature as divine while living and conducting very modern lives.

Mawphlang

The Himalaya are the youngest mountain range on the planet and home to some of its highest peaks too. They divide the Indian subcontinent from the Tibetan Plateau in a 2,400 km long arc from west, north-west to east, south-east. Nanga Parbat in Kashmir is their western anchor and Namcha Barwa in remote south-east Tibet their eastern sentinel. Namcha Barwa rises at 7,782 m above the river Yarlung Tsangpo, which turns sharply northwards before flowing south, where it enters Arunachal Pradesh in India as Siang. Its waters flow further south-west as the mighty Brahmaputra. In essence, the Himalaya stretch between the Indus in the north-west and the Brahmaputra in the south-east. Both rivers trace their origins to the Mansarovar Lake area in Tibet. But both rivers take completely different courses, flowing through different altitudes and topographies, forging awe-inspiring landscapes along their paths. While the Indus flows through the cold desert of Ladakh and onwards through the valleys of Gilgit–Baltistan towards Pakistan, the Brahmaputra crosses the Tibetan Plateau and eventually flows through the lush green mountains and thick jungles of Arunachal Pradesh. It becomes a giant, ocean-like river as it travels through the vast plains of Assam before turning further south towards Bangladesh near the Garo hills of Meghalaya in India's north-east.

Meghalaya is a Sanskrit word, literally meaning 'abode of clouds'. The average rainfall in the state is as high as 11,500 mm annually, which makes it one of the wettest places on earth. The state is largely a mountainous plateau, abundant in forests, minerals, flora and fauna. Ranging from 150 m to 1,961 m in height, its hills form the lush green foothills of the mighty Himalaya. Its forests are among the richest in biodiversity in Asia, constituting 70 per cent of the state's geography. Meghalaya is chiefly divided into the Garo Hills, the Khasi Hills and the Jantia Hills, each of these deriving its name from the tribes that call those hills their home.

I had visited Meghalaya as a teenager for a short holiday with family, spending a few days in the state capital, Shillong. But I never really had the chance to explore the state until an invitation from the government of Meghalaya in 2012, which asked me to advise the government in its livelihoods and entrepreneurship mission. This entailed travelling to the state and interacting with its people almost every quarter. On one such occasion, I visited the village of Mawphlang. It is a Khasi word and means 'grassy stone'. The village is known for its monolith stones and its sacred grove forest of 78 hectares. Sacred groves are virgin forests left undisturbed and untouched by local communities, largely due to their spiritual and natural significance. The groves are a treasure trove of biodiversity and are fine examples of the age-old culture of living a life of reverence towards nature. Meghalaya has 125 such sacred groves, of sizes ranging from 0.01 hectares to 900 hectares.[2]

The sacred grove at Mawphlang is more than 500 years old. Entry to the grove is only possible when one is accompanied by a member of the local community, who also serves as a guide for the fascinating walk through this unspoilt forest. There is a nominal fee for this, which enables the locals to maintain the natural beauty of the area. The sacred grove at Mawphlang was traditionally used by the Khasis of the village for various rituals. The Khasis believe that the grove is protected by the deity Labasa and they take on the role of guardians for the grove. No one is allowed to so much as pick a single flower or leaf from the grove, and logging and deforestation are out of the question. Speaking with authority and conviction, your guide will tell you that to take anything from the grove or to pollute it with any extraneous materials will anger the deity and the spirits of the forest. The community believes that their forefathers had the wisdom to live in harmony with nature and that this is a tradition to be cherished and protected. My local guide walked me through the grove, pointing to trees that cure cancer and trees like the rudraksh, which are of spiritual importance. In the spring, the forest floor blushes with pink and red rhododendrons. The grand old trees are covered in green moss throughout the year. I was told that this particular sacred grove was home to 453 different species. As we walked towards the centre of the grove, I started to notice the monolith stones. My guide explained each of them and their unique purpose in the Khasi rituals.

At the heart of this old forest, protected by the gods and nurtured by humans, I felt a sense of healing and hope. The Khasis, who call it their own, do so with love and pride. The sacred grove is a vital part of their lives, even though many of them work in government offices or banks or farm their lands. I began to decode the wisdom of the Khasi elders. For them, life was about living in reverence to nature, regarding it as divine and combining community care with care of nature. In this way, the Khasis of Mawphlang had achieved a sustainable future, for both humans and nature, in their immediate habitat. It made me wonder whether this devotion to nature was unique to the Khasis and Changpa as they were tribal societies and whether nature is revered in other parts of India too.

Revering Nature

India has approximately 14,000 recognized sacred groves across the country;[3] although it is believed in some quarters that there could be as many as 100,000. In Karnataka, for instance, they are known as Devarakadu, literally, 'God's own forest'. In ancient Indian literature, sacred groves find mention in the Vrikshayurveda, a classical ancient Hindu text, authored by Surapala. The text is a medical science manual for trees and their well-being. Hindus traditionally categorized their forests into three kinds: mahavan—a grand natural forest where all species dwell; tapovan—a forest where sages and spiritual masters seek truth and knowledge; and srivan—a forest for the prosperity of the community. The sacred groves fall in the category of srivan.

In ancient times, centres of learning called rishikuls would be set up inside tapovan forests. Forests and trees have been central to Indian rituals and the Indian way of life. In the four stages of life prescribed for a Hindu, the third is vanaprastha, where a person gradually retires from his householder duties and transitions into a life of spiritual pursuit, culminating in a hermit-like existence. The word vanaprastha literally means 'journey to the forest'.

Irrespective of their moorings, Indians have traditionally held nature in reverence. Much science and literature over thousands of years has been dedicated to it. Many Indian spiritual teachings, like the Buddhist Jataka tales, are based in the natural world. Buddhists worship the Bodhi tree, under which the Buddha is believed to have achieved enlightenment. Hindu gods and goddesses have animals and birds as their vahanas (vehicles) and every deity has his or her favourite tree or flower. Indian literature, the Indian performing arts, painting, weaving and handicrafts use the natural world as inspiration. The Panchatantra tales are a fine example of this. A collection of animal fables, written originally in Sanskrit, they have been translated into every Indian language and into as many as fifty foreign languages. The tales have travelled far and wide, in both ancient and modern times.

Rivers are given the stature of goddesses in India and are regarded as life-givers. During the Hindu festival of Mahakumbh, millions gather on the banks of India's holy rivers every few years and take a dip in their waters and offer prayers for salvation. The festival is touted as the largest religious gathering in the world, and UNESCO regards it as an intangible cultural heritage of humanity. Indian fishermen offer adulations to the seas before they set out fishing even today. Many tribes in India continue to worship nature-deities. In the north-east of the country, the Lepchas and Bhotias of Sikkim worship the Khangchendzonga or Kanchenjunga, the tallest peak in India and the third highest mountain in the world. Such is the importance of nature in the Indian way of life. Culturally, for Indians, nature is not an external environmental factor that merely dictates weather and offers scenic solace to the eyes. On the contrary, nature for Indians is both personal and integral to life; it is a giver and taker of life; it is the genesis of life and it is life itself. We revere the power of nature as the manifestation of the divine.

This ability to revere nature and work in cooperation with it for a harmonized existence may have been prevalent across the world before the rise of the industrial age. But in many parts of India, it exists even today. Perhaps this enables Indians to accept with ease the scientific findings on climate change. In a SAP and Qualtrics survey fielded in January 2020, titled 'Toward a more Sustainable World: A Global Study of Public Opinion', people in thirty countries were asked, 'How much do you trust what scientists say about the environment?' Eighty-six per cent of Indians surveyed said that they trusted what scientists said about the environment; the highest in the basket of thirty countries, followed by their South Asian neighbours of Bangladesh and Pakistan. Contrast this to the 45 per cent of those surveyed in United States, 25 per cent in Japan and 23 per cent in Russia who responded affirmatively to the same question. Further, 53 per cent of the Indians surveyed felt that protecting the environment should be a priority, even if it meant slower economic growth[4]—again, this was the highest percentage from among the thirty countries surveyed.

As Sir David Attenborough commented at Davos, if we can begin to respect and revere nature, it would allow us to see how much we depend on it and how much it contributes to our survival and growth. Therefore, it is encouraging that most Indians have an attitude of reverence towards nature and trust the science on environment in large numbers. But, does this mean we show respect for nature in our daily lives? Has this acknowledgement of the *Power of Nature* allowed us to lead a life more in harmony with our natural surroundings and with other species?

Desecrating the Divine

India is a nation blessed with geographical and natural diversity. From the shores of the Indian Ocean, the Arabian Sea and the Bay of Bengal to the mighty Himalaya, from the vast sand dunes of the Thar Desert to the massive wetlands of the Gangetic plains, nature has manifested her full glory in India. Indians enjoy six seasons traditionally, and we have festivals that celebrate nature, the seasons and the planet. In fact, the natural world of India is a treasure—not just for itself but also for the world at large. And so I am compelled to share some statistics—India has 2.4 per cent of the world's landmass but is home to 8 per cent of the earth's flora and fauna; 54,000 species of flora and 1,02,718 species of fauna are found in

India.[5] This makes India one of the seventeen most mega-diverse countries in the world.

Out of the thirty-six biodiversity hotspots in the world, four are in India.[6] The Western Ghats that run along the western coast of India for almost 1,600 km are one of these biodiversity hotspots. But in the past ninety years, they have lost 35 per cent of their forests. Their degradation began when the British cleared forests for coffee, tea and rubber plantations in the 1800s. Over the decades, an increase in population, environmentally unscientific road projects and rampant deforestation have led to substantial biodiversity and forest loss. This has further precipitated floods and landslides in the monsoons and has created perilous conditions for the human and animal populations who live in and around the Ghats.

Indians revere the river Ganga as divine. But in the Gangetic plains of northern India, we see this goddess of salvation and purification reduced to a pollutant-rich water body. Near Kanpur, one of Uttar Pradesh's mega-industrial centres, almost 450 million litres of daily sewage was being dumped into the holy river. In 2019, a project under the Namami Gange Programme diverted the sewage from thirteen out of the sixteen main drains of Kanpur into a common effluent treatment plant.[7] But this is inadequate. Years of disregard for the Ganga have left the river polluted and her waters unfit for human and animal consumption along most of its course in the Gangetic plains. How can the same people who venerate the Ganga as a purifying force of the divine pollute her with human and industrial waste? This remains a baffling question.

The more macabre display and after-effects of human greed and ambition are visible in India's large cities, including the national capital, New Delhi. Pollutants from Delhi's industries foul the waters of the Yamuna, which runs along the city's eastern periphery. Here, the river foams from the poisonous chemical discharges into its waters. The air pollution in the National Capital Region (NCR) due to vehicular carbon emissions and industrial activity reaches its zenith during the months of October and November as the early winter cooling of the atmosphere coincides with the burning of paddy crops in the neighbouring states of Punjab and Haryana, creating a vortex of pollution that drops the air quality in the city to hazardous levels.

When Alok and I moved to Gurugram in Delhi NCR in 2016, we were unprepared for this polluted air. In early October, I found myself gasping for breath, and my asthma, which had been latent for fourteen years, returned with a vengeance. Our eyes would water and burn frequently. Alok, who had spent large part of his childhood in Delhi, could not fathom how a city once so green and full of open spaces had now become a gas chamber. It forced us to reconsider our life choices. We always wanted to live in the Himalaya in the latter part of our lives, but Delhi NCR's pollution, coupled with the horrific data on water tables in Haryana, pre-empted that plan by a decade. We began looking for a place to live, and Alok decided to venture into regenerative agriculture in the mountains of Uttarakhand.

The following year, we rented a village house in the Munsyari block of Pithoragarh district in the state and found a small piece of land to construct our forever-home and also some land to do regenerative agriculture. While living there for almost eight months of the year, we became proximate with nature in a manner that is not possible in the cities. But even though the air was devoid of pollution and skies were a sunny blue, the impact of climate change was visible even in these remote areas. For instance, Alok had to first engage in apiculture to mitigate the dwindling population of Apis Cerana Indica—the Indian honey bee. Without the bees, there was no hope of catalysing natural pollination in the area. And without pollination, there was no hope for reviving any kind of nature-based regenerative agricultural practices.

While Alok focused on nature-based solutions in small farms with the local farmers, I looked at the interlinkages between deforestation, global warming and glacial loss. The more I observed and researched, the clearer it became to me that something had to be done urgently to save the natural forests of the Himalaya from logging and plunder. Awareness at a global level was needed to mitigate glacial loss in these mountains. The Himalaya are widely acknowledged as the planet's 'Third Pole'. The vast reserves of freshwater stored in their icy glaciers and in their perennial layers of snow accord them this status. Their reserves are the highest after those found on the other two poles of the planet. But this snow is melting fast with the earth warming at a heightened pace over the past five decades. Many Himalayan glaciers face existential threats and scientists predict that by the end of the current century, the Himalaya could lose anywhere between one third to two thirds of their ice and snow.[8] This would bring precarious water crises to the population of more than 1.5 billion who depend on the ten river systems that originate and are sustained by the Himalaya.

Our own valley, known locally as the Johar Valley, and the Gori river basin are home to more than twenty-five glaciers and they are the chief water source for the Gori river and many mountain streams that provide water to the locals. Munsyari receives extremely heavy rainfall for three months of monsoon but most of this rain water is not harvested. Therefore, the source of water remains the snow and glacial ice. Over the past three years, we have seen the snow on these mountains lessen at an alarming rate. We have also observed that the western jet streams that make their way from Europe and Central Asia and cause precipitation and snow in the Himalaya carry with them pollutants, carbon particles and dark black deposits of particles from burning oil wells and industrial waste—so much so that in the higher reaches we have started seeing the glacier sheets turning dusty grey-brown at times.

The Himalaya are closer in proximity to the equator than the two poles of the earth are to our planet's midriff. While this creates special conditions for biodiversity, it does not spare the Himalaya from the risks of global warming. The depletion of their ice is caused by human activity near and far. The interlinkages between rising temperatures, which cause massive forest fires in their mountains, and the melting of their ice are being studied by scientists. But, sadly, the communities that live in the Himalaya have not been made aware of this. They are unaware of the fact that their own actions and those of others far away are accelerating climate change, causing nature crises in their immediate habitats. They worship the Himalaya as divine and call their own state 'Dev Bhoomi', literally 'land of gods' but they continue to cut trees for firewood and poach animals for fur or body parts. They hunt animals by lighting forest fires and replace the existing biodiverse oak, birch, horse-chestnut and rhododendron forests with monoculture of pine trees. The degradation of the Himalayan natural ecosystem is a sordid example of human greed. Communities in these mountains need more interventions such as the one at Hemis, where modern tools are available for a shift in livelihood, where a life in reverence to nature can be in sync with the livelihood aspirations of the people.

What has led us to disregard the same rivers which we continue to worship? What has led us to uproot our forests that nurture life and nourish our civilization? What has led us to silently witness the ebbing of our glaciers in the Himalaya, the same mountains we revere as the doorway to emancipation? It compels us to ask some uncomfortable but necessary questions about our relationship with our natural world. We must be persuaded to acknowledge that despite revering nature as divine, we have through our actions weakened our bonds with it. And that our relationship with nature is broken, albeit not irrevocably.

Mending Broken Bonds

India's national anthem (*'Jana Gana Mana'*) and national song (*'Vande Mataram'*) both pay homage to the country's natural world. Over the years, there have been significant and undeniable movements for environment protection, wildlife conservation and biodiversity in India. India's success in protecting the endangered snow leopard in high numbers inside the Hemis National Park is one such example. In the past decade, India has multiplied the number of tigers and lions in its forests. The presence and protection of thousands of sacred groves like the one in Mawphlang in Meghalaya continue to reinforce that all is not lost in our age-old relationship with nature. So, we may ask: why it is that we succeed in protecting and regenerating nature in some areas and not in others?

At the heart of this conundrum is the issue that man and nature have been separated. We no longer believe that man is an integral part of nature. While we revere nature in our traditions and culture, and respect its divine power, the laws and institutions we have established in our republic for nature are anthropocentric, i.e., they look at nature from a human-centric view point. Some of these laws have been inherited from the British Raj and were made to extract from nature, rather than nourish it. But for several decades post-Independence, we didn't modify these laws to reflect the sensibilities of our traditional deep bonds with our natural world. In fact, the anthropocentric idea of man being the centre of existence was discarded by Gandhians such as J.C. Kumarappa as early as in the 1930s, who believed that a sustainable life is one that is lived in cooperation with nature.

If we want to rethink our approach towards nature and the efficacy of the legislations that govern our natural heritage, we need to reclaim our powers of living in concord with nature; we need to salvage our belief that nature is a manifestation of the divine and that human beings are an intrinsic part of the natural world. Most importantly, we need to co-opt nature itself in this endeavour. The unprecedented crisis and tipping point that the planet is approaching as far as its natural ecosystems are concerned make it necessary for all of us to transform our way of life back to one of collaborating with and living in unison with nature. How do we do this? By engaging in life and livelihoods that are nature positive and by adding more back to nature than we take from it.

In May 2019, the Intergovernmental Science-Policy Platform on Biodiversity and Ecosystem Services (IPBES), an intergovernmental body of 140 member states, released a report written by 145 leading experts from fifty different nations, and with contributions from 310 authors. The study spoke of the dire state of the natural world on our planet. The report highlighted: '1 million of the planet's 8 million species of plants and animals are at risk of going extinct in the near future.'[9] The report went on to elaborate that human activity was adversely affecting the well-being of the natural world through deforestation, loss of habitats, unsustainable agricultural practices, overfishing, excessive mining, air and water pollution, wildlife poaching and trade, climate change and global warming. It stressed that we cannot mitigate the climate crisis without actually addressing the nature crisis. We need to take a larger natural ecosystem view for the long-term survival of our planet and our species. The report led to widespread awareness about why we need to shift our attention towards our natural world.

The Living Planet Report 2018 of the World Wildlife Fund (WWF) states that nature provides services worth USD 125 trillion to humanity annually.[10] Without a robust natural world, our chances of survival are dismal. Campaign for Nature, an initiative supported by the Wyss Campaign for Nature and National Geographic, has said that it would be important to protect 30 per cent of the planet from all human activities by 2030 if we want to sustain human existence.[11]

For such an ambitious target to be achieved, it will be vital to create a road map for human beings to live in harmony with nature. This would be no different from what we have seen the villagers of Hemis National Park or the Khasis of Meghalaya do. But for this, we need to understand and accept at a national scale that we are not separate from our natural world but are an integral part of it, just like the Changpa of Changthang do.

Nature-based Solutions

India is fully committed to the Paris Climate Agreement of maintaining the global temperature rise well below 2 degrees centigrade and working towards limiting the rise to 1.5 degrees. This is not possible unless we protect our forests, our biodiversity hotspots and our natural carbon sinks, and focus on regenerative agriculture. If we genuinely want to go back to our way of life in partnership with nature, we will need to make some changes in the way we legislate, implement our policies, invest in our businesses, educate our young people and carry out the affairs of our republic. We will have to turn to science as well as tradition and weave them together to find the road ahead. More importantly, we will need to use *nature–based solutions* to heal and strengthen nature.

The International Union for Conservation of Nature (IUCN) is the global authority on the status of our planet's natural world and on the measures needed to safeguard it. India became its member in 1969, and IUCN has had an office in the country since 2007. At its World Conservation Congress organized in 2016 in Hawaii, United States, the IUCN adopted a definitional framework of 'Nature-based Solutions'. The IUCN defines nature-based solutions as 'actions to protect, suitably manage and restore natural or modified ecosystems that address societal challenges effectively and adaptively, simultaneously providing human well-being and biodiversity benefits'.[12]

When I first heard of the definition at a session on nature and business at the WEF annual meeting in Davos, I couldn't help but correlate it with what I had witnessed at Hemis National Park. Alok too was curious about this new framework as it seemed it was something he was trying to do with his nature-based agriculture initiatives in the Himalaya. Therefore, we requested the experts, post the session, to give us more information. We learnt that the IUCN further divides nature-based solutions into three categories: [13]

1. Nature-based—where we partner with nature to restore ecosystem benefits; for example, what Alok is doing with the revival of Apis Cerana Indica—the Indian honey bee—to catalyse nature-based agriculture.

2. Nature-derived—where we source energy from nature; for example, wind and solar energy.

3. Nature-inspired—where we come up with solutions that involve innovative design and which are modelled on biological processes.

As we thought more about it, we were clear that from regenerative agriculture, and forest and species conservation, to sustainable fishing and mining, circular economy ventures, investment in renewable energy, nature-positive business processes, waste resource management … there are countless opportunities for nature-based solutions to achieve nature-positive growth and development.

Alok and I came back from the annual meeting in Davos empowered with knowledge and tools we could use to support nature conservation through nature-based solutions in our little Himalayan village. But our challenge came when we started discussing the way forward with the villagers. At first it was hard for them to see how climate crisis and nature crisis were interrelated. How could nature with all its divinity be at risk? The idea that humans could endanger the divine was hard to digest for these simple folk. As we persevered, we realized that if nature-based solutions had to materialize at scale in our country, we would need mass awareness supported with standards and tools that transform these solutions into action on the ground. The fact that culturally Indians respect the power of nature is a strong foundation to build on.

In his book *Standards: Recipes for Reality*, Lawrence Busch points out: 'Standards are the means by which we construct realities … Standards shape not only the physical world around us but also our social lives and even ourselves.'[14] Under the Food Safety and Standards (Packaging and Labelling) Act of 2006, all packaged foods and toothpastes sold in India need to identify whether they contain lacto-vegetarian or non-lacto-vegetarian ingredients and products. A green dot enclosed in a green square indicates a vegetarian food product and a brown triangle inside a brown square indicates a non-vegetarian food product. Recently, a symbol for vegan foods has also been introduced. By mandating these labels, the Indian government has set standards for consumer behaviour. Today, what began as a government action has now impacted processes all across Indian food businesses. A unique cultural aspect is now a market standard, and therefore a market reality. Was it implemented to drive vegetarianism? We cannot tell for sure. But such is the power of standards that Indians now take these labels for granted. Therefore, what we need to do is to create standards for nature-based solutions. The standards for emission have transformed automobile manufacturing across the globe today, therefore this is doable.

The International Union for Conservation of Nature (IUCN) has already suggested a standards framework for nature-based solutions. We can use it in its entirety or adopt it to our national context. But having standards for nature-based solutions will bridge the gap between our civilization, which reveres nature as divine, and the workings of our republic, where a re-think and redesign of our environment and conservation policies is urgently warranted. As far as our relationship with nature is concerned, until now our policies and institutions have pushed the raft of the republic in opposition to the natural flow of our civilization. When we have standards for nature-based solutions and a nature lens in every policy decision, we will begin to truly follow a more nature-positive development path.

The residents of Hemis, the Changpa of Changthang and the Khasis of Mawphlang are all testament to the fact that revering and respecting nature and becoming an integral part of its powerful essence can transform lives for the better and ensure continuity of communities and their natural world. With standards for nature-based solutions, we can, as a society and as a collective, begin to reconnect with a way of life that is more in collaboration with the power of nature.

Mukti of Binsar

It was the winter of 1985 and Mukti Datta was all of twenty-two years. She had returned from Oxford in England for a break, to the place she had called home from her infancy—the forest of Binsar near Almora in present-day Uttarakhand. Back in those days, it was still part of the state of Uttar Pradesh. While walking in the forest, which she had come to befriend from early childhood, she noticed a few porters carrying carcasses of deer shot on a hunt. The sight deeply upset Mukti. She realized that the timber mafia were cutting trees inside the Binsar forest, many of them hundreds of years old, and resin factories were cutting oak trees as old as half a millennium for coal that came from oak wood. She says, 'It got my goat.'

Oxford became history and Mukti decided to pen a letter to the then Prime Minister of India, Rajiv Gandhi in March 1986. As we sipped ginger tea in her old English-era home in Kasardevi, a short drive from Binsar, she shared what followed.[15] In the letter, she had requested the prime minister to declare Binsar as a wildlife sanctuary, citing that it was a unique forest that warranted protection from poaching, hunting, logging and other extractive and illegal activities. She vividly remembers the day she received a response to her letter. The postman, who had walked fourteen miles in order to deliver the letter, was running up the rugged forest hill, shouting at the top of his voice that a letter had come from the prime minister's office. In the letter, Mukti was applauded for taking up the cause and was asked to come and see the prime minister when she was in Delhi.

Mukti promptly went to Delhi and met with the prime minister, who assured her of his full support. She returned to Binsar, full of optimism. Little did she know that the story of her letter, the prime minister's response and her meeting with him had made it to the ears of the local timber mafia, contractors, corrupt politicians and government officers. They ganged up against her and tried every trick in the book to deter her. She faced political protests, personal character assassination, death threats and even attempts on her life. But instead of giving up, she just pushed harder. It was at this point that she realized that Binsar was not her forest alone. It was home to several rural communities and she decided to co-opt them into her mission. She met with the thirty-five gram sabhas (village councils) in the vicinity of Binsar forest and formed a Jan Jagaran Samiti (a committee) for the cause. The postman who had delivered the letter from the prime minister became its treasurer. The committee had seven office bearers and over 100 members. Its main thrust was that the forest of Binsar belonged to the local communities and not to the timber contractors and government officials. It proposed that the forest produce should be harvested without any deforestation or

other harmful effects and that the earnings from the harvest should
go directly to the local communities instead of to third parties who
were plundering the forest.

Mukti then undertook a signature campaign, demanding that the
forest of Binsar be declared a wildlife sanctuary. She got over 1,000
signatures from the local villagers. She used the economic case of
forest produce for the benefit of villagers to incentivize them to join
her movement. Unknowingly, she was using a nature-based solution
to protect her local natural ecosystem and support local livelihoods.
She also used the spiritual standing of Binsar as the sacred forest
of Bineshwar Mahadev (a local name for the Hindu god Shiva)
and Golu Devta (a local patron deity of the Kumauni people) to
rally support. In doing so, Mukti was calling upon the traditional
reverence for nature and its divine aspects to support her cause.

With the local forest department at odds with her, Mukti was
advised to go to Delhi and meet the then environment ministry
secretary, T.N. Seshan. He took an interest in what she was doing
and organized a small grant of Rs 8 lakh from the ministry for her
to set up forest nurseries involving the local women. This gave the
initiative a new ray of hope. But the felling of trees in the forest
still continued. So Mukti decided to take the matter to the state
government in Lucknow. There she began advocating the cause of
declaring the Binsar forest as a wildlife sanctuary. She even went
to Delhi to meet the Union minister for environment, Z.R. Ansari,
who, instead of helping her, tried to take undue advantage of her
vulnerability.[16]

It was a terrible time for a young woman who was trying to save
her forest. For Mukti, Binsar was what the forest of Seoni was for
Mowgli in Rudyard Kipling's famous *Jungle Book*. Binsar was a home
she shared with age-old oaks and blooming rhododendrons, deer
and leopards, and birds of all kinds. This was not a political fight;

for her, this was a personal fight, a fight for what she considered her own—the forest of Binsar.

Two years since her first letter to the prime minister, the fight for Binsar still continued. Mukti turned her attention to advocacy in Lucknow again. By now, word of her tireless pursuit for protection of the Binsar forest had travelled far and wide within the government system. The coverage of her struggle by media houses also helped. The state forest secretary was aware of Mukti's struggle. He empathized with her, and in fact he paved the way for Binsar to be declared a wildlife sanctuary. Finally, in 1988, the forest of Binsar was declared a wildlife sanctuary by a decree of the Governor of Uttar Pradesh. With that, nearly 45.59 sq. km. of forest was protected from poaching and plunder while the local communities had the right to use sustainable, nature-based methods to earn from the forest produce. Ahead of her times, Mukti had acted to protect, suitably manage and restore a natural ecosystem while addressing societal challenges effectively and adaptively, and simultaneously providing for human well-being and biodiversity benefits. She had indeed implemented a nature-based solution to protect the forest of Binsar. How wonderful it would have been if the government and forest department of the day had the mandate to act on implementing standards for nature-based solutions at that time!

As you drive from Almora towards Binsar, the hills are covered with the monoculture of pine forests, but as soon as you enter the gates of the sanctuary, the scenery changes. Oaks, birches and rhododendrons make an appearance. Today, Binsar is home to twenty-five different types of trees and twenty-four types of bushes. It is home to musk deer, leopard, red fox and the red giant flying squirrel, to name a few. More than 200 species of birds call this dense forest their home. Villagers in the area continue to access the forest for sustainable forest produce and prayers continue to be offered at

the temples of Bineshwar Mahadev and Golu Devta. When tourists
visit, the revenue from their entry fees helps to meet part of the
expenses of maintaining the area.

Mukti still lives inside the Binsar forest, where she retreats to
when the buzz of Kasardevi gets too much for her. While sitting
by her small hut-like home perched on a hill inside the forest and
listening to her journey as a crusader for the forest of Binsar, I
noticed bright blue and brown Eurasian jays flocking on the forest
floor. On the eastern horizon, the Himalaya, from the Chaukhamba
Peak in the Garhwal region to those in Nepal almost 300 km
away, with the mighty Nanda Devi Peak right in the middle, were
soaking up the morning sun. I looked at Mukti in awe and admired
her bond with this beautiful forest. But I also felt ashamed that I
had no such bond with the Sanjay Gandhi National Park on the
outskirts of Mumbai.

Mukti Datta is a believer in the power of her natural habitat: the
Binsar forest. Maybe that is why she was able to fight against all
odds for its well-being. She is truly empowered and strengthened by
her belief that nature is sacred and should be revered and preserved.
As for me, I do believe that apart from envisaging and charting a
nature-positive development path and creating standards that
include nature-based solutions as a tool for transformation, if India
truly wants to bring back a way of life which is in partnership with
nature, then we need to be ready as a nation and as a society to raise,
educate, inspire, empower and support millions of young sentinels of
nature. These young people may engage in cleaning rivers and lakes
or in protecting glaciers or wildlife, on the land or in the oceans, or
passionately commit to saving species of birds or butterflies. They may
rise for the forests, jungles, wetlands, urban green cover or the mighty
Himalaya. They may innovate products and services that regenerate
nature. Our obligation should be to equip them with knowledge
and skills, support them with nature-positive policies and standards

for nature-based solutions, and encourage them to come up with innovative ways to nurture and nourish their natural heritage. Only then will we mend our broken relationship with nature and restore our erstwhile wholesome way of life—one of reverence and respect for nature. Only then we will have communities like the Khasis of Mawphlang who are able to marry traditional wisdom with modern tools. That is when we will truly strengthen our republic with our civilizational power of nature.

4

Power of Heritage

A Ballad in Stone

The Satpura and Vindhya mountain ranges run across the midriff of the Indian land mass from west to east, a natural boundary dividing the country into north and south. These mountain ranges form the upper boundaries of India's Deccan Plateau, an inverted, raised triangle, known colloquially as 'dakshin'—the Sanskrit word for south.

In late April of 2014, Ejji, Mahesh, Venkatesh and I were driving across this vast plateau. We had been on the road for over six weeks by then, having started our journey on 16 March from Chennai. During these weeks we had driven through India's Eastern Ghats, along its eastern coast and then drove to the north-east and north India, all the way to Kashmir. From there we had turned southwards, driving through Punjab, Rajasthan, Gujarat, Maharashtra and, finally, reaching northern Karnataka.

On that summer morning, as we drove out of Bijapur in north Karnataka, the sun was rising on the horizon, a fiery orb of deep amber, its rays lighting up the massive expanse of the plateau almost magically. Mahesh turned to me with the giddy expression of a joyful child and started to talk about the geological origins of the plateau.

He explained, 'The Deccan Plateau originated from Gondwanaland, a supercontinent which began to break up around 180 million years ago. The name Gondwana itself is inspired from a region inhabited by the Gond tribe in India.' This reminded me about our interaction with the Gond women on their market day in the Eastern Ghats. Mahesh continued, 'The Deccan Plateau is rich with basalt and granite rocks and boulders of all sizes and shapes. Many of the rocks and boulders can be geologically dated to 65 million years ago.'

'So, you are saying that these rocks and boulders are in a way a natural heritage of the Deccan, the Indian nation and the planet—a kind of intergenerational wealth of the local people,' I said. He nodded and continued, 'In fact, the Deccan has been the womb of India's most significant empires and dynasties. The Pallava, Chola, Satavahana, Vakataka, Pandya, Gajapati, Chalukya, Chera, Rashtrakuta, Kakatiya, Maratha and Vijayanagara empires rose and fell with the tides of time out here. These kingdoms left a civilizational heritage of epic proportions, expressed in architecture, language, dance, music, spirituality and affairs of the state. Temples, monuments, palaces and forts were made with incredible vision and passion. Many of them survive till date and tell a story of an era rich in the arts and steeped in tradition.' At this point Ejji interjected, 'And nowhere is the manifestation of this structural heritage more visible than in the ruins of the once-famed city of Hampi, the seat of the Vijayanagara empire.'

As we drove towards Hampi, Mahesh pointed to the massive boulders scattered across the landscape. He explained that it was

through the carving and chiselling of these boulders and stones that
the great monumental heritage of Hampi had been brought to life. Ejji
knew Krishna Devaraya, the nineteenth descendant of the Aravidu
dynasty which had once ruled the mighty Vijayanagara empire.
Krishna had kindly agreed to spend some time with us and take us
around Hampi. His personal story left a deep impression on me.

Krishna was raised in Hospet near Hampi. He completed his
school and college education in India. But after dabbling in an
automation business in the 1990s, Krishna left for the United
States in 2002. There he admired how certain neighbourhoods
in Washington DC did not permit the construction of modern
buildings in an effort to preserve the heritage structures in the area.
His moment of reckoning came while on a visit to Philadelphia to
meet a friend who took him to see the Liberty Bell. Krishna recollects
waiting for more than thirty minutes in the queue of visitors.
However, when he finally saw the Bell, he was pretty disappointed;
he had expected something grander. But he was impressed with
how committed Americans were in preserving their heritage. He
strongly felt that in India, and in his own ancestral city of Hampi,
there was so much history and culture worth preserving. And he
was deeply anguished that Indians thought little of conserving their
public heritage.

In 2008, Krishna's father passed away and he finally returned
for good to India. Upon his return, he decided to continue his
family traditions in Hampi and Anegundi. The archaeological sites
of Hampi are situated around the river Tungbhadra's banks and
Anegundi is located on the northern bank of the river. Krishna
settled in Hospet again and embarked on the ambitious project of
restoring his ancestral home in Anegundi. The traditional home of
the royal family—Heere Dewan Mansion is spread across 9,000
sq. ft. Initially, Krishna found it hard to hire an architect who was
willing to use the traditional lime-and-mortar technique used for the
original structure. After two years of searching, he found an architect

in Auroville and a construction expert from Mumbai who agreed to come on board. However, the process hit another snag in the tedium of getting the building plans approved by the Hampi World Heritage Area Management Authority. But Krishna persevered in his mission, and he was ultimately able to restore his ancestral home. He feels much of Anegundi and Hampi can and should be restored in this manner. No wonder, then, that Ejji insisted that we meet him in order to understand how he was resurrecting Hampi's rich heritage.

As evening approached, Krishna asked someone to take us on a walk to one of the still-standing mandapas (watchtowers.) As we climbed up a small, sparsely vegetated hillock littered with boulders, a stone mandapa came into our line of sight. It was strategically positioned for sentries of a bygone era to keep vigilance over the city. Once atop the hillock, we entered the mandapa and stood in the middle of it. Nothing could have prepared me for what I saw next. Spread as far as my eyes could see were the ruins of this once-great city of Hampi: the remnants of marketplaces, boulevards, army stores, palaces and, of course, the iconic silhouettes of Hampi's world-famous temples. The builders of Hampi had done an incredible job in weaving religion into art and art into heritage. Centuries later, the ruins stood there, still telling the stories of a time long past. Standing there, completely stunned by the architectural grandeur and audacity of this ancient city, I felt that Hampi was like a ballad sung in stone.

The next morning, Krishna invited us to visit the Heere Dewan Mansion. Krishna's grandfather, Durbar Raja Krishna Devaraya, had been the last king of Anegundi, at the time of India's Independence in 1947. By then, Anegundi was a very small jaagir (feudal land), with only ten villages. But Krishna is acutely aware and immensely proud of the fact that his forefathers ruled large areas of the Deccan more than 500 years ago. Sharing with us the tales of the very beginnings of the Vijayanagara empire and the foundation of Hampi, Krishna spoke with the pride and passion of a man who is fully aware of his own heritage and the power it has had over his life. I felt he was humble about his intergenerational legacy and was committed to passing it on to his next generation.

Krishan shared that the Vijayanagara empire was founded by the brothers Harihara I and Bukka Raya I of the Sangama dynasty in 1336 CE. Many different dynasties held its reins through the centuries. But it was Krishnadevaraya, the third ruler of the Tulava dynasty, who accorded the Vijayanagara empire and its capital Hampi a grandeur and influence that was unparalleled in the sixteenth century CE. This was a period of triumph and splendour, and it is believed that during his kingship, Hampi was the second largest city in the world after Peking (modern Beijing). Krishna Devaraya transformed Hampi with grand architecture and patronized arts of all forms. His was a golden age of artistic expression and Hampi was the chief beneficiary.

With a tinge of sadness, Krishna told us that the British took over Hampi from his ancestors in 1824, handing them a monthly pension.[1] But, despite his sadness about it, Krishna was equally delighted that the traditional linkages of the family to Hampi and Anegundi had continued regardless of the political upheavals of the subsequent centuries. He fondly remembered going to Hampi from Hospet with his father as a child and taking part in the annual Rathotsava Temple festival and also their weekly visits to the Virupaksha Temple. His father often talked about preserving the heritage and culture of the lost Vijayanagara empire, though as a child Krishna did not comprehend that idea fully.

Today Hampi is recognized as a UNESCO world heritage site. It spans approximately 41 sq. km. and has 1,600 monuments. Its majestic temples, its city ruins and its extraordinary architecture leave the visitor in complete awe. One can only imagine the days when Hampi was not merely a collection of beautiful ruins but the bustling capital of a powerful empire. Legend has it that the original scale and splendour of Hampi was such that the Bahmani invaders who fought the Vijayanagara empire had to stay in the capital city for nearly six months, just in order to burn and plunder it completely.

Hampi is now a sought-after destination for travellers who want to explore the structural arts of India. But Krishna laments the lack of passion and commitment among the various stakeholders who are in charge of Hampi and its preservation. From his time in the United States, Krishna had seen how important the role of community and local stakeholders in preserving local heritage is. He emphasized the urgency of bringing this model to Hampi—and how the local people, the government and experts needed to work together to resurrect Hampi's glorious past and restore its ruins.

Otherwise, he said, Hampi may fall into further decay and lose its appeal for tourists and art enthusiasts. This would result in a massive loss for the local economy and local employment. It would ruin the fight these monuments have put up for centuries and end their resplendent past in tragic decay. More significantly, apart from being a personal loss to Krishna, it would be a civilizational loss for India. Listening to Krishna, I could not help but feel his helplessness. I felt a strong urge to support him somehow. I told him that during one of my visits to India from the United States on a summer break from college, I had been pleasantly surprised to learn what my fellow citizens in my own city of Mumbai had done to protect their heritage and that I would be happy to introduce him to some of the key people who ideated and implemented the Mumbai 'Heritage Mile'.

The Heritage Mile

Growing up in Mumbai, I was quite aware of the relatively recent history of my city in comparison to other cities such as Delhi or Madurai. In 1999, when I was home on a college vacation, I read

an article in a local daily about how a few passionate citizens of
Mumbai had come together to protect the heritage buildings located
on Dadabhai Naoroji Road (D.N. Road).

Mumbai is one of the world's most populated cities and D.N.
Road is located in its busy Fort area. The heritage buildings that
line the road on both sides are constantly exposed to traffic—both
vehicles and people. Over the course of their time in India, the
British built the Fort area of Mumbai (then called Bombay). In
so doing, they incorporated several architectural styles from neo-
Classical, Victorian, neo-Gothic and Indo-Saracenic to Edwardian,
experimenting with materials from bricks to stone and metal. Today,
these buildings stand cheek by jowl with modern constructions and
are occupied by banks, companies, newspapers and other commercial
establishments.

The Heritage Regulation of Greater Bombay Act 1995 recognized
D.N. Road as a Grade-II A heritage streetscape, and that paved
the way for its revival and restoration. At that point in time, urban
activity, billboards and signboards threatened to swallow the original
façade and structures of these buildings. The Mumbai Metropolitan
Regional Development Authority (MMRDA) initiated the
Dadabhai Naoroji Road Heritage Streetscape Project with the
support of committed citizens. To further augment conservation
activities, a public trust by the name of MMR Heritage Conservation
Society was set up. Architect Abha Narain Lambah was requested to
lead the documentation of the buildings. Under her able leadership,
by 1999, a team of architects and several undergraduate students
were able to document these buildings.[2]

Individual shopkeepers, offices, banks and newspapers pitched in,
along with the city government, to voluntarily remove signboards
and replace and redesign the street furniture. The initial success of
this project led to the formation of the Heritage Mile Association, a
citizens' body with individuals and organizations that occupied the

D.N. Road buildings. Together with Mumbai Metropolitan Region Development Authority (MMRDA), they co-created a mechanism to raise funds, carry out restoration, revive the streetscape and ensure cleanliness and security. It was a path-breaking example of how citizens and government can work together to revive, restore and celebrate heritage, even in the busiest and most populated places. Their efforts were recognized by UNESCO, and MMRDA was awarded the Asia-Pacific Heritage Award of Merit in 2004.[3]

Thus, a public–private partnership between local community, heritage conservation experts, architects, urban planners, students and the government administration transformed D.N. Road into what it is fondly called today—The Heritage Mile.

As you stroll down the iconic Heritage Mile from its northern end at Crawford Market to its southern end at Flora Fountain, you come to realize what a massive task this committed group of citizens and public officials took up and what an achievement it was to have succeeded on the scale that they did. Each building on the Heritage Mile now bears a small navy-blue plank with gold letters at its entrance, describing the history of the building. Shops operate and sell everything from clothes to laptops; street vendors sell books and newspapers, and the cacophony of busy traffic is on through the day. In fact, the Heritage Mile Walk is part of several walking tours of Mumbai, with guides regaling visitors with interesting anecdotes about the heritage buildings and their erstwhile occupants. It is also wonderful to see that many of those signing up for the walking tours are citizens of Mumbai themselves.

Mumbai has been fortunate to have this kind of involved and aware citizens' action. Mumbaikars, as the citizens of Mumbai are popularly known, chose to collectively preserve, sustain and celebrate their intergenerational wealth. They chose to activate their power of heritage. I suggested to Krishna that he too could do the same in Hampi. He could call upon his power of heritage to convene like-minded stakeholders to begin conversations for restoration and conservation of Hampi. His ancestry could be his biggest ally in the process, and his modern education and exposure to the world would come to his aid as well. If Hampi, like Mumbai, is able to restore its collective heritage through a participative public–private effort, then we will have a unique model for heritage conservation and continuity in the country. In Hampi's case, the basics are already in place as there are local authorities, interested experts and a strong local community leadership of people like Krishna. However, for many other historic monuments across India, the story is very different. Despite India's incredible heritage and the power this intergenerational wealth has over our way of life, the country faces a loss of vision, direction and action when it comes to preservation of its heritage.

Mysterious Unakoti

The dense jungles of Tripura, India's third smallest state bordering Bangladesh in the north-east, hide many a secret. These thickly forested hills are shrouded in mystery. One such spectacular mystery is the site of the Unakoti bas-reliefs. Located in the north of Tripura and approximately 178 km from the state capital Agartala, Unakoti is often regarded by avid travellers as the Machu Pichhu of India.

While on the north-east leg of our trip in 2014, I suggested to Ejji and Mahesh that we meet with Pradyot Bikram Manikya Deb Barma, the current head of the Tripura royal family. Pradyot belongs to the Manikya dynasty, which had ruled the erstwhile kingdom of Tripura since the early fifteenth century. I had met him several times earlier at the Young Leaders Connect conference and also in Shillong, Meghalaya, where he has a home.

As we drove from Meghalaya to Tripura, we discovered that the roads were in a terrible condition. It was already dusk and reaching Agartala before nightfall was looking nearly impossible. Pradyot suggested that instead of coming to Agartala to meet him, we stop for the night at Kailas Sahar and visit Unakoti, which was nearby. Even though Ejji, Mahesh and I had spent so much time in the North-east earlier, none of us had heard of Unakoti. Therefore, we decided to take Pradyot's advice. Since the only local tourist housing provided by the state government was already full, we stopped at a trucker's lodge for the night.

The next morning, we rose early and set out for Unakoti. The entrance to the site had a worn-out board giving an overview of its history, stating that it is under the protection of the Archaeological Survey of India (ASI). As we walked down the half-broken concrete steps to the site, the tree cover gave way to the gigantic faces and images of Hindu gods and goddesses carved out of the rocky surface of the hills themselves.

The Unakoti bas-reliefs date back to between the seventh and ninth centuries CE or even earlier,[4] when ancient Tripura was under the rule of what was ancient Bengal. Indeed, Unakoti itself is a Bengali word, meaning one less than 1 crore or 10 million. According to the Rajmala, the royal chronology of Tripura,[5] the origins of Unakoti are shrouded in a mysterious tale. Legend has it that the god Shiva was on his way to his abode in Kashi (some versions have it as Kailash) with 99,99,999 gods and goddesses. The entourage stopped over at Unakoti for the night. Shiva asked everyone to wake up before dawn so that they could cover the distance to their destination faster. The next morning, finding that no one had woken up, an angry Shiva cursed them, turning them to stone. Thus, the Unakoti bas-reliefs came into existence. Obviously, there must have been a historical human endeavour that resulted in these carvings, but no such record exists and so the legend takes prominence.

The most striking of the reliefs is the 30-foot-tall face of Shiva himself, known as Unakotishwara Kal Bhairava. It is considered to be the largest bas-relief of Shiva in India depicting only his face. Mahesh and I stood mesmerized by the sheer scale of the Shiva bas-relief, whilst Ejji was busy spotting other reliefs. The site has three enormous carvings of Lord Ganesh, over which a waterfall gushes into a pond. At other places, there are life-sized images of goddesses carved on the rocks. The bas-reliefs bear a unique resemblance to the local tribal traditions of decoration and anatomy and stand out from concurrent architectural styles of those times in other parts of India. There are many carvings that have only been partly recovered and quite a few are in mutilated condition. The locals say that Unakoti has been a pilgrimage centre for Shiva devotees for centuries. We saw local Tiprasa families worshipping the main bas-relief of Shiva at the site and we also ran into a few tantric yogis meditating in some nooks in the vast area. But, apart from these few people, the site was desolate.

On our way from Unakoti to Aizawl in Mizoram, we kept discussing how incredible the bas-reliefs were. We wished we had an entire day to explore them. Mahesh was also livid at the mismanagement of the site by the ASI. But Ejji insisted that Unakoti would only get its due when the locals took full ownership of their own heritage. He felt that their just performing rituals at the site was not enough. Unakoti needs further excavation, restoration and maintenance. For a monument to be maintained well, it needs funds. We were told that some funds had been set aside for Unakoti's preservation by the state government. But we felt that such efforts could not make up for the callous attitude with which successive governments at both the Union and state levels have dealt with this extraordinary heritage of the people of Tripura.

We pondered on the question of whether more tourist footfalls could change the fortunes of Unakoti. It could possibly help the local economy, for one. The local community could be trained to run homestays and to work as guides at the site. But, as Mahesh was quick to point out, an excess of tourists can also endanger a heritage site. The question of the best approach to ensure optimal management of heritage sites and monuments, and the importance of engaging local communities in the process, kept us occupied for some time. However, we wouldn't get a clear answer to our questions until after a few weeks, when we reached Jaisalmer.

The Collapse at Jaisalmer

The state of Rajasthan has been a tourism attraction for decades. Its palaces and forts, and its colourful folk arts, lure tourists to the state from within and outside the country. The 'Golden Fort' of its western frontier town, Jaisalmer, is a case in point, where tourism has become a bane for the more than 850 years old structure. Touted as a 'living fort', the citadel has homes, hotels, palaces and markets functioning inside its walls with 4,000 plus occupants! Tourists come to see the fort's sandstone walls light up with golden sunshine, matching the vast sand dunes of the Thar Desert that encircle the town.

When we were there, a few local youngsters explained the challenges of heritage preservation in Jaisalmer to us. High footfalls put huge pressure on the sandstone structure. Tourism also encourages greed to manifest into illegal hotel constructions. Overlapping of jurisdiction further complicate the life of this ancient monument. The external walls of the fort, for instance, come under the ASI, but the inside of the fort comes under the local district management and municipal corporation.[6] These organizations do not work in coordination. The badly planned sewage system drains the water into the fort walls, leading to a situation verging on complete collapse. Indeed, seventeen of the fort's ninety-nine bastions have already crumbled, while many others are propped up by illegal and unsafe structures. As a result of this thoughtless planning, this ancient citadel has weakened considerably.

To add to the miseries of this structure, climate change is further weakening it. Rawal Jaisal's workers built the fort and many of its

interiors in the twelfth century CE, with the burning summers of
the Thar Desert in mind. They topped most of the buildings with
mud, nearly 3 feet deep, in order to insulate the interiors against the
heat. Climate change now brings excessive rains, which turn those
same roofs into sludge, causing entire buildings to collapse.[7] More
than eighty-seven structures inside the fort have already succumbed
to the onslaught of both man and nature. To our surprise, we
learnt it was the local community that rose up to protect their
own heritage. They came together to stop illegal construction
inside the fort. Much like the citizens of Mumbai or like Krishna
at Hampi, this community was trying to bridge the gap between
their ancestral heritage and their modern needs, fully aware that the
power of their heritage and their deep-rooted bonds with it made
this a worthwhile endeavour.

As I listened to the young volunteers at Jaisalmer telling me
about the challenges they faced in protecting their beloved fort, it
occurred to me that India's power of heritage symbolizes India's
intergenerational wealth and legacy. This intergenerational wealth,
legacy and heritage are a kind of our intergenerational equity.
What do I mean by that? Intergenerational equity is a concept
that rests in the idea of fairness and justice between generations.
Nurturing our heritage, restoring it and allowing for its continuity
is to ensure that future generations are not lacking in knowledge of
their roots. Our neglect towards our collective heritage can amount
to being unfair and unjust to our future generations and will risk
breaking the continuum of our civilization and the bequest of our
intergenerational equity.

Strengthening Our Roots

Indians value their personal heritage immensely. Stories and objects
of our ancestry have a special place in our psyche. Don't we all have

that one sari, painting, carpet, book or piece of old furniture that we inherited from our ancestors and which we hold very dear? Every Indian household will have stories of its own family heritage. Every village will have its own traditions around its monuments or crafts. Every region or state will have its own unique civilizational heritage. The sheer diversity of India's heritage attracts people from across the world. Travellers of the past and present continue to marvel at the continuity of our civilization and the grandeur of our heritage.

Our deep connection with our heritage and the stories that are woven around it also give us a unique power: the power of knowing who we are and where we come from. This *Power of Heritage* gives us the exclusive identity we enjoy as an ancient people who value traditions and foster civilizational continuity. When we live out this power to its full potential, we recognize and celebrate our roots and the very foundations on which our way of life is built.

In fact, every object or monument of heritage is a fulcrum of stories and ideas that define the community that inherited it. Therefore, when communities come together to protect their collective heritage, they pay unconscious tribute to the legends that define them. Even by performing simple daily rituals at Unakoti, I felt the Tiprasa were keeping their heritage alive. In a way, they were deepening their roots so that future generations could continue to benefit from their ancestral past. If our power of heritage is harnessed appropriately, it can generate employment and enrich our civilizational legacy, in the same way as it has done for the dwellers of the Jaisalmer fort—and as it could for the people of Tripura who live near Unakoti. It can give us the impetus to convene the way the citizens of Mumbai did for the Heritage Mile and inspire individuals like Krishna to reclaim their roots. It can allow us to foster our intergenerational equity with modern-day tools.

In fact, Article 51 A(f) of the Indian Constitution provides for this when it says: 'It shall be the duty of every citizen of India to value and preserve the rich heritage of our composite culture.'[8] But when entire communities are disengaged from their own heritage, a certain apathy sets in when it comes to preserving, restoring and celebrating that heritage, whether it comes in the shape of a monument, craft or art. This is the difficulty that Krishna is trying to resolve at Hampi. But even in the case of the more famous monuments of India, such as the Rajgir walls or the Qutub Minar, one finds evidence of pervasive disregard. Graffiti finds an open canvas on the palace walls of Rajasthan's grand Rajput homes and pilferage continues at the archaeologically seminal sites of the Indus civilization. Many forts succumb to even greater disregard and become spots for alcohol and drug addicts to gather. Temples, if still functioning, are spared the horror of mutilation. This is baffling for a nation that takes great public pride in its ancient civilizational heritage.

Some would argue that all this is the responsibility of the government. The governments, at the Union and state levels, are bound by Article 49 of the Indian Constitution, which states: 'It shall be the obligation of the State to protect every monument or place or object of artistic or historic interest, (declared by or under law made by Parliament) to be of national importance, from spoliation, disfigurement, destruction, removal, disposal or export, as the case may be.'[9] Apart from the ASI, which is funded by the Union ministry of culture, there are several state-level authorities specifically dedicated to heritage sites such as Hampi. But they seem to lack resources, in terms of skilled people and funds. Often, they lack a larger vision for the cultural and modern-day continuity of the monument(s) they protect. In fact, most of the laws that concern our heritage have chosen to pay only lip service to the role of community in preservation of our heritage. As citizens, we have also not created platforms for wider community engagement like the Heritage Mile Association. This has resulted in sites such as Unakoti being forgotten, discarded as relics of the past instead of being celebrated as living, breathing pieces of our continued civilization.

The ASI only covers 3,691 monuments of 'national importance', and only those that are more than 100 years old. A report in 2014 by the Controller and Auditor General of India (CAG) held the ASI accountable for the disappearance of ninety-two of the 1,655 monuments that were surveyed in the audit.[10] It is believed this number would be higher if all 3,691 moments under the custody of the ASI were to be surveyed! The government is considering expansion of the list of monuments under the ASI and the Union government's purview.[11] But, given the large quantum of India's monumental and structural art, we are destined to lose many of these to climate change, pollution, encroachment, et al, unless all of us follow the example of the Heritage Mile Association.

On our way from Hampi to Goa, Ejji pointed out to me that the success of Mumbai's Heritage Mile was possible because the local government had also shown an interest in the project and had taken some initiative. But what would happen to the monuments in those areas where there was neither government nor political support for their preservation? I told him of the incredible story of community-led heritage revival I had come across during one of my visits to Leh, the capital of Ladakh, and how it had made me believe that just as the heritage of a people had anchored their community to its past, that community could be an anchor for its heritage in the present.

The LAMO Way

As you walk up the old town in Leh towards the Lachen Palkar (Leh palace), a small pathway down from the main road leads you to the Ladakh Arts and Media Organisation (LAMO) Centre. It consists of two historical houses restored by LAMO, which have been converted into a space with art galleries, offices, a library and

reading room, a screening room, a conference room and an open-
air performance site. The Centre conducts outreach programmes,
lectures, film screenings, research and documentation projects,
and workshops and exhibitions that showcase Ladakh's culture,
performing arts and literature.[12]

In 2011, while visiting Ladakh for a visioning exercise for the
erstwhile state of Jammu and Kashmir, I came across LAMO. One
of the two houses where the Centre runs, earlier belonged to a
Munshi family who were ministers to the king. In early 2000s, the
British conservation architect John Harrison who has been involved
in restoration activities in the Himalaya since 1985, introduced
Monisha Ahmed, Co-founder of LAMO, to the Munshi family.[13]
The Munshis had lived for several generations in this seventeenth-
century home but had now moved to other areas of Leh in order
to access modern amenities. Since the Munshi family's departure
from the main building, the house had been occupied by a caretaker,
but otherwise it lay virtually abandoned. The area around the house
was filthy with dumped garbage, human and animal waste. Many
rooms had fallen into disrepair and in some places the roof had caved
in. But vestiges of its external beauty, especially its lovely wooden
balconies, remained. A year into its restoration, Stanzin Gyaltsen of
the adjoining Gyaoo house contacted LAMO for the restoration of
his family home as well.

LAMO intended to demonstrate the resurrection of a heritage
building in order to bring it back to life for the community. Monisha
Ahmed and her team at LAMO were able to restore the Munshi and
Gyaoo houses in a manner where they were not merely reminders
of the past, but could also play a role in anchoring arts and allied
interests for the local community.

The LAMO Centre is especially attractive to the local youth as
they feel they have a space to express themselves artistically. When I
visited, there were paintings done by young children on a mud wall

of a passage in the building. These children had definite ideas about how they wanted to see their town of Leh develop. The Centre also houses exhibits of contemporary modern art by Ladakhi artists. LAMO organizes art workshops, and digital tools are integral to their work. During my visit, I saw young local women sitting with laptops and working on something intently. Behind them, the intricately carved seventeenth-century balcony with its wooden frame provided a view of both the old and new parts of Leh town. It felt surreal to see these women at complete ease with their heritage. I felt elated to see intergenerational equity being passed on, right in front of my eyes. LAMO had managed to claim the intergenerational legacy of the local people by restoring the houses, and the people of Leh, who engaged with the Centre, were ensuring that it was passed on to the next generation.

When it began, LAMO wanted to prove that a twenty-first-century public space could be created inside a heritage structure, and I feel they have succeeded with aplomb. LAMO has been working with the local government and communities to make them aware of the historical importance of the old Leh town for Ladakhis. The reason LAMO is so unique is that it doesn't differentiate between the arts of the past and the arts of the present, and gives equal space to both. In its ability to see the present as a continuum of the past and the future as the next page of the story, LAMO achieves what many have failed to do. It has brought together community, artists and experts to live their heritage and not just merely protect it. It has proved that when local communities take leadership, either with or without government support, then spaces such as LAMO can rekindle and strengthen the bonds that communities share with their collective heritage. It has proved that our collective power of heritage and our intergenerational equity is ours to claim, nurture and pass on. We have only to figure out the tools by which to do so.

The real joy of preserving a heritage structure or restoring a painting lies in sharing it and passing it on to the next generation. Indian families have tremendous respect for their ancestral homes, furniture, heirloom textiles, paintings, artefacts, utensils and rituals. Why should these not be celebrated and shared with the world through local efforts like LAMO? The power of heritage is truly experienced when our personal heritage and collective heritage are interwoven to create lasting imprints of our civilization.

Peoples' Museum

Apart from using the space for activities, the restored houses where LAMO operates also give visitors a peek into the traditional Ladakhi way of life. In a way, LAMO also serves the purpose of a living museum. It has an old Ladakhi kitchen with traditional utensils, old yak horns and door frames. Walking through the Centre, one clearly gets a feel of how a Ladakhi family must have lived in the seventeenth and eighteenth centuries. LAMO is therefore also serving the purpose of being a capsule of time so that Ladakhis themselves, as well as tourists, can have a glimpse of the past of this region and its peoples. In a way, it is a 'peoples' museum'.

LAMO reminded me of my visit to the house of Albert Einstein, my hero from the world of physics, in Bern, Switzerland, in 2005. The house is now a museum, but Einstein lived there when he was working at the local patent office. This was where he came up with the idea of the Theory of Relativity. As a visitor, one gets to walk through this restored house-museum, which has photos and other memorabilia. The lighting is perfect, enough for one to see by but not so strong that it might damage the objects on display. There are self-guided audio tools and brochures for visitors. The signage is illustrative but not obstructive. All-in-all, it transports one back in time and gives one a feel of what it must have been like when Einstein was living there.

Walking through the restored houses in Ladakh, I felt LAMO too had diligently used natural lighting to give visitors the warm feeling of walking through a home. They have used furniture that blends with the architectural style of the houses they have restored. Perhaps they don't have the access to the technology and funds on the same scale as the Einstein house-museum in Bern might have, but they have certainly made a laudable attempt. But I feel that many museums in India are managed with such apathy and lack of interest that visitors walk out feeling more frustrated than impressed. An example is the Indian Museum in Kolkata.

The Indian Museum in Kolkata is the oldest museum in India, established in 1814. It is also the largest, with over 1,00,000 artefacts in its collection, six sections and thirty-five galleries. Earlier known as the Imperial Museum of India, it also has the distinction of being the ninth oldest museum in the world.[14] But while it may be one of the oldest museums in the world, it is certainly not in the list of top twenty most visited. In 2017, when I visited it for the first time, I could understand why. Upon disembarking from the yellow Ambassador cab at the entrance of the museum, I had to struggle with the lack of tourist-friendly ticketing. Once I made it past the entrance, the museum enthralled me with its collection, only to disappoint me with its lack of interactive information tools and unfriendly floor plans for a walk-through. I empathized with it for its lack for funds and resources. I could not help but feel sorry for the few exceptional people who continue to strive to make a visit to this museum a more pleasant experience. Nevertheless, when I walked out after a few hours, I felt disenchanted.

India has close to 1,000 museums which house artefacts from our rich, ancient civilization.[15] From bronze, copper and marble objects to textiles and paintings of varied styles on canvas and cloth, and ancient manuscripts, there is so much of our heritage that is not structural in nature. Many of these items can be moved and kept in museums as capsules of our glorious past. Unfortunately, and because they were portable, many of them were taken by the British during colonial times to museums in England in large numbers. There has also been rampant theft of many of these artefacts post-Independence for sale to art and antique collectors across the world. Of whatever remains, sadly, India's museums continue to struggle to preserve artefacts from our past even today. Also, for most Indians, the experience of visiting a museum is limited to a school trip.

There is an opinion that our callous attitude towards our museums has its roots in our in-built belief in the impermanence of everything, because of which we think that everything is transitory. This is far from the truth. Tradition and heritage are twin strands of our DNA. The truth is that Indians value heritage greatly. There is immense power in our ability to connect to our heritage and we carry it with us wherever we go. Across the world, the Indian diaspora is involved in building temples, or in pursuing Indian classical music and dance, and of course in following Indian spiritual teachings. This would not happen if we did not value our heritage. But, just like our monuments, our museums too have been kept apart from the very communities they are located amongst. Whenever there has been involvement on the part of citizens, museums tend to do well. For example, Mumbai's Chhatrapati Shivaji Maharaj Vastu Sangrahalaya (CSMVS) is largely run by private donations from citizens. In 2007, Sabyasachi Mukherjee, a well-known museology expert, was appointed as its director general and secretary. He brought much-needed attention to the exhibits and walk-throughs using technology and design principles and forged partnerships with international museums, increasing the annual footfalls multi-fold.[16] The CSMVS is quite unique in its very genesis as it was a 'peoples' museum' from the very beginning. A few prominent citizens of Mumbai had come together in 1904 to propagate the idea of a museum, and in 1922 the museum was established. This year as India celebrates seventy-five years of Independence, the CSMVS is celebrating its centennial year.[17]

There are also private museums, like the Kiran Nadar Museum of Art in Delhi, the Piramal Museum of Art in Mumbai and the Kasturbhai Lalbhai Museum in Ahmedabad, whose patrons have brought out their personal collections for public viewing. They also provide space and opportunity for other collections and contemporary artistes. These private museums have, in fact, expanded the traditional role of a museum into being an anchor for the arts in society.[18] Then there are notable public efforts like the Gandhi Smriti in New Delhi, the Sabarmati Ashram in Ahmedabad and Mani Bhavan in Mumbai, which give us a glimpse into the life of Mahatma Gandhi.

Technology now makes it possible for organizations such as The Heritage Lab to focus on making India's museums more accessible and engaging. These organizations are making museums accessible digitally so as to generate wider public interest in them.[19] They use interactive tools like games, puzzles, social media and creative competitions to attract attention to and celebrate India's heritage. Organizations such as the Bengaluru-based Rereeti even take exhibitions to schools to create better awareness of the country's heritage among children.[20] The private sector not only brings funds but also brings ideas, skills and knowledge to India's museums. But it is keen interest from communities and citizens that is the life force for bringing these capsules of time alive. Think about it. When was the last time you visited a museum in India?

In the small Himalayan hamlet of Munsyari, where Alok and I now live for the most part of the year, there is a small museum. Started by noted historian and author Sher Singh Pangtey, the Tribal Heritage Museum of Munsyari is a three-room endeavour.

It showcases the history, culture, traditions and lifestyle of the Bhotia/Shauka people, an ethno-linguistic group residing in the upper Himalayan valleys. Before its establishment in the year 2000, Pangtey spent several years travelling to local villages in the higher Himalayan valleys for collecting artefacts, utensils, clothes, tools used in daily life, documents and other memorabilia. He then carefully curated it all. When you enter the museum—housed in an old home built in the local Kumaoni style—the receptionist behind a small counter starts an audio tape in Hindi. As you walk past the displayed items from the daily lives of the Bhotia/Shauka community, the recording gives you information about the objects displayed. There are even life-sized human dolls in traditional clothing. The jewellery of the local women and other decorative items are also on display. One wall displays the local herbs, grains and legumes of the area. The second room of the museum has old maps and trade agreements made between the Bhotia/Shauka and the Tibetans, who traded with each other until the Indo-China War of 1962.

In his small but committed way, Sher Singh Pangtey has shown that if we want to connect with our powerful heritage, we have only to have the intention and dedication. He took no support from the government and took the effort to visit the villages to collate items for the museum. I feel proud of the villagers too, who partook in his venture by donating their own personal heritage so that their collective heritage as a people could be preserved, shared and celebrated. What a marvellous way to pass on intergenerational equity! Communities are not just important but are the essential core when it comes to preservation of heritage. The LAMO way is a great way. If citizens can access local government support, as the Heritage Mile Association did, that would, of course, be ideal. In the (more likely) absence of government support, citizens can start on their own, as Krishna has in Hampi. Like heritage monuments, museums too thrive when they belong to the community and when they are in truest sense peoples' museums, like the Tribal Heritage Museum of Munsyari.

The Manganiars of Hamira

When I first met my Aspen co-fellow Mukti Datta at her home in Kasardevi, I was impressed by the fact that her mother, a French-Belgian, had come down to India in the 1950s to document the songs and ballads of the Kumaoni people for UNESCO and travelled across the region to do so. She had even documented the famous ballad '*Rajula-Malushahi*', a love story about a Shauka princess called Rajula and a Katyuri prince, Malushahi. During my visit to the Tribal Heritage Museum started by Pangtey, I thought how lovely it would be if there was a room in this building where local people could engage in their traditional arts and women could sing ballads like the '*Rajula-Malushahi*' for visitors. It made me think about how India's intangible heritage is wider, deeper and even older than its tangible heritage.

The tradition of Vedic chanting; the Ramlila performances of the Ramayana; the Koodiyattam Sanskrit theatre; Ramman, the religious festival and ritual of Garhwal, Uttarakhand; Mudiyettu, the dance-drama form from Kerala; the Chhau dance of West Bengal and Jharkhand; Buddhist chanting from Ladakh; the Kalbelia folk songs of Rajasthan; the traditional brass and copper crafts of the Thatheras of Jadiala Guru, Punjab; the Sankirtana of Manipur; Nowruz, the New Year of the Parsis; Durga Pooja celebrations in Kolkata; Yoga and the Kumbh Mela … all have been included in UNESCO's global list of the intangible cultural heritage of humanity.

In addition to the UNESCO list, Indian ministry of culture has decided to further include diverse intangible heritage from across the country in its National List of Intangible Cultural Heritage (ICH). From the Kalamkari paintings of Andhra Pradesh to the Shamanic

songs of Arunachal Pradesh and the Kinnar Kanthgeet of the
transgender communities of Delhi, the list is exhaustive and is still
being expanded.[21] The hope is that this will lead to the protection,
celebration and continuity of these traditions.

Conventionally, many of these arts, crafts and traditions
were passed on from one generation to the next in a family as
intergenerational equity of sorts. They chiefly received patronage
from royalty, spiritual and religious institutions, and wealthy patrons
who cared for their continuity. But in the past century, this support
has been dwindling, and in many cases is no longer available. Artists
and craftspersons are struggling to make ends meet and their children
are choosing to leave the traditional occupation of the family for
better avenues. I became more conversant about the struggle of these
communities when, during our visit to Jaisalmer, Mahesh's friend,
Prakash Detha, a Rajasthani folk traditions expert, took us to meet
the family of Sakar Khan.

Sakar Khan, of the Manganiar community of Rajasthan, was
awarded the Padma Shri—India's fourth highest civilian honour—
in 2012 for taking the traditional music of his community to global
audiences. He hails from the village of Hamira near Jaisalmer. As we
left the hubbub of the main city of Jaisalmer and drove through the
burning sands of the Thar Desert, Hamira emerged on the horizon
approximately 25 km later. Sakar Khan lived here with his family
until his death in 2013, doing the only things he knew: singing and
playing the kamaicha, the Rajasthani version of the Persian musical
instrument of a similar-sounding name.

The Manganiars are a community known for their musical
traditions. Sakar's father too was a well-known kamaicha player and
all his sons and grandsons also sing and play musical instruments. A
kamaicha is almost like a rabab. It is a string instrument consisting
of a goatskin-covered body and three or four main strings and over

fourteen sympathetic strings. The Manganiars have been singing for centuries, and their songs are passed on from one generation to the next. The songs narrate the stories of the desert and its long history, its warrior princes and beautiful queens. Then there are devotional songs that tell the story of the Hindu god Krishna and describe episodes from his life. For the Manganiars, music is part of their existence and their life, whether on stage or at home.

When we reached his home in Hamira, Sakar Khan's sons welcomed us in their humble sandstone abode. We were invited to sit on a cot in the open front yard, while Khan's sons laid carpets on a small platform and began tuning their instruments. As the sun set on the dunes of the Thar Desert, three generations of Manganiar men began to indulge us with their traditional art. The kamaicha led the way, accompanied by the dholak, shehnai and khartaal (a type of castanets). The singing slowly began and we were transported to an era when Rajput kings fought gallantly for the cause of their land, their people and their pride. These royals were the earliest patrons of the Manganiars. As times changed, wealthy merchants also started supporting their art. But Sakar Khan knew that unless he took his family's music tradition to the world, it would die and the livelihood of the family would cease. Therefore, he went out into the world, performing with Grammy Award-winning artists and lending the melody of his kamaicha to the music of the world.

A lot needs to be done for the artists, craftspersons and practitioners of our many traditions. There are some great examples of individuals, organizations and communities that have taken a lead in creating spaces and festivals that celebrate India's vast intangible heritage and make it relevant for our youth, but the one that stands out for me is the Hornbill Festival of the Nagas.

The Festival of Festivals

The north-eastern state of Nagaland is home to different tribes. All of these tribes have their own ways of dressing, eating, speaking, dancing, singing and celebrating. Being predominantly an agricultural state, most of the festivals of the tribes here are agriculture-related. Different festivals happen at different times of the year and the tribes are spread across the state. It would take an entire year for a visitor to fully comprehend the Naga culture and all its traditions.

Nagaland has experienced armed conflict and insurgency for years and therefore has had significant challenges in attracting tourists. In the year 2000, the state government decided to address this by organizing the Hornbill Festival. Named after the great Indian hornbill, a bird that features in the tribal folklore of Nagaland, this is a festival for which all the Naga tribes gather. Dance and music are performed by every tribe; a tourist can savour food from every corner of the state and buy handicrafts from different tribal stalls. Over the years, prime ministers, foreign ambassadors and Union cabinet ministers have inaugurated this festival of vibrant colours, foot-thumping music and mouth-watering Naga food. It begins every year on December 1 and ends on December 10. It is now touted as the 'Festival of Festivals'.

The Hornbill Festival has brought large tourist footfalls to the state and has also helped restore cultural pride among the Naga youth. As you walk around the Naga heritage village of Kisama, the venue of the festival, the bold and bright colours of the various Naga tribes enliven the mountainous winter landscape. The vast cultural heritage of the Naga people is curated and beautifully presented to outsiders. Young men and women from the various Naga tribes participate in the festival, which has now become part of Naga tradition. The local people look forward to it as it not only brings economic benefits and but also generates cultural pride among them. The artists love it as they get a platform to showcase their talents.

Many state governments across India have been trying to revive their traditional cultural festivals in order to attract tourists and boost livelihoods. But Nagaland is special and noteworthy in having created an entirely new festival that harnesses the culture of the state to attract tourists and generate livelihoods. It has called its power of heritage to action, created new ways for the old ways to continue, and is passing on its people's intergenerational equity with élan.

The Heritage Mile Association and the Hornbill Festival are great examples of how efforts to invigorate our heritage can happen at scale. But to do justice to our power of heritage, we will need to raise funds and create capacity, even in terms of skills. Vinod Daniel is the Chairman of AusHeritage and the only person of Indian origin to be on the board of the Paris-based International Council of Museums (ICOM), an apex body representing over 43,000 museum professionals and 20,000 museums from over 140 countries. He spends a few weeks in India every year to give his time pro-bono to the country's marquee museums. He sums up India's skill and knowledge gap in the field aptly when he says, 'India, if it wants to be self-sufficient in conserving its collection, needs a pyramid model with 1,000 people on top who are degree holders with good analytical skills; and a cadre of 9,000 conservation technicians with a diploma or certificate, working on specialized categories, be it wall painting, metals or textiles. Every state should have people at both these levels. Unfortunately, we don't have more than 200 in the top-end category and not more than 500 in the second.'[22]

Due to lack of awareness and skills, many Indians remain unaware of the opportunities in the fields of conservation, restoration, museology and antiquity. The career path is not clear and there is information blindness about this field in the society at large. LiveHistoryIndia, founded by journalist Mini Menon, is an excellent example of how modern media can create awareness on a mass scale about our history, heritage and culture.[23] The platform is committed to bringing India's history alive through research, storytelling and visuals. Through its social and digital presence, it dives into India's rich heritage and helps bring awareness about it to a large number of people.

Skills, finance, awareness, government, corporate, and pro-bono efforts, can all fail if there is no initiative from communities to anchor the monuments, museums and traditional arts and crafts they have inherited. As we have seen in the case of LAMO, the Hornbill Festival and the Heritage Mile, if there is purposeful engagement from communities, then, more often than not, all else follows in train. If there is leadership and passion in each one of us to protect and resurrect our power of heritage, as Krishna Devaraya of Hampi, Sher Singh Pangtey of Munsyari and Sakar Khan of Hamira have shown, then nothing is impossible. Our power of heritage is our intergenerational equity, and passing it on is not just our privilege but also our obligation to future generations.

Lawrence of Arunachal

Lawrence Koj hails from the state of Arunachal Pradesh. His ancestors were followers of the Donyi Polo path of nature worship. He is now a Christian by faith. His home state has tribes and clans of different kind, who speak different dialects and practise unique traditions. Lawrence attends church but also continues to participate in his tribal traditions. He is also the 'chief volunteer worker' for the world's tallest naturally formed Shivling—a monolithic representation of the Hindu God, Shiva.

In 2014, as we were driving from the north bank of the mighty Brahmaputra through mountains covered with thick jungles and gushing waterfalls, Mahesh informed us that Lawrence was coming to meet us from Itanagar, the state capital. We were on our way to Ziro in the Lower Subansiri district of Arunachal Pradesh. The Ziro Valley is home to the Apatani tribe, which continues to follow nature worship and other tribal traditions. After reaching Ziro and interacting with the Apatani natives, we met Lawrence at a local home.[24] A fire burnt in the traditional kitchen of the small Apatani hut, but there was no electricity. By the dim light of a furnace, Lawrence began to share how he came to be associated with the world's tallest Shivling.

In the village of Kardo in Ziro Valley, on a piece of farmland owned by a local man called Nada Buda, stands a 25-foot-tall naturally formed Shivling. Its discovery was accidental. In 2004, while trying to cut a tree, a local labourer found it. Hindu priests were called from the main town to ascertain what had been discovered. Subsequently, a committee was formed for the protection and consecration of the Shivling. Describing the process of restoring this Shivling, Lawrence excitedly explained how he and the committee members had visited different temples in India, including one at Rameshwaram on the southern tip of India, approximately 3,500 km away. They met with experts and discussed a way forward for the Shivling and the entire lingalayam. They brought 108 priests to Kardo for prayers and for consecration of the linga. Thus, this naturally formed and accidentally discovered Shivling became Shree Sidheshwar Nath Temple.

When prodded about his own belief in nature worship and in Christianity and how it may have clashed with the Hindu worship of the Shivling, Lawrence answered with ease and authenticity. He said, 'First and foremost, the Shivling is found here, so it is part of our collective heritage.' He also explained that there are common threads running through all three faiths. He pointed out that Donyi Polo, Christianity and Shiva worship are ultimately all about meditating and connecting with the Almighty. It was heartening to see how in a small village, in a far-off corner of the country, a group of people from different faiths had come together to protect and resurrect their collective heritage. They did so without any force or invitation by any state actors. They did so of their own accord and put in the time and resources to ensure that they left no stone unturned (metaphorically speaking!) in the rightful resurrection of their discovery. This was possible because they value heritage: their own and those of others. It is evident that they consider their heritage as a powerful force for societal good and recognize it as their collective intergenerational equity.

There is an acute need for a national vision combined with local action if we are to do justice to our country's magnificent heritage. Our power of heritage can only be enhanced if we break the barriers between public and private and join hands to rescue our monuments from decay, create engaging experiences in our museums, continue to celebrate our cultural traditions and preserve our arts and crafts. This cooperation between state and citizen can help create a way forward for passing on our collective heritage as intergenerational equity to our future generations.

India has a unique position in the world. It has managed to nurture and continue its way of living for more than 10,000 years. It has been able to nourish its traditions despite invasions and cultural assimilations. The river of civilization continues to flow through the ravines of time. This is our superpower. Every generation has only added to this power of heritage and it is our turn now to protect it and pass it on.

5

Power of Creativity

Majuli

We were standing on the south bank of the mighty Brahmaputra, near Jorhat in Assam. The river flows through the state of Assam, splitting the land into twin shores—the north bank and the south bank. A rickety barge was anchored to a sandy patch on the shore. Ejji and Mahesh were in an intense discussion with the barge operator on how to load our black Mahindra Scorpio onto it without making the entire thing unstable. Venkat was filming people and other boats on the river, and I was searching the horizon for a glimpse of our destination that day—Majuli, one of the largest inhabited river islands in the world.

In 2014, when we crossed the Coronation Bridge over the Teesta river and entered north-east India, Mahesh had insisted that at some point we must visit Majuli, home to some of the oldest satras of Assam. Satras are institutions founded in the Ekasarana tradition of Vaishnavism, unique to Assam. There are hundreds of satras in the state today, where rituals of daily worship and monastic life and cultural programmes are conducted. They were first founded in Majuli in the sixteenth-century CE by Srimanta Sankaradeva, a social reformer of Assam.

The barge finally sailed. The Mahindra Scorpio—which we had fondly named The Beast—had been loaded onto it. I sat in the Beast through the ride, as the balance of weight in the vehicle had to be maintained so as not to tilt the barge. Mahesh and Venkat stood on the edge of the barge, filming the massive expanse of the Brahmaputra. Ejji leaned on a bike with an orange life jacket firmly fastened over his chest. He had been told these barges have a high probability of overturning, and he wasn't going to risk his life! As we approached Majuli, a white sand beach came into sight. When we disembarked, we saw, to our pleasant surprise, that the island was lush green and densely vegetated. Mahesh had arranged for us to stay in a local hotel, which was built out of bamboo in the traditional style of the homes of the Mising tribe (there is a sizeable number that lives on the island).

After freshening up, Ejji, Mahesh and I set out to visit the satras. A single-lane road lined with farm fields led us to the first one—the Dakshinpat Satra. We walked towards the main prayer hall, known as namghar or kirtanghar, a rectangular structure with two rows of pillars along its length. The pillars and wooden panels had intricate carvings, colourfully painted with various symbols of this unique tradition. A panel carved with the images of Garuda—the eagle demi-god, often worshipped as the vehicle of Vishnu—was at the other end of the hall. During the visit we interacted with a Bhakat, a celibate monk at the satra. He explained to us several nuances about the functioning of the satras and their unique way of life. To me, what stood out most in our conversations with him was that every satra, apart from being a religious institution, also anchors the ancient tradition of curating, preserving and propagating artistic forms. For example, the Auniati Satra is famous for the Natua and Apsara dances; the Dakshinpat Satra patronizes the Raasleela; the Kamalabari Satra is a centre of art, culture, literature and classical studies, and is known for the crafting of beautiful boats, and the Samaguri Satra is famous for its mask-making tradition.

The next day, we visited the Samaguri Satra and were treated to an enthralling theatrical performance by one of the Bhakats depicting a story from the Ramayana. Using different masks, he played different characters for us. One of his fellow Bhakats was busy giving finishing touches to a mask, and we asked him what motivated him to commit to a specific artistic tradition with such dedication. He replied almost instantaneously, 'It is through these creative pursuits that we are able to discard the mundane and access the realm of divinity. The arts allow us to shed our identity and become part of a collective that is in pursuit of the divine.' I couldn't have agreed with him more.

Later that day, we were fortunate to see the Gayan Bayan dance performed at the Uttar Kamalabari Satra. This is a type of dance performed with khols (a percussion instrument) slung from the necks of the Bhakats and is accompanied by cymbals. The Bhakats are dressed from head to toe in pure white and dance in complete unison, playing the drums as they dance to invoke the Lord. During the Gayan Bayan performance, the entire hall was charged with the energy of devotion and passion. It was clear to me that the Bhakats of the satras of Majuli use their *Power of Creativity* to access a world beyond this one. They do this not in private, but publicly, in front of thousands of people, thus taking them along in their pursuit of the divine. The fact that each of these satras has held on to its unique power of creativity through its arts and traditions for more than five centuries is simply awe-inspiring.

At night, when we returned to our quaint Mising huts, I lay in bed thinking about my own power of creativity. Had I expressed it enough over the years, or had it been subdued? I remember being fully aware of it when I was learning Bharatanatyam at Guru Mani's Kalasadan in Mumbai during my childhood. But what had happened of my pursuit later on? I wasn't sure. Did my education in science and maths keep me away from my inner power of creativity? Did I consider my passion for dance a distraction as I prepared for my college exams? What about students in my school who wanted to pursue the arts as a career? How had they gone about it? What had we done as a society to stoke our power of creativity?

Traditionally, many art forms in India were connected to spiritual and religious institutions. Artisans were engaged by kings or queens to build temples of grandeur. Dancers and performers would perform stories from Hindu epics in the courtyards of these temple complexes for the common people. The religious centres in ancient India, therefore, had always been centres for the arts and creativity. This practice was seen in Buddhist and Jain places of worship too. The Sanchi Buddhist stupa in Madhya Pradesh and the Palitana Jain temples of Gujarat are fine examples of this. Over the centuries, Islamic rulers, especially the Mughals, brought their own arts to India. These were merged with local styles to create new versions of artistic expression in architecture, crafts, couture, music, theatre, et al. Royal patronage of literature, of writers and of poets, too continued through the centuries. Some of our greatest literary works have been commissioned by or dedicated to the kings of yore. Historically in India, the anchors for our powers of creativity lay in places of worship, spiritual centres and the royal courts. The cultural wealth produced by our myriad arts, crafts and literature made India a truly incredible place for any visitor who knocked at our doors.

Although the Ganpati and Durga festival mandals, Ram Leela performances, Sufi qawwali immersions and bhajan/kirtan satsangs are modern-day examples of how creativity still finds its anchor in spirituality or religion, the creative and performing arts are no longer solely linked to spiritual life in India. We are witnessing individual creativity express itself in our dance forms, music, street theatre, films, and even our TV shows. Talent shows on various TV channels often run competitions for singing, dancing or other special talents, and these shows continue to enjoy some of the highest viewership rates among audiences. Indians intensely crave personal creative expression, and it can be observed in the way we build and decorate our homes, tractors, cars, autos, buses and trucks. In recent years, social media platforms and digital apps have given much impetus to our individual expression of creativity. People record songs, dance routines and even skits, and publish them on social media, and many of these even go viral.

In a manner of speaking, social media platforms have opened up the flood gates of the individual power of creativity in Indians from all walks of life. But much before their arrival, Indians have been expressing their personal power of creativity with exuberance in their daily lives.

Trucks and Tanks

One sight that stands out for most foreign visitors driving across India is that of our colourful and artistically decorated trucks. The first truck that came to India during the British rule was a simple vehicle, painted in one colour. But at some point, we Indians decided to unleash our power of creativity on this humble goods carrier, thus beginning a uniquely creative tradition of truck art across the Indian subcontinent.

Most trucks across India used to carry the words 'Horn Ok Please' painted on them. As a child, I would ask my father what it meant. He would explain that it was the request of the truck driver to the vehicles behind his truck to honk. The painted phrase would be framed by intricate motifs of animals, birds, men and women, etc. Each truck would be a riot of bright colours, with designs reflecting the truck driver or owner's beliefs, personality and preferences. The phrases written on the trucks were often in different languages in unique, stylized fonts. Some bore social messages, and others religious ones. But every truck was an individual work of art. No two trucks were the same. As a child, I found this fascinating.

The words 'Horn Ok Please' are banned now in many places, in an attempt to curb noise pollution, but the colourful truck art remains. Perhaps this creative expression on their vehicles helps drivers cope with the long and tiring journeys they make across the country. Perhaps it reminds them of home. Whatever the case may be, the art on every truck is its owner's pride. Over the decades, truck art has become a standalone business, and workshops and artists specializing in this craft are found across the country. But its most celebrated and skilful practitioners can be found in the north Indian state of Punjab.

Driving through Punjab with Ejji, Mahesh and Venkat in April 2014, I had the opportunity to view the state and its people through the eyes of three south Indian men. They would point out things that I had never thought of as very unique. On the day we were driving from Amritsar to Gurdaspur, Ejji suddenly exclaimed, 'Hey guys, I see an airplane on top of a house.' Mahesh, who had been engrossed in reading his notes, suddenly looked up. I was lost in mapping our route ahead. But when I looked out, I found that our car was parked in front of the main gate of a house. I looked at Ejji and Mahesh and they both pointed to the roof of the house, which had an airplane made of cement, approximately 5 feet long and 4 feet tall, coloured in red and white, firmly placed on top of it. I burst into a roar of laughter; little did my south Indian friends know that the airplane they were pointing at was actually a fully functional water tank.

I tried to explain to a completely zapped Ejji that this was a unique feature of Punjabi homes. Each has a functional water tank atop it designed to reflect the home owner's personal choice, hobby or profession. A chef might have a pressure cooker for a water tank; a football enthusiast a football and a non-resident Indian an airplane! None of my co-travellers could fathom this at first. What was the need, they wondered, for such elaborate work for a simple water tank? I explained that this was one of the ways in which the Punjabis expressed their creativity. Water tanks were almost a status symbol across the state. It was similar to how women in Tamil Nadu might create kolam art (a type of design made with rice paste drawn on the ground in front of homes or outside the main door), each of which was unique and personal.

For the rest of our drive and stay in Punjab, Ejji, Mahesh and Venkat would keep spotting water tanks atop houses. Some were in the shape of eagles painted in gold with symbols of the Sikh faith displayed prominently on them. Some were in the shape of animals, others in the shape of humans, war tanks or rockets. But each was brightly painted and intricately designed. We even stopped at a water tank workshop, where water tanks of various sizes, shapes, designs and colours were being made. The owner, a water tank artist himself, gave us a deeper understanding of the practice. He said, 'Tank art is a way for the Punjabi to say what he feels in his heart.' Tank art to Punjabi homeowners is as personal as truck art is to truck drivers and owners, or the kolam is to a south Indian woman. They are all expressions of the personal power of creativity of these people. This power of creativity is not expressed on a grand scale, as we see in our monuments; nor is it nurtured institutionally, as we see in the satras of Assam, but it is fully expressed in the spheres of personal influence of the people who indulge in it. These individuals have nourished their own sense of creativity, expressing it through their homes and professions.

Supressing Creativity

Driving through the hinterland of India, whether through the Thar Desert, remote Himalayan hamlets, the backwaters of Kerala or the plains of Haryana, you notice homes painted with bright, saturated, almost neon colours. The sight may be slightly numbing to those with more subtle tastes, but to those Indians who are the proud owners of these homes, they are expressions of themselves and their own creativity. Indians are a naturally creative people. In music, dance, painting, writing, theatre and the crafts—India's power of creativity is omnipresent. Yet India's creators are abandoning their art forms for jobs in factories and call centres. Our master artists are dying without being able to pass on their crafts to the next generation as their young are not interested in work that will fetch them only meagre earnings. They willingly subdue their creativity for more mundane careers because those jobs pay better.

While in Majuli, we came across a mother–daughter pair who was weaving sarees on traditional looms. The mother was only school-educated, but the daughter was pursuing a bachelor of arts in the nearby college. When we asked her about her craft, she said, 'I only learnt it to please my mother and help her make ends meet. But this is not what I want to do for the rest of my life.' When we prodded her a bit more, she admitted that she loved to weave. She saw colour patterns in her dreams and even wanted to weave modern designs, such as for a scarf or skirt, for more contemporary use. But she knew that weaving would not earn her as much as a clerical job in a local government department would. When I mentioned the satras, she quipped, 'But I don't want to live a monastic life!'

I felt sad hearing her words. What had we come to? Why were we boxing all our young people into pursuing only a few streams of education? Why couldn't this young woman study fashion design? Of course, for that there should be a local college that would have to teach it in the first place. Most rural colleges will teach courses such as political science and sociology. She was studying the latter, but that was not what her heart desired. I thought about my class in school and how most people took up science or commerce because the arts offered no sustainable career path.

This kind of systemic suppression of our creativity is like rafting the boat in opposition to the current of the civilizational flow. Decades of such systemic suppression has led to societal conditioning where parents are reluctant to have their children pursue the creative arts for a career. I know of people in my own family and friends' circles who would have loved to be singers, writers or painters but were now running businesses or working as a teacher or in administrative jobs. Perhaps the fault lay in our education system itself. How many Indian families can afford to have their children taking up arts outside of the school system? I was fortunate that my parents were able to afford a dance class for me; my mother was fortunate that her parents were able to afford a painting class for her, and my father was lucky to have his father support his acting and participation in theatre while he was in college. But most families in India cannot afford to provide their children any creative or artistic education. We may then say that the school system needs to include more outlets for a child's creativity. But when a school can barely afford one teacher or even a proper classroom, how are we to make arrangements for creative pursuits?

Therefore, the question arises as to what can we do to unleash our individual power of creativity and nurture our collective power of creativity as a society. Does creativity have a place in a world that is moving towards massive digitization and automation? Will it have a market? Will it earn a livelihood for our artisans? Is there opportunity for India to make an economic case for its creative products and services? Can there be a thriving creative economy in the country?

Creative Economy

'Creative Economy' is a concept first presented by John Howkins, a British author and entrepreneur. He mooted the idea that a creative economy is one where people use their creativity to increase the value of an idea, a product, an art form or a service. It is an economic system where the creativity of individuals or a collective group creates economic value that goes beyond the traditional resources of land, labour and capital.[1]

The United Nations Conference on Trade and Development (UNCTAD) has been working to shape the global understanding of creative economy since 2004. In its Creative Economy Outlook report published in 2018,[2] it highlights that creative economy continues to increase its share in global trade; the size of the creative economy trade increased from USD 208 billion in 2002 to USD 509 billion in 2015 worldwide. Among the top ten exporters of creative goods worldwide, India was ranked eighth, with exports of USD 17 billion in year 2015. UNCTAD identifies creative goods as 'advertising, architecture, arts and crafts, design, fashion, film, video, photography, music, performing arts, publishing, research and development, software, computer games, electronic publishing, and TV/radio'.[3]

If India wants to bring the power of creativity of its people to markets, we would need to deep-dive into each of these categories and see where we stand among other nations. We will need to arrest the institutional gaps and change societal mindsets. There have been a few policy and infrastructure interventions to augment our creative economy potential, especially in the spheres of animation and VFX of late, but that is a limited view of the vast landscape of the creative economy system.

A strategic roadmap for growth of the creative economy in India can be supplemented with ideas as to how our power of creativity can be applied in sectors beyond the arts and crafts. The World Economic Forum's The Future of Jobs Report of 2018[4] predicted that creativity, along with ideation and innovation, would be key skills required for jobs of the near future. Many leadership surveys have consistently identified creativity as one of the most important traits of successful leaders. Should this not be an impetus for us to revise our approach to even school education? Should we not enhance the creative skills of our children—after all, it may help them get a decent job when they grow up!

Creative economy goes beyond the sphere of creative goods and influences our approach to sustainable development as well. Therefore, the United Nations' seventy-fourth General Assembly in 2019 declared 2021 as the International Year of Creative Economy for Sustainable Development.[5] In India, we need a roadmap for how we can explore our inherent power of creativity through education, markets, technology, policy and innovation. This roadmap can articulate how we can call our power of creativity to action even for the new frontiers of the fourth industrial revolution, such as artificial intelligence (AI), machine learning, and the internet of things (IoT).

For decades in India, we moved towards economic activity focused on productivity. The time has now come to pay heed to our inherent power of creativity and establish a vibrant creative economy ecosystem for it within the country. It is time to transition from being producers to becoming creators. This would be in sync with our natural affinity towards creativity; and will demand a complete rethink of our societal mindset, education system, markets and policies.

Bloom and Boom

Creativity is an inherent strength, a conduit to experiences beyond our physical limitations. Artists and craftspersons have the ability to visualize or craft an intangible idea into something people can see, hear, experience, touch and feel. When William Shakespeare or Premchand wrote, they shaped a reality for the reader through their words. When Leonardo Da Vinci or Raja Ravi Varma painted, they took the mundane and transformed it into something magical. In the India of yore, one would find schools dedicated to specific creative arts, and students would specifically study those arts under masters or gurus. When the Western formal education system was introduced, it brought massive opportunities for large-scale education. But with this model, we also inherited the nineteenth-century industrial age-thinking of the West, where the whole purpose of education was to equip humans for standardized, non-creative process jobs in the private and public sectors. Productivity reigned supreme, and out-of-the-box thinking was dismissed as a distraction.

Even in the twentieth and twenty-first centuries, the education system in India continued, and is continuing, along this pattern, where children are pushed to memorize rather than to learn, and to conform rather than to create. A certain bias has developed—for rewarding students who have the ability to reproduce what they have read in textbooks rather than apply critical thinking and come up with creative and innovative ideas. The arts and the humanities have been dismissed in favour of maths and science with zest!

If India is to unleash the power of creativity of its people and benefit from the worldwide growth in creative economy, we will need to start by rethinking our education system first. We will have to give sizeable weightage to the arts—including digital forms of visual art skills—in our curriculum. The era of visual storytelling is upon us. Even if a child eventually ends up as a manager in a bank, she will need visual storytelling skills to present her ideas or a project at the workplace. We may have to nurture creativity, just as we do computer skills, as a core capability. This will mean that concepts such as design and ideation, and skills such as writing, video-creation and editing, will need to be given focus in both the curriculum and teaching methods. Theatre can be an effective tool in teaching, and videos are a great way for students to express their understanding of a concept. What we call basic good education needs to be redefined. Accordingly, school infrastructure, faculty and resources will all need to meet the standards of this new paradigm. India's education challenge is huge, but with such a reorientation, we will be able to apply fresh thinking and avoid the mistakes of the past.

As a next step, the foundational education at the school level must be married with higher-education possibilities for students who want to pursue the creative arts as a career. India has several prestigious colleges for the creative arts, but students there would also need exposure to technology and/or marketing, for instance. Our college system today is not designed for cross-pollination between different faculties and subjects. When I went for my undergraduate studies to the United States, I had the option to take courses in music, philosophy, theatre and history along with my major subjects of maths and business. We need to design a new system where an IIT engineering student can take classes in MS University, Vadodara, in the arts, and vice-versa; we need a robust, flexible system where communications students at MICA, Ahmedabad, can take an accounting class at a college in Chennai. With the massive strides in online learning tools, this is absolutely doable if we put our minds to it. Where local options for such cross-pollination are available, we may not even need online classes. Even within various art forms, there needs to be a confluence of different art streams and an environment of collaboration should be fostered. Until now, little thought has been given to the confluence, convergence and co-creation of art forms with other faculties on our academic campuses.

While we rethink our education system, we can also focus on reskilling or retraining people already in the workforce in creative skills. Companies like Adobe have workplace tools that make this process easy. Companies that come up with training pathways for their workers and leaders to explore their creative potential will be able to improve on their innovation roadmap. Individual and team creativity is the basis for product or service innovation. Companies that encourage and reward a creative approach to work will win the day with more motivated employees and larger market shares.

We can also equip our artisans with digital skills that can help them redesign their products and repurpose their crafts for modern-day usage. Hand-crafted products can have a price premium, and fashion and clothing designers can nurture and propagate traditional Indian weaves. Much of this is taking place quite naturally in the private sector. But what we need is a policy-level rethink on how we approach our traditional arts and crafts in order to bring them back into vogue. How do we create better access to markets for these products, and how do we help our artisans renew their crafts and creativity?

In 2012, I came across a small start-up in Kashmir called Kashmir Box. They were initially an e-tailing venture that sourced produce from Kashmiri artisans and sold them online. But, as time progressed, they ventured into giving design inputs to the artisans and bringing innovative products to the markets through their traditional crafts. They not only trained artisans and gave them design inputs but also shared their profits with them. When I chose to invest in this venture, I realized that they had allocated 10 per cent of their equity for the artisan community. To me, Kashmir Box and the likes of it are fine examples of what is possible when we marry modern tools and skills with traditional creative arts and crafts. Such amalgamations can lead to a renaissance of the arts in the country. There have been encouraging signs lately. Young Indian adults are looking for traditional crafts in a modern mould for their homes. Many are open to using sustainable, impact-driven goods that come from smaller artisan communities.

For our creative economy to boom we must nourish and nurture our inherent power of creativity and bring it to bloom. We can create a system of education, skilling, market access, collaboration, cross-pollination and innovation that will serve this purpose. Such a system would need to be supported with policies and laws that protect our artisans and our creative workers and ensure that they are rewarded well in the marketplace. One of the ways to do this is to strengthen the ecosystem around our copyright, patent and geographical indication laws.

GIs and Copyrights

Geographical indicators (GIs) encourage the preservation of local methods, produce and crafts, and help communities pursue sustainable development. They are like intellectual property rights or patents, in that they accord collective rights to the local communities that produce a specific agricultural or art/craft item. They protect both biological and cultural heritage and, more importantly, they bring stakeholders together across value chains.

Article 22(1) of the World Trade Organization (WTO) Trade-Related Aspects of Intellectual Property Rights (TRIPS) agreement defines GIs as 'indications which identify a product as originating in the territory of a WTO Member nation or a region or locality in that territory, where a given quality, reputation or other characteristics of the product is essentially attributable to the geographical origin'.[6] The geographical indication is a type of indication of source. It acts as a certification that the product for which it is awarded possesses attributes due to its geographical origin. Globally, it is the World Intellectual Property Organization (WIPO) that administers use of GIs through a number of international treaties. Each country has their own process of registering domestic GIs and may choose to recognize GIs of other countries as well. GIs that are recognized in foreign geographies in addition to their domestic one, are said to have been applied in foreign jurisdiction.

In India, GI registration is administered under the Geographical Indications of Goods (Registration and Protection) Act of 1999.[7] India has more than 350 GIs—for products as diverse as Darjeeling tea, Lucknow chikankari craft, Madurai malli (jasmine), Kashmiri walnut woodcarving, the Chanderi saree from Madhya Pradesh, Channapatna toys from Karnataka and Muga silk from Assam, to name a few. Many of the GIs are for specific crafts. And quite a few of them are for agricultural produce, such as Gir kesar mango of Gujarat. Yet, very little awareness or marketing has been done to leverage this GI tagging to help local creative communities earn from their crafts or produce.

In 2019, when I was looking for handicrafts from various regions of India for our home in Munsyari, I was shocked to discover that in some cases the artisans earned only one fifth of the market price of the retailed product. It seemed very unfair to me. Some of these craft products take months and much patience and diligence to produce. Many have GIs accorded to them, but the artisans are neither aware of it nor benefit from it economically. Actually, if applied appropriately, GIs can help remote communities reach markets and sell their produce at a premium. But law enforcement of GIs in the domestic Indian market is abysmal and needs a more well-deliberated system of identification, application and protection. As one of the largest markets in the world, India itself makes for a huge domestic market for these products, in addition to the opportunities they have for export. We need to build awareness among the artisan communities as well in the marketplace, and we also need to nurture ventures such as Kashmir Box, which not only ensure that artisans are paid well, but also train them, give them design inputs and a share of the profits too.

We may feel elated that India has more than 350 GIs, but when we compare our listed GIs with those of countries like Germany and China, we are way behind. Data received from the fifty-four national/regional authorities that shared their information with WIPO reveals the existence of approximately 42,527 protected GIs worldwide as of 2016. Approximately 49 per cent of these were in force domestically, and the remaining 51 per cent in foreign jurisdictions. Germany had the largest number of GIs in force (9,499), followed by China (7,566).[8]

Our roadmap for a creative economy can include new ideas and methods to create a robust system for a vast number of India's traditional crafts to receive GIs. But we must not stop at according them GIs. We must carry their value to the market eventually. Once these GIs are established, it would be prudent to build an ecosystem of research, innovation, application and modern-day market-oriented applications of these products. We need to build value chains and bring varied stakeholders together to translate the GIs into economic opportunities. Training communities that engage in these specific crafts can be an important first step. It may seem that this would be a very niche intervention for a small number of people in the country. But the official estimate of the number of artisans in India is 7 million, the unofficial estimate being 200 million.[9] The gap in the numbers is due to the unorganized nature of the entire sector.

While GIs can help us protect what we traditionally create or produce in a community in a specific geographical location, we need a vigorous copyright system that allows our creators to protect what they create anew. We have musicians, dancers, writers, directors, actors, et al, producing massive content, both offline and online, across the country. Their work needs a more robust system of copyright protection. According to the Music Consumer Insight Report, 2018,[10] released by the International Federation of the

Phonographic Industry, 96 per cent of Indian consumers listen to music on their smartphones, the highest proportion in the world. They favour local genres of music, with new and old Bollywood songs and Indian classical music as their top three choices. Close to 96 per cent of this music is licensed. There is a steady rise in the number of consumers who pay subscriptions on OTT platforms to consume content in the country. The number of creators using social and digital platforms to create and collaborate on productions of an eclectic nature is also increasing. Digitization allows for wider reach and faster market penetration of content but lowers the income that creators can earn from such distribution. Additionally, many of these platforms are companies headquartered outside India and earn a percentage of revenue from the content sold on their platforms through advertisements or subscriptions. But despite the massive reach and impact of its creators, India has no such indigenous platform of its own. Our creators are putting much of their creativity out there, but not only do they earn less, the distribution income of their content also does not accrue to our own GDP. This must change so that we are able to actively shape the prospects of our own creative economy.

Copyright allows creators to monetize their content for a few decades before their creations are available free for public use, and also motivates creators to constantly develop new content. India's Gross Value Addition (GVA) from copyright-relevant industries was INR 89,000 crore in 2016–17, at a 0.58 per cent share of total value added to the Indian economy and a tenth of the global average.[11] We need new digital tools and platforms, and laws or processes, that incorporate the new reality of content creation and distribution globally. If we want to create a thriving creative economy, we need to ensure that our creators are incentivized to create and are remunerated for it adequately. The domestic Copyright Act was last amended in 2012, and warrants constant adaptation to match the new developments in the global creative economy.

Given the significant work ahead of us in charting a long-term strategy and short-team actionable plan for our creators, artisans and creative economy stakeholders, one pauses to ask if this will be a worthwhile exercise to undertake at all, given how drastically digitization and automation are going to transform livelihoods and economies. What will be the future of creative economy in the age of artificial intelligence and robots?

Man and Machine

In the vastly popular movies of *The Matrix* franchise, the 'machines' are a highly advanced population of artificial intelligence and are portrayed as the major antagonists. The movies of *The Matrix* series explore a future where the machines have managed to overpower the humans. Their storyline revolves around conflicts between 'man' and 'machine' and how human society copes with it.

In the new era of coexistence of man and machine, it is imperative to understand what sets us humans apart from the machines. Kai-Fu-Lee is a computer scientist, businessman and writer from Taiwan and a world-renowned figure in the field of AI and deep learning. Lee firmly believes that human attributes such as expressions of creativity and emotions such as love set humans apart from artificial intelligence. He has also predicted that in the next fifteen years AI will take over half of the human jobs that exist today.[12]

For a country like India, with a vast young population that adds millions to the job market annually, this can be a scary proposition. What will our young people do? Are we equipping them with skills that will help them keep their jobs? If creativity is one such skill, then we need to act fast, in terms of redesigning our education system and retraining our young people. This would need to be supported by a dynamic creative economy.

India can also combine its power of creativity with its prowess in the field of information technology to create new models of co-creation, employing both man and machine. In his book *Creativity Code*, professor and mathematician Marcus du Sautoy explores the creative capacity of AI and leaves the question open as to how human creativity will keep pace with the creativity of the machine's.[13] Musician David Cope has created an AI algorithm called Emily Howell; it creates music in its own style.[14] Cope is no exception. Musicians across the world are using IBM's Watson and Sony's Flow Machine to co-create new works.[15] This collaboration between AI and humans is now spreading to dance, theatre, painting, cooking, design and writing. The Japanese novel *Konpyuta ga shosetsu wo kaku hi*—literally, *The Day a Computer Writes a Novel*—was fully written by an algorithm![16]

If we want to explore this new frontier of collaboration between man and machine, we will need to create opportunities for cross-faculty studies, projects and education, as discussed earlier. When our best creators are exposed to the knowledge of machines and our best engineers get to explore their creative side, we will be able to create a cohort of young people adept at riding this new wave of growth.

The more I think about the potential of creative economy, the more I feel that it is also up to each one of us to go back to that one creative pursuit which we indulged in when we were children but left it because of other demands in our lives, like our studies or our jobs. Whether this pursuit was writing, singing, dancing, painting or cooking—if it was anything where our imagination took charge, nudged us to think out of the box and goaded us to break barriers, then it should ideally make a comeback in our daily lives. Having creative pursuits is no longer about work–life balance but about survival and life skills, if experts like Lee and Marc are to be believed. A change in our approach to our own creativity, individually and collectively, is the need of the hour.

From the tank art of Punjab to the satras of Assam, our power of creativity is alive and kicking. For it to reach new heights, we must rethink education, markets, GIs and copyrights. We must also reimagine the role of digital platforms and explore new avenues for man-and-machine collaboration. The era of man and machine must not disempower our youth. Instead, we can be ready to exploit its potential at scale. We can use our power of creativity to fuel a thriving creative economy. Today, many of our creators are leaving the country in search of better ecosystems to create their works abroad. We can arrest this talent drain by taking a strategic approach and devising a well-thought-out roadmap for our creative economy.

Aditya Patwardhan

When his film *Red House by the Crossroads* was selected to be shown at the 2015 Cannes Film Festival at the Cannes Short Film Corner, Aditya Patwardhan was elated. The film was a story set around a Polish-Jewish Holocaust survivor and his family. Aditya was barely twenty-six when he made the film. The film was adjudged the Best Short Film at the Los Angeles Independent Film Festival Awards. In his thirty-three years on this planet (as of 2022), Aditya has directed twenty-seven films and videos, written for ten and produced nineteen, many in languages as diverse as Portuguese and Korean.[17]

Based in Los Angeles in the United States, Aditya fondly remembers his childhood in Mumbai and Jaipur. As a young child, he loved the beat of drums and was encouraged by his parents to learn the Indian percussion instrument, tabla. As he grew up, he developed a great affinity for music. Filmmaking was not on the horizon. He thought of becoming a music director for some time.

Ideally, he would have loved to pursue a bachelor of arts in English literature. But, as it was with many young people of his generation, he took up engineering instead for his undergraduate studies and also managed to get a job with the prestigious IT firm Tata Consultancy Services (TCS) upon graduation. At that point he felt a nagging in his heart. Engineering was not his calling. He wanted to pursue the arts, especially music. His parents were supportive of the drastic change he wanted to make in his career path and he decided to work with a jewellery company in Jaipur, Rajasthan, to enhance their branding and marketing. During this time, he was approached by a local band to direct a music video for them. The video received more than 100,000 online views and likes, and this started Aditya's love affair with the camera.

Aditya remembers his passionate search to find the best course in filmmaking. But the more he researched different institutes in India, the greater was his disappointment. The National Film Institute in Pune was India's finest, but he was not happy with its curriculum and the teaching methods. He wanted to explore the world of filmmaking and try new techniques, make films in different languages and of different genres, and live out his power of creativity by donning different roles of director, writer, producer, actor, composer, et al.

Finally, he found a course offered by the New York Film Academy in Los Angeles, and in 2014 Aditya flew to the United States. The environment there was very supportive of his creativity and allowed him to think out of the box. He felt he could stretch his comfort zone and experiment with techniques, stories and form. It was not easy at first. He didn't come from a film background. He came from a traditional Maharashtrian family of professionals and businesspersons. His education was in engineering. But his creative zeal got him through, and soon he found an agent and started working on several projects.

Aditya went on to direct *A Touch of Aurora (Um toque da Aurora)*, a Portuguese-language Brazilian drama about a visually impaired couple—Luis, an ex-football star, and Sara, a school teacher. *A Touch of Aurora* features Brazilian film celebrity and star Thaila Ayala, who received critical acclaim for her role in the film. The film has received over forty nominations and awards, the prominent ones being the North American Film Awards Jury Prize (USA); Best Short Film, Rolda WebFest (Colombia); Best Art Direction, 41st Guarnicê Film Festival (Brazil); Best Director of Photography, 1st Festcine Pedra Azul (Brazil); Best Actress, 1st Festcine Pedra Azul (Brazil); Best Actor, São Paulo Film Festival. It was shown at prominent film festivals across the world, 41st Guarnicê Film Festival, Cannes Le Petit Film Festival, Albuquerque Film and Music Experience, Hollywood Boulevard Film Festival, Figueira da Foz Film Festival, 10th Maranhão na Tela Festival in Brazil, Offcine 2019, to name a few.

Aditya made his debut in Korean cinema with his film *And the Dream that Mattered* (꿈의의미). The film won the prestigious award for best independent film at the twenty-sixth Korean Cultural Academy Awards. His Spanish-English film *I.C.E Cream* has found much acclaim, and his all-American feature film *Transference* is a horror movie that saw him working with some of the best creators in Hollywood. His most recent film, *Nomad River,* has been shot in India. It tells a story woven around India's rivers and a woman's quest to know herself.

When I asked him if he would ever make a film in India, his answer was a resounding *yes*. He told me that he had been looking at several stories, but didn't feel ready yet. At this young age, and with a career span that has been relatively short for his industry, Aditya has explored a wide variety of genres and has even dabbled in documentaries. He has had the opportunity to work with actors, artists and professionals from across the world. His only regret is that he has had to do this away from his family and his home country.

Aditya's documentary *Eastern Shores of the Western World* follows the culture and lifestyles of Eastern Europe and the Baltic countries, drawing genetic and linguistic parallels between the Indian and European civilizations. He admits with a sense of exasperation that such a project may have not happened had he been based in India. He wishes now—as he had when he was in India—that a creative ecosystem of academia, training and openness to new ideas existed here in India. Why should a filmmaker be confined to only a certain type of cinema? Why does a young man like him need to leave India to pursue his creativity? Why can't we provide that environment for young people like him right here, when we have no dearth of talent, ideas, creativity and market?

Aditya was fortunate to have a family that supported his creative passions. He was encouraged. But many young Indians continue to be discouraged from pursuing creative careers. The accelerated growth of technology and digital media has somewhat changed that, but our society continues to be plagued by the idea that creativity is a side pursuit and cannot be the mainstay of our careers. In the context of the advent of machines and rise of the global creative economy, we ought to reflect upon this false notion and discard it sooner rather than later. India is an immense storehouse of creativity, and our power of creativity can be put to use to create jobs, support our artisans and creators, increase economic growth, create social and cultural continuity and provide new ways for man and machine to coexist. The choice is ours as to whether we will embrace this opportunity or squander it. The choice is ours as to whether we will move the raft of the republic forward or capsize it with our outdated thinking and disregard for our power of creativity.

6

Power of Knowledge

Nalanda

In 2014, driving along a two-lane road from Purniya to Bodh Gaya in Bihar in eastern India, I saw the countryside most of us tend to associate Bihar with—mud houses, cows, cow dung, agricultural fields and poverty. Talking to the locals, I noticed a shift in the attitude of the people of Bihar from what I had encountered on my earlier visits in 2005 and 2010. They spoke of better governance, better healthcare and better education. In fact, it was eye-opening to see a large number of schools and schoolgoing children in the state. Clearly, lack of wealth had not deterred the residents of Bihar from pursuing education—for themselves and for their children. This delighted me, and I told Mahesh about it. He was driving the car and looked at me in the rearview mirror with a knowing smile on his face. 'Bhairavi,' he said, 'then, you don't know Bihar at all.'

It was already post-noon that day, and while our original destination was Bodh Gaya, Mahesh decided that in order for me to fully comprehend Bihar's love affair with learning and knowledge, we needed to visit Nalanda first. So we took a detour and drove through many villages and towns before we reached the archaeological site of Nalanda Mahavihara, believed by many historians to be the world's first residential university.

It was nearly evening when we arrived at Nalanda and the burning rays of the setting sun beamed through the entrance of the complex. The sight made me stop in my tracks. Somehow, I had the feeling of walking into light. Mahesh, Ejji and Venkat caught up with me and Ejji exclaimed, 'Hey, Bhairavi, do you know that this is the fourteenth time that Mahesh is visiting Nalanda?' I was stunned. I looked at Mahesh for an explanation, and he obligingly told me that he had spent years understanding the Silk Road, China, India's influence on China and the spread of Buddhism across the Far East. He had always looked at Nalanda from the perspective of Xuanzang, the Chinese monk who came to Nalanda in the seventh century CE. 'Imagine, Bhairavi,' Mahesh exclaimed, 'we have been driving on the road for 7,000-odd km already, but this man *walked* all the way from China, crossing deserts, rivers and snow-clad mountains. Weathering storms and hardships, he came here with the sole objective of learning. Can you imagine what the glory of Nalanda must have been that this man came that far, risking his life to seek knowledge?' At that point, our guide Pradeep started explaining the genesis of this great ancient university.

Based on the excavations at this UNESCO Heritage site, the time of establishment of Nalanda has been estimated, by most historians, as early fifth century CE, though some other sources point to the university existing in some form or the other since the third century BC. As we walked through a passageway lined with red brick walls more than 25 ft high, Pradeep explained that by the time

Xuanzang came to Nalanda to study, the university already had over 1,500 faculty members and more than 10,000 students from eight to ten different countries. Scholars believe that it was the Gupta king Kumaragupta-I who laid the foundations for transforming what may have been a small gurukul-like school into an institution of higher learning. And so it was that in the early days of the institute, a residential complex of learning and knowledge took shape. After the decline of the Gupta dynasty, it was the emperor Harsha of Kannauj who donated land, built viharas and even made nearby villages contribute food and supplies to the students so they would not have to seek alms. They could, instead, concentrate on their studies, and the institute's faculty would be well paid. Successive kings supported its expansion. Ejji intervened, 'Bhairavi, what you see today is only 12-odd hectares of excavated ruins, but the university was spread over for miles on end. Much more is left to be discovered.'

We walked through the ruins and came to a section which had small rooms lined next to each other in a quadrangle. I was told these had originally been dorms for monks to stay; they even had wall alcoves for lamps. Adjacent to this group of small rooms was a larger room where a resident faculty member would stay. Pradeep explained that students were grouped on the basis of the subjects they pursued. Nalanda offered Buddhist studies, a subject of prime interest to seekers like Xuanzang. It also offered subjects such as astrology, philosophy, mathematics, logic and literature—to name a few! Students from far and wide—from Central Asia, Tibet and the Far East—came to study at Nalanda. Its faculty consisted of some of the most respected academics and its students were some of the brightest. Therefore, in its time, it was a true global centre for learning and knowledge—a medieval Ivy League college, if you will.

We walked over to a large structure with ascending steps. Pradeep explained that this was what was left of a temple. Nalanda had many temples. It also had stupas and libraries. In fact, there was an entire area earmarked for libraries. There were three main libraries: the Ratnasagara (Ocean of Jewels), the Ratnodadhi (Sea of Jewels), and Ratnaranjaka (Jewel-adorned). Each was a multi-storeyed structure and had once housed some of the most precious manuscripts in the world during Nalanda's heydays. No one knows the exact number of books or manuscripts that Nalanda's libraries housed, but it would not be amiss to surmise that during the 800 and more years of its functioning, this university would have accumulated thousands at the very least.

Pradeep then took us to a map on the premises showing the expanse of the excavations, and I was pleasantly surprised yet again. The university was not just a barren monastic facility but it had also been organized to provide learning on a large scale. It had separate cooking areas, an underground clay oven for cooking, water wells, dorms, study halls, libraries, stupas, temples and more. What most impressed me was that from the fifth century CE until its destruction by the armies of Muhammad bin Bakhtiyar Khalji in the thirteenth century CE and its cessation a century later, the people of Bihar, then the erstwhile kingdom of Magadha, had actively supported and fostered this centre of learning. I realized that Mahesh was right. I didn't know Bihar at all. If a community could stay committed to nurturing a global centre of knowledge for more than 800 years, then they must value, no, they must *worship* knowledge.

Nalanda was not the only institution of higher learning in ancient India. Shardapeeth in Kashmir, Vikramshila, also in Bihar, and Takshashila in Taxila are some other examples of ancient centres of knowledge in India. The Indian sacred texts are full of stories of great seers running their own schools—gurukuls—deep inside forests where children from all walks of life came to study. It is clear that, traditionally, Indians accorded great importance to knowledge, education and skills.

Ancient Indians believed that knowledge—vidya, in Sanskrit—was a divine boon. Even today, irrespective of their moorings, Indians worship knowledge as a powerful force. They actively covet this power and give it priority over many material aspects of life. The person who gives you knowledge is called your guru—a Sanskrit word, which means dispeller of darkness. The guru is worshipped on the day of Guru Poornima, sometime in July/August. On Teachers' Day in India, which falls on September 5, children give small gifts, such as flowers, to their teachers. Hindus revere Goddess Saraswati as the goddess of knowledge and wisdom, and worship her on the festival of Basant Panchami.

Basant Panchami

Every year in late January or February, on the occasion of the Hindu festival of Basant Panchami, the dargah (shrine) of the Muslim Sufi saint Hazrat Khwaja Nizamuddin Aulia in New Delhi is drenched in all things yellow. Devotees gather wearing mustard-yellow head covers, scarves, saris and other garments. When I was in the process of moving to Delhi to work at India@75, I was nudged by some friends to visit the Nizamuddin shrine on Basant Panchami. It was early February of 2011. There was still a winter chill in the air. We covered our heads with yellow shawls before making our way to the shrine. As we walked through the narrow alley that led to the dargah, my friends told me that the shrine has been celebrating the Sufi Basant festival since the thirteenth century CE. I was curious. Why was a Muslim shrine celebrating a Hindu festival dedicated to spring and Saraswati, the Hindu goddess of knowledge?

As we entered the shrine, a shower of yellow flowers greeted us. The air was filled with the sound of people singing songs. The lyrics of these songs were about welcoming the spring in all its beauty. My friend introduced me to someone who was part of the organizing

committee of the shrine. The man from the committee told us that
when Khwaja Nizamuddin lost his nephew, he fell into an abyss of
sorrow. He forgot to smile. His disciple and devotee, Amir Khusrau,
himself a renowned poet, searched for ways to make his master
smile. On the day of Basant Panchami, Khusrau saw women dressed
in yellow, singing songs as they walked along the streets. When he
asked them what they were doing, they replied that they were on
their way to a temple and were singing songs to make their deity
smile. Khusrau was delighted. He too dressed in yellow and went off
to Khwaja Nizamuddin, bearing mustard flowers and singing. His
appearance made the saint laugh. Thus, a Hindu festival celebrating
the spring was institutionalized in a Muslim establishment. Nodding,
I remarked that this was a cultural connection and had nothing to
do with Basant Panchami being dedicated to the Hindu goddess of
knowledge. The man from the committee quickly responded, 'Sister,
our Khwaja ji was a saint of the Chistiya Silsila, which is one of the
four major Sufi orders of India. He was a firm believer that Sufis
must possess *Ishq*—love, *Aql*—wisdom, and *Ilm*—knowledge. He
would have been thrilled that his shrine celebrated a festival that
venerated knowledge.'

Although people celebrate Basant Panchami popularly as a
festival to herald the spring, many Hindus across India also worship
Goddess Saraswati on this day, and children are made to write their
first words or say their first hymns on this day. In many schools,
students worship Saraswati and perform rituals. The goddess is often
depicted holding a book and a veena. Some Buddhist traditions
celebrate Saraswati as the goddess of music. The festival and some
of its rituals are a reminder that revering knowledge is an ancient
Indian tradition.

Perhaps it is this reverence for knowledge and knowledge-givers
that kept the people of ancient Bihar committed to supporting
Nalanda. When we were strolling through the excavated site, I

noticed that there was no litter at all and the place was very clean, even though it was a tourist attraction. I complimented the security and administrative staff for maintaining it well. One of them responded humbly, 'Madam, this is a temple of knowledge. Maybe there are no more students and teachers here and there are no books to be found here anymore, but for more than 800 years this was an abode of knowledge. I feel greatly privileged that I can look after it.' If I had any doubt that the Bihari people worship knowledge even today, it dissipated with this one remark.

Sarawati's Seekers

On our way to Bodh Gaya, I kept thinking about the relationship Indians had with knowledge. The Bihari people were no exception in their reverence for knowledge. It was amply clear to me that Indians worshipped knowledge and sought the power of knowledge, but I was wondering whether, over the years, we had subdued it? Did colonization have anything to do with it? Our current state of primary education in schools, or even the state of our higher education, barring a few exceptions, makes me wonder whether we stopped pursuing excellence in knowledge or stopped valuing it once we were enslaved.

Approximately 400 km from Nalanda, as one travels south-east, one reaches Shantiniketan in the state of West Bengal, home to Visva Bharati University. This educational institution was established as a centre for cultural education with the objective of exploring the arts, language, humanities, music, etc. It received much fame as its mentor, Gurudev Rabindranath Tagore, was driven by a mission to make it a place for global cultural exchange. Another example of a colonial-era premier institution is the Indian Institute of Science in Bengaluru. The British and many prominent Indian citizens continued to build educational institutions throughout the nineteenth and early twentieth centuries. It was clear to me that India's love affair with knowledge and learning had continued even during colonial times. But have we given enough importance to education post-Independence?

Post-Independence India saw the founding of many institutions of higher learning—the Indian Institutes of Technology and the Indian Institutes of Management, for example. For a new nation struggling with poverty and hunger, it was remarkable that so much emphasis was given to higher learning. In the past seven decades, towns and cities like Coimbatore in Tamil Nadu, Pune in Maharashtra and Ahmedabad in Gujarat have become centres of higher education. Towns like Kota in Rajasthan have created an entire economy by attracting students from across the country to come there in order to study for various competitive examinations. In the late 1990s, the advent of the computer and IT jobs led to the mushrooming of engineering colleges in states like Andhra Pradesh and Telangana. Philanthropists and corporate houses too have ventured into education, with BITS Pilani in Rajasthan being set up by the Birla family and the Tata Institute of Social Sciences in Mumbai by the Tata Trusts. But it seems our school education did not receive the same focus and resources.

Even seventy-five years post-Independence, India's public-school system suffers from poor infrastructure, teacher absenteeism, an inadequate number of teachers, and poor student retention rates. In 2012, a Right to Education Act was passed by the Indian Parliament, giving every child the right to a school education. Since then, there has been greater focus on school education. It is not that the people of India had shunned school education post-Independence. Even today, the wealthy in Indian cities line up outside prestigious schools to enrol their children there and the poor postpone health-related issues, simply to put a child through school. But, despite many efforts and even though our K-12 education system is the largest in the world[1]—our education system and institutions have continued to underserve the super-high expectations Indians have of them. There is also a major gap between the quality of education in rural and urban areas. Well-performing students often have to leave their villages to pursue secondary education in nearby towns. Girl-student enrolment is up, but retaining girls at the higher-secondary level is a challenge. Fewer people are taking up teaching as a profession. Many schools have closed down and in the wake of the Covid-19 pandemic, millions of children who had no access to the internet by means of smartphones or computers suffered massively on the educational front.

India has a total of 1.5 million schools, with 250 million student enrolments,[2] but there is a huge demand for private schools rather than for public schools. What ails the Indian school education sector is the quality of education. The Program for International Student Assessment (PISA) undertaken by the Organisation for Economic Co-operation and Development (OECD) conducted an assessment of fifteen-year-old students from the states of Tamil Nadu and Himachal Pradesh in 2009. Among the seventy-four countries assessed, India ranked seventy-third! And up until 2022, India has kept away from this assessment.[3]

Even though we have more than 40,000 colleges and over 900 universities, many of our higher learning institutions (barring a few exceptions) have become breeding grounds for corruption. Educating new aspirants has become a commercial 'trade', and despite the high demand for education and many interventions, India has very few institutions that can rival their ancient predecessors such as Nalanda.

Quality continues to remain the major challenge for our education system at both school and college/university level. A large number of public and private actors continue to strive to improve the state of education in our country and there are some examples of improvement, but a systemic shift is still far off. The new education policy has been unveiled and aims to address the issues of learning outcomes in school education. There are significant donations by Indian philanthropists and huge contributions through corporate social responsibility programmes made towards improving school education. Even then, Saraswati's seekers are being underserved and their thirst for knowledge remains unquenched. The accelerated pace of transformation so badly required is still elusive.

The world is fast-tracking towards a new order which is going to be driven by the knowledge economy. As the fourth industrial revolution creates new ways of learning, India stares at a massive opportunity, given its people's high regard for knowledge and a large, young population. In fact, some of these new technologies can help us bridge the gaps in our current education system. During the pandemic, the haves and have-nots in the context of education were those who could access online education and those who could not, respectively. We need to learn from this and create infrastructure for digital learning on a large scale, as it has many advantages, especially for schools that struggle to get teachers and for colleges that have difficulty in offering more streams. We are heading towards a future where knowledge-driven interventions will impact society on a huge scale. We need to be ready for this shift. It is time we call upon our *Power of Knowledge* and put it to action to benefit fully from the emergence of the knowledge economy at the world stage.

Knowledge Economy

In a more generic sense, a knowledge economy is an economic system which is increasingly based on knowledge-intensive activities, where the system of production and consumption is driven by intellectual capital and human skills. The World Bank has identified four critical pillars necessary for a nation to be able to participate in the global knowledge economy:[4]

- Education and training—the population has access to quality education and skills so as to create, share and use knowledge.
- Information infrastructure—new technologies are deployed to constantly improve communication, dissemination and processing of information and knowledge.
- Economic incentive and institutional regime—the regulatory and policy environment fosters an economic system that attracts investments in knowledge and technology, encourages entrepreneurship and provides for free flow of information and knowledge.
- Innovation systems—basically, a robust network of universities, centres of higher learning and research, think-tanks, public and/or private groups that are engaged in spurring innovation and applying global innovations locally.

It would be unfair to say that India has not moved on any of the above. In fact, in some of the 'pillars' and areas mentioned above, India has done impressive work; but gaps remain. For example, in education and skills, our challenges remain despite the introduction of the National Skill Development Corporation (NSDC), which is a public–private initiative. Additionally, there is a ministry dedicated to skills, state-level skills councils and sector skills councils. In fact, working at India@75 gave me the opportunity to deep dive into the skills ecosystem in India. In 2010, Prof. C.K. Prahalad's ambitious target of training 500 million Indians in world-class skills by 2022 was publicly accepted by our former prime minister Manmohan Singh.[5]

At India@75, we worked on prototyping India's first skills portal with the NSDC. We partnered with them to launch a competition called 'Power to Empower', designed to encourage young entrepreneurs from some of India's best-ranking educational institutes to come up with ideas that could help accelerate the skills ecosystem. I recollect visiting over forty institutions across the country to hold interactions with some of our brightest young minds. The session at IIT Kharagpur, for instance, was scheduled at 9 p.m., and yet the auditorium was packed to the brim with over 400 students. At IIT Guwahati, the students refused to leave the session as there were so many ideas to explore. At IIM Kozhikode, we spent time with the students discussing ideas even after the session was over. At XLRI Jamshedpur, students wanted to know more about India's upcoming skills ecosystem. Apart from the odd IIT or IIM, we covered them all, visiting their campuses and interacting with the students.

During the interactions there were several questions on the target number to be skilled, and many of the arguments on this matter have held true over the years, but there was no doubt in anyone's mind that India can and should train a larger number of its people in world-class skills. When I look back on the exercise, I realize that these students were second to none in the world in their ideation and innovation capabilities. In my heart I thanked the first prime minister of India, Jawaharlal Nehru, and his education minister, Maulana Azad, for having the foresight to build some of the best institutions in the world for our young. Unfortunately, the policy and regulatory ecosystem created to set up these institutions did not percolate to other areas, such as school education, non-technical education, etc. And these institutions themselves ended up becoming islands of excellence. Overall, the first pillar of the knowledge economy (as identified by the World Bank) remained stunted until the mid-1990s, when there was a bourgeoning of engineering colleges to meet the demand of a flourishing IT industry. India has made significant strides in making its mark in the global knowledge economy through its tech expertise. Whether it is the Indian IT giants or the multinational IT campuses in India, India's bright young minds who left the country to work in the IT sector abroad or India's tech start-ups—we have done justice to our inherent power of knowledge in this aspect.

India has also acted reasonably well as far as the building of information infrastructure (World Bank pillar #2) goes. A comparison of mobile data charges in 228 countries done by cable.co.uk shows that India has the lowest average mobile data prices in the world, at an average USD 0.09 for 1 GB of data, whereas the United States is ranked at 188, with an average mobile data tariff of USD 8 for 1 GB.[6] This low cost of data is today the backbone of the massive digitization programme of Digital India by the government of India. But we have been abysmally slow in bringing digitization to our learning needs and have not grasped the need for computers and hand-held devices in hinterland India. Some low-cost innovations were made here too, but they could not be scaled. Given our strength in the IT sector, this should be something we can solve if we put our minds to it.

Recently, there have been important policy changes (World Bank pillar #3) in India for building skills for the knowledge economy and for fostering entrepreneurship around digitization, artificial intelligence, machine learning, data science, etc. The new National Education Policy unveiled by the Indian government in 2020 is partly designed to build the foundations of a knowledge economy ecosystem.[7]

In creating an innovation system (World Bank pillar #4), India is making significant progress, but again, not on a large scale. An innovation ecosystem needs much more than just a skilled and educated human workforce. There are several aspects—such as the number of researchers, the number of patents filed, the number of publications in scientific and technical journals, research and development expenditure as a percentage of GDP, trademarks and industrial design application filings, hi-tech exports—to a good innovation system. In terms of researchers per million, for example, as of 2019–20, China had 1,206 researchers, the United States 4,313, and India only 216. Our patent system remains slow and dismal in its functioning. Indians filed 45,000 patents, against 1.33 million filed by the Chinese between 2019 and 2020. As of 2020, smaller nations such as Israel and South Korea spent around 4.5 per cent of their GDP on research, whereas the corresponding figure for India is only 0.62 per cent.[8] Our universities don't rank among the top 100 globally, even though many of them feature in the top 500. Recently, it was only IISC Bengaluru, IIT Delhi and IIT Bombay that made it to the top 200 QS ratings.[9]

The Indian government is now offering incentives to global giants to establish and augment their R&D facilities in India. There is also a special focus on knowledge-based start-ups. These are all positive signs—but what remains difficult to achieve is wide-scale awareness about the prospects of knowledge economy among citizens and co-opting them into building a thriving knowledge and innovation economy.

Moonshots

In 2017, I was invited to participate in the Action Forum organized by the Aspen Institute in the United States. It was a four-day programme, with my Aspen Global Leadership Network (AGLN) co-fellows from across the world converging at the institute's campus in Aspen, Colorado. As part of its Public Leadership Series, the programme included a session titled 'Re-igniting Citizenship: Reviving the Moonshot'. The purpose of the session at the Action Forum was to discuss what ideas in present-day democracies could garner mass-scale citizen engagement; and how leaders could unite citizens around ambitious national goals. I was to bring to the Forum the learnings from my Yi and India@75 experiences to look at how to make a 'moonshot' work.

The term 'moonshot' was originally coined to describe NASA's mammoth task of putting a man on the moon, which would take several missions. But, over time, after the United States achieved this goal, the word 'moonshot' became synonymous with an extremely ambitious mission undertaken to achieve a monumental goal.[10]

Prepping for my session early in the morning, sitting on a bench outside one of institute's seminar buildings, I thought about the Aspen Institute itself. It was the vision—an ambitious one—of Walter Paepcke, a Chicago businessman who was the chairman of Container Corporation of America. He wanted to create a space where artists, leaders, thinkers and musicians could gather. The scenic mountains of Aspen in Colorado seemed perfect for such a rendezvous. Paepcke organized the first Aspen festival on the occasion of the 200th birth anniversary of the German poet and philosopher Johann Wolfgang von Goethe in 1949. The festival attracted 2,000 prominent participants for the seminars and it lasted for twenty days.[11] Paepcke wanted to create a place where the human spirit could flourish for the collective good of humanity, in the midst of the churns of modern society. He founded the Aspen Institute on the outskirts of the then depleted and deserted silver mining town of Aspen for this very purpose. He was personally inspired by the Great Books programme of the University of Chicago, from which the Aspen Institute Executive Seminar took inspiration.

I looked around, and it seemed that even after almost seventy years the mission of the institute to foster a good society was very much at work! I recollected my own first seminar in December 2010 with three wonderful moderators—Keith Berwick, Peter Reiling and Ferial Haffajee. When introducing the Aspen Global Leadership Network (AGLN) to us, Peter had remarked that he liked to call it 'the inter-galactic army of the good'. As part of the AGLN fellowship, each fellow is expected to launch a venture emphasizing leadership and personal stretch. Today, AGLN has over

2,500 fellows in fifty-one countries who have launched projects and ventures, and have sometimes transformed their whole lives to create a positive impact and take forward the idea of a good society. As the aspen trees around me swished in the mid-summer breeze, I could not help but think that moonshots were not just about nations and societies but also about individual action for the collective good.

When I think about what ails India's knowledge and innovation ecosystem, it is clear to me that there has been no call-to-action for individual citizens in our knowledge economy journey. If we want to be global leaders in the knowledge economy, then we have to proclaim it as our moonshot. And we need to inspire everyone to pitch in. Our first moonshot should be to co-create a robust education system. Our second moonshot should be to ensure every learner has access to digital learning tools. Our third moonshot should be to rethink our approach in policies and laws that govern the knowledge economy, and our fourth moonshot should be to allow the mushrooming of high-quality research, higher-education and think-tank institutions. And we need to do all of this pronto, as the world is moving fast towards a new reality, a knowledge age if you will, and we should not lag behind. In fact, there is a clear risk of our people becoming knowledge slaves if we don't take immediate steps to strengthen our knowledge economy pillars.

In his address at Rice University on 12 September 1962, President John F. Kennedy proclaimed, 'We choose to go to the moon. We choose to go to the moon in this decade and do the other things, not because they are easy, but because they are hard, because that goal will serve to organize and measure the best of our energies and skills, because that challenge is one that we are willing to accept, one we are unwilling to postpone, and one which we intend to win ...'[12] Seven years later, on 20 July 1969, NASA astronaut Neil Armstrong took his first step on the surface of the moon. This is the power of moonshots.

From the time President Kennedy proclaimed the moonshot of setting a man on the moon, NASA and the United States government worked diligently on their plans, with a singular focus of becoming the first nation to do so. During those years, schools and universities in the US also joined in the mission. Science projects, research and conversations took place around the ambitious goal. Corporations and private-sector think-tanks pursued the goal by augmenting their own research and brought innovative ideas to the table. The ambitious moonshot captured the imagination of an entire nation. In terms of its sheer size, it was one of the biggest financial commitments by the US government until then.

When I was sixteen, Neil Armstrong visited Mumbai. I love astrophysics, and my father, who knew of this passion, managed to get me an invitation pass for one of his interactive programmes in the city. I listened to him, wide-eyed and fully attentive. After the talk, I went up to him to get his autograph. I remember asking him, 'Sir, did you always know you would go to the moon?' He looked at me with a gentle smile and said, 'Young lady, often your whole life is a preparation for that one moment, one event that can transform humanity. I think my education, my training and my interests all came together in that one moment when I put my foot on the lunar surface. Never underestimate the small steps we take for that major milestone.' His advice has stayed with me all my life. I continue to believe that small steps lead to the big moment—to the realization of the moonshot.

I think if India wants to use its power of knowledge to achieve the moonshot of being the world leader in the knowledge economy, we will need leadership that inspires collective citizen action; we will need ideas that capture the national imagination, and we will need to put our financial and human resources at work towards that ambitious goal. As Neil Armstrong advised, we will need to take small steps towards the final moment of glory. These small steps cannot simply stem from an idea or imagination. We will need to take good stock of where we are and comprehend how the pace of technology and innovation is changing the twenty-first century world order before we take up the challenge of treading and then transforming our path.

4IR

Founder and executive chairman of the World Economic Forum Klaus Schwab coined the popular term '4th Industrial Revolution (4IR)' in his article for *Foreign Affairs* in 2015. Describing the advent of 4IR, he said: 'We stand on the brink of a technological revolution that will fundamentally alter the way we live, work, and relate to one another. In its scale, scope, and complexity, the transformation will be unlike anything humankind has experienced before.'[13] Indeed, a 4IR world will be a world driven by data, interconnectedness and seamless connections between humans and machines. It will be a world shaped by the power of knowledge. Technologies such as block chain, internet of things (IoT), artificial intelligence, 3D printing, smart autonomous transport and vehicles, cloud computing, 5G wireless, quantum computing, nano-technology, machine learning and robotics are all examples of the technological revolution that Klaus Schwab referred to.

This new world of 4IR will be a significant leap for mankind as it will impact not just industrial activities but will also change the very manner in which human beings live, work and interact. This is not some far-fetched future that can only be experienced in the present as a figment of fiction. Many of the technologies listed above are a reality today. They have penetrated many industries and are also impacting many aspects of our lives.

In 2013, I was in Belgium to interact with the next-generation members of Flemish business families. I decided to spend a few days exploring Brussels and its museums. At the Museum of

Musical Instruments, I came across a simple, early-generation IoT application that left me awestruck. The museum gave you a gadget with earphones to carry along on your tour of its galleries. When you stood in front of an exhibit, the gadget recognized the instrument you were viewing and started playing audio information about the instrument, including a recording of how the instrument sounds when played. The censor on the instrument was recognized by the gadget and its software, which then picked the relevant information to play to me. This is a simple explanation from a novice like me but it gave me a peek into what a world with connected devices that seamlessly spoke to each other could mean. That was nine years ago. Today, smart homes, smart appliances and gadgets such as Alexa are commonplace. This is the accelerated wave of change that we are riding.

Although 4IR, like its preceding industrial revolutions, offers opportunities for income growth and technological advancement, there is another massive parallel shift the world is witnessing—climate change. This—coupled with the pandemic that the world is experiencing, and a frictional geopolitical environment—means that we are looking at challenging times for sure. How every nation navigates this road to 4IR actualization will be different. Those that are able to lead in development, deployment and adaptation of 4IR tech on a large scale will tend to lead and shape the global order. Countries like China and the United States have some of the highest number of research and innovation projects happening in the field of 4IR technologies. Although India lags behind in this field of research, it has an opportunity to make a mark.

An analysis conducted by the Organisation for Economic Co-operation and Development (OECD) of the Microsoft-owned code-sharing platform GitHub shows that India has surpassed even the United States in AI code writing.[14] Facebook, Google, Microsoft and IBM have their AI labs in India. Indian prowess at writing AI code and developing commercial applications using AI is second to none in the world. Years of investment by the Indian IT sector and companies in training our software engineers in upcoming 4IR technologies are now showing results. There is also significant investment flowing into India for funding AI-driven start-ups. The WEF has also set up a centre for 4IR in Navi Mumbai. There is also much impetus given to 4IR tech in the Indian government's Digital India mission.

These are all good foundations on which to build a more nuanced and focused strategy for India's 4IR future. But let us not forget that for a knowledge economy ecosystem to thrive, we need to address the long-standing inadequacies of our education system, which will be the crucial cornerstone of our moonshot. A 4IR future is a foregone conclusion. What we need to determine is what that future will look like for India. How will it affect our education, healthcare, climate and agriculture? We definitely need to have a more detailed plan for this new reality that awaits humanity. Also, we have to ensure that access to knowledge that drives 4IR development is not a privilege of the few but is accessible to people from all walks of life in the country. Some may ask whether it's not too early for India to make these decisions. Should we not first digitize everything, set up frameworks for data protection and privacy, change our educational curriculum and *then* draw up a plan for 4IR? The truth of the matter is that if we wait to do all of this in sequence, or organically, we may miss the boat in playing a global leadership role in the new knowledge economy. The pace of development of new technologies is unprecedented. If we don't want to miss the bus, we are going to have to jump from the aircraft and build the parachute along the way. That may sound crazy, but maybe it is time for both moonshots and 'loonshots'[15].

Loonshots

In 2020, just when the Covid-19 pandemic had begun to spread across the world, I got myself a fascinating book written by Safi Bahcall, a second-generation physicist (son of two astrophysicists), a biotech entrepreneur and a former public-company CEO. In this bestseller *Loonshots – How to Nurture Crazy Ideas that Win Wars, Cure Diseases and Transform Industries*, Bahcall describes a 'loonshot' as a widely dismissed idea whose champions are often written off as crazy. He emphasizes that post the ideation stage, loonshots need large groups of people to give them shape and make them successful. He uses the science of phase transition to give us a slew of examples and some principles on how to structure teams that make loonshots succeed. Many of these principles, I strongly feel, we can imbibe here in India to ensure we are leaders of disruptive innovation era rather than its victims. As someone who was already inspired by the idea of a moonshot, I found Bahcall's book an invigorating read.

Among the key ideas he writes about, one stands out the most to me. It is the principle that the success of loonshots does not depend on the culture of the organization in which they are anchored but on the structure of those organizations. This makes me wonder, if becoming a knowledge economy leader is our moonshot then what should be our loonshot? Given that India continues to struggle with education, healthcare, poverty, climate change and livelihood generation, may be our loonshot could be about using 4IR tech to achieve India's sustainable development goals. Then the next question arises, as to how we can organize ourselves so that we are successful in our loonshot. What should be the role of the government, of the private sector and of the citizens in this endeavour? Imagine calling our power of knowledge to action for the overall development of the nation by organizing ourselves in a manner where success is possible. Imagine, rallying the entire nation to collaborate in that mission.

Imagine, 1.38 billion people empowered with skills and organized as a team to realize the dream of an inclusive and developed India. Challenging enough? Yup!

Despite the significant progress in pan-India digitization and the low cost of data in the country, many Indians remain unaware about the coming of 4IR. If we were to follow the advice of Neil Armstrong, then our first step should be to create nation-wide awareness about this new wave of change imminent upon humanity, and let people know that India will be no exception. Perhaps our students in schools and colleges should have a subject that talks about 4IR and its impact on the future of work and society. Perhaps our college students need to be given special grants to explore the use and application of 4IR technologies in their area of work. Currently, much of this focus is based on either simple innovations at school-level labs or through programmes in engineering colleges. We need to broad-base 4IR tech and innovation pertaining to it. Therefore, students of music, art and history must also be equally encouraged to learn and apply 4IR tech in their work as students of science, engineering and mathematics are.

India is an agrarian economy. It is time our farmers are made aware of and empowered with skills that allow them to use technologies like block-chain and IoT at the farm level. This means a complete shift in our farmer training programmes. We may think of exposing our micro, small and medium enterprises through MSME tool rooms across the country to 4IR technologies that can help in their businesses. In fact, we may think of transforming MSME tool rooms into centres of 4IR for MSMEs. We can train our teachers and educators to avail of cloud and automation technologies to deliver quality education to a larger number of students in a shorter period of time than is currently possible. Smart classrooms are a reality of today, but classrooms that use augmented reality (AR) can completely shift the learning experience.

We can think of training our healthcare professionals—doctors, nurses, ward boys, ASHA workers, Anganwadi workers, etc.—in 4IR tools such as IoT and AI applications in order to make quality healthcare available at affordable prices even in remote places. We can use the powerful force of 5G networks to connect remote communities, small traders, homemakers and even the retired elderly, with modern markets, products and services. As far as technology is concerned, we need to leapfrog over some incremental stages of the tech journey to ensure that citizens' experience of government and their participation in governance is drastically improved by using 4IR tools. These would form the necessary aspects of our loonshot.

While all the actions mentioned so far can help us engage citizens on a mass scale with 4IR reality, we need to take significant steps in structuring our organs of innovation in a way that can fire up loonshots, as advised by Bahcall in his book. Currently, our grants for innovations are based on the success rate of a project or programme, but maybe we need to accept failures first. If we set up our innovation funding with a bias towards funding successful outcomes, then we may not see the mushrooming of loonshots, for they need an environment where failure is normal and even important. The nation-wide lamenting of the failed lunar landing of ISRO's Chandrayan-2 is the kind of hysteria around failure that we need to avoid. Was it really a failure? Weren't there other learnings and advantages of the mission that we didn't notice because we were all hung up about the landing? Was it a false failure then? Bahcall says that recognizing false failures and continuing to back innovations is an important test of whether we can incubate loonshots. This also brings us to the question of what kind of leadership can make some of this happen. Bahcall throws some light on this too. We need to find leaders who nurture innovators and are not hungry for fame themselves; leaders who create systems that fire the maximum loonshots will be people happy to be behind the scenes. Have we seen such leadership before? Does India have the tools to fire loonshots? Yes, indeed!

ISRO

The Indian Space and Research Organisation (ISRO) is India's national space agency. It was established as the Indian National Committee of Space Research under the Department of Atomic Energy in 1962,[16] the same year Kennedy spoke about the 'moonshot' at Rice University. In 1962, India was a poor developing nation. The launch of a space programme invited much criticism within and outside the country. Many called it a 'crazy idea'. To those detractors, the first chairman of the space agency, Vikram Sarabhai, responded with confident yet measured words: 'There are some who question the relevance of space activities in a developing nation. To us, there is no ambiguity of purpose. We do not have the fantasy of competing with the economically advanced nations in the exploration of the Moon or the planets or manned space-flight. But we are convinced that if we are to play a meaningful role nationally, and in the community of nations, we must be second to none in the application of advanced technologies to the real problems of man and society, which we find in our country.'[17]

The early years of ISRO were difficult and the scientists had to make do with limited resources, but their aspiration to create an Indian space programme that served India's developmental needs—a loonshot indeed—took them past those limitations. India's first rocket flight was launched in November 1963 from a beach in Thumba, a northern suburb of Thiruvananthapuram in Kerala on the Arabian Sea coast. In fact, in those initial years, the scientists worked out of a makeshift office in the nearby non-functional church of St Mary Magdalene, as it was one of the few concrete buildings around the beach. With a promise to the local fisherfolk that the sanctity of the altar would not be compromised, the pioneers of India's space programme assembled their rockets in the church's main hall in the company of pigeons. And the bishop's quarters served as an accommodation for visiting scientists.[18]

If Vikram Sarabhai were here today, he would be proud of what ISRO has accomplished so far. It has the distinction of becoming the seventh national space agency to possess full satellite launch capabilities. It has the world's largest network of remote sensing satellites and has sent two satellite missions to the moon and one to Mars. But more importantly, as envisaged by Sarabhai, ISRO has made mammoth technological advancements, making its innovations available for India's developmental needs. In areas as varied as civil aviation, biodiversity information systems, telemedicine, academia, agriculture, earth sciences, defence and telecommunication, technologies or platforms developed by ISRO are being used for the nation's progress and well-being.[19]

ISRO was a loonshot from the word go. Firstly, it was a space agency in a country where there were famines. It was set up under the Department of Atomic Energy but it functioned separately, in Bengaluru, a location far away from the seat of the Union government in New Delhi. ISRO had the good fortune in its formative years to be headed by a leader who was humble in his expectations but ambitious in his vision. Sarabhai created an environment where scientists and innovators were given room to fail and the support to explore. Even though the Department of Space over the years has remained under the prime minister of India, the chairman of ISRO has always been a scientist and innovator—just like Sarabhai. This structure allows much more flexibility than would have been possible if it had been operated as a government department headed by someone from one of the mainstream government services.

ISRO is not one facility operating out of a single location. It is an organism of space exploration and innovation with a

national presence, and with several sister organizations under the
Department of Space that help in research as well as in application of
its innovations. It has several facilities spread across the country for
research, in areas as varied as atmospheric research, semi-conductor
innovation and space applications. It has a few construction and
launch facilities, one test facility and several tracking and control
facilities. What amazes me most is the network of training, education
and research infrastructure that ISRO possesses. Apart from the
Indian Institute of Remote Sensing at Dehradun and the Indian
Institute of Space Science and Technology at Thiruvananthapuram,
ISRO has six active incubators spread across the country, along with
Regional Academy Centres for Space at different universities and
a fully equipped Space Innovation Centre. In essence, ISRO is
structured to fire 'loonshots' such as the Mangalyaan-1 mission—
the only mission to the orbit of Mars to succeed in its first attempt.[20]

ISRO is a fine example of what India can achieve, should the
country call its power of knowledge to action and pursue the loonshot
of using 4IR tech for the country's developmental challenges.
Such an ambitious 'loonshot' can consist of several moonshots.
But foremost among the moonshots must be a global leadership
in knowledge economy. This moonshot will serve as our compass
for the transformational changes needed in our education, skills
and innovation ecosystem. India's former president A.P.J. Kalam,
more popularly known as Missile Man of India, was an aerospace
scientist who worked at both ISRO and DRDO (Defence Research
and Development Organisation). He once famously said, 'Dream,
Dream, Dream. Dreams transform into thoughts and thoughts
result into action.'[21]

As a nation of 1.38 billion and growing, it is time that we begin
to dream of a loonshot once again. Today, we have much stronger
winds beneath our wings than we did when ISRO came into being.
Culturally, we worship knowledge as a supreme power. Now it is

time we gave it strategy, structure and strength for its twenty-first century actualization. That is when, as seekers of Saraswati and connoisseurs of Ilm (knowledge), we will do justice to our power of knowledge. If we could nurture a centre of knowledge like Nalanda for over 800 years, then we can nurture a knowledge economy that engages citizens at large. There is no doubt that this will be hard and we will fail along the way too. But to paraphrase what the US president Kennedy said, we need to do this because this challenge is one that we are willing to accept, one we are unwilling to postpone, and one which we intend to win.

7

Power of Food

The Naga Chef

The winter in Nagaland ushers in sunny days, clear blue skies and a biting chill. In December of 2014, the air was abuzz with excitement in Kohima, the state capital. Prime Minister Narendra Modi was coming to inaugurate the annual Hornbill Festival. People lined the road from Dimapur airport to Kohima to greet him. The prime minister of India was gracing the Hornbill Festival after a long hiatus. The Hornbill Festival is a kaleidoscope of Naga culture. Tribes from across the state bring their artwork and handicrafts for display and sale, as well as entertain visitors with their performing arts.

Hekani and I reached the venue of opening ceremony on 1 December, the inaugural day, well ahead of time. The opening ceremony itself was a celebration of Naga traditions and the Naga way of life. The prime minister spoke with passion and shared his

164

vision for not just Nagaland but for the entire north-east region. I would have loved to spend more time watching the colourful Naga dances, but Hekani said we had to rush to the Naga Chef competition.

On our way to the venue of the Naga Chef contest, Hekani told me that her husband, Alezo Kense, had begun work on this contest the previous year. The chief minister at the time, Neiphiu Rio, and his advisor, Abu Metha, had come up with the idea of Naga Chef to create awareness about Naga cuisine and culture. The contest design took inspiration from Master Chef Australia, which was by then a rage on television.

On the way to the venue, I was thinking about whether it was possible to create the same excitement around Naga Chef that Master Chef Australia had managed. When we reached the venue, I was pleasantly surprised. The set-up looked very professional. The contestants were cooking various tribal dishes, some even innovating new dishes on the spot. I was amused to see vegetarian dishes being cooked too, because traditional Naga food consists largely of meat. Alezo explained to me that the purpose of Naga Chef was to expose people from far and wide, and with varied dietary preferences, to Naga food. I was a bit curious. What was a young man from a prominent business family doing with a chef competition?

Alezo shared with me that his intention was to give people an experience of Naga culture through Naga food. He explained to me that Naga cuisine is quite unique in taste and in its preparation. There is very little use of oil, and not very many ingredients are mixed together. Most of the recipes call for the steaming, roasting or boiling of meat and/or vegetables, and the original flavour of the ingredients is thus preserved. Each Naga tribe has its own special dishes. Recalling the first Naga Chef competition of 2013, Alezo told me about the innumerable challenges they had faced. Organizing a competition that did justice to the vast repertoire of

Naga food would entail sourcing of more than 200 ingredients. Alezo and his small team of young enthusiasts at Synergy Group (Alezo's company that organizes the Naga Chef competition) had to create their own kitchen and pantry. They had to design the contest— think about how the competition would play out on the ground and who would judge it. They watched several cookery contest shows and also took inputs from experts. They reached out to colleges, especially hotel management institutions, to seek candidates for participation. They wanted to make sure that the best and brightest participated, and to this end they partnered with local newspapers and village-level organizations. They also advertised widely. In the first season, the prize money was a modest Rs 5 lakh. And despite the many difficulties along the way, they managed to get thirty-four participants. And so began a journey of culinary expression and celebration.

Alezo said his team learnt many lessons in the first year itself. For example, some dishes would take a long time to get done, making it difficult for the organizers to decide on a suitable time limit for the participants. The chefs themselves were not all skilled in the culinary arts, even though they knew their food quite well. Alezo wanted the competition to be open to anyone who had culinary skills—from a homemaker in a village to a young aspiring chef from Kohima. The idea was to create excellence in Naga cuisine and to introduce it to the world. When it was launched, Naga Chef was the first-of-its-kind culinary competition in the north-east of the country.

By 2019, Naga Chef was in its seventh season. When I last spoke with Alezo,[1] he was brimming with satisfaction as he described his journey so far. He told me that before Naga Chef, there were a few restaurants outside Nagaland selling Naga food, but what the competition had done is that it had made Naga cuisine fashionable. It had also created an impetus for the local chefs to refine their skills. Many had found new livelihood opportunities and had started catering businesses and restaurants. Some had even published cookbooks. Alezo proudly informed me that the winner of the first season now works for the Taj Bengal, a five-star hotel in Kolkata.

Not one to rest on his laurels, Alezo now wants to take the success of Naga Chef further and aspires to make Naga food part of the global culinary map. He believes that Naga food is not only unique but is also representative of the Naga people and their culture. He wants the world to know Nagaland through its cuisine. In order to do this, Alezo wants to institutionalize the Naga Chef competition, invest in research and offer culinary courses for people to upgrade their skills and innovate new dishes based on traditional Naga ingredients and methods. He wishes to introduce refinement and further diversity to Naga food by engaging experts, such as celebrity chefs and nutritionists, to create more awareness about Naga cuisine. When I asked him about his big audacious goal for Naga Chef, Alezo gushed, 'I want our food to be part of people's everyday food choices around the world, just like pasta, pizza or burger. That is the only way for people everywhere to know Naga culture.'

In the argument that food is a gateway to cultural immersion, Alezo is absolutely right. Food allows us to experience a different people and their ways more intimately without having to travel to their lands. When I was studying at Miami University in the United States, food was my way to experience culture, especially since I was staying with people from eighty different nationalities. Every weekend was a culinary bonanza, where dishes from different countries would be cooked and stories about them shared with love and nostalgia. During those years, I also came to the conclusion that the eclectic nature of Indian food makes our cuisine very unique. There are many cultures that have rich culinary traditions, but Indian cuisine has a richness of diversity and taste that is quite special. The same lentil has varied preparations across the country and every community has its own version of a roti or a vegetable dish. Sweets and savouries, pickles and chutneys, too, vary in preparation, and are prepared with unique ingredients in different parts of the country. In India, food is a powerful medium through which we convey our emotions, beliefs and traditions. Our food preparations and habits are also rooted in a deep and ancient science, ensuring a good and healthy life. Indeed, there is no better example of a well-thought-out Indian food tradition than the ubiquitous thali.

The Thali

The concept of the thali is unique to India. It comes from the idea that your food plate must be diverse for it to be a balanced and nutritious meal. Ayurveda espouses the idea that 'you are what you eat'. Hence, a huge amount of focus and work has gone into defining what should be eaten with what, and when and how each item should be prepared, served and consumed. This traditional science identifies six tastes, or rasas. They are: madhura (sweet), amla (sour), lavana (salty), katu (pungent), tikta (bitter) and kashaya (astringent). Ayurveda states that each of these rasas plays a vital role in our physiology, health and well-being. In essence, the thali is a well-balanced representation of our ancient science of food where every one of the six rasas is present in appropriate proportions, cooked using methods that retain and enhance the nutritious qualities of the food.

The word 'thali' literally means a plate. There are many versions of the thali, depending on which region of India is on your plate! Alezo's ultimate goal is to create a Naga thali that is as famous as its Rajasthani or Gujarati cousins. Thalis can be very modest, as served in temples, or very elaborate, as served at weddings. They can be vegetarian or non-vegetarian. But every version of the thali is a representation of the six tastes and contains the appropriate proportions of proteins, carbohydrates, fats, fibre, minerals and vitamins. In addition to the six tastes, a variety of textures is also incorporated in the thali, such as softness of boiled rice, or crunchiness of the deep-fried pakoda. The items in a thali also call for different cooking methods, such as steaming, frying (both shallow and deep), roasting, smoking and grilling. The entire focus of the thali is to deliver an ideal meal, achieving several objectives: a nutritionally balanced and diverse meal, portion control to avoid overeating only one rasa, and using a variety of cooking methods and local ingredients. In a manner of speaking, the thali is a truly delicious, nutritious and sustainable meal.

The science of food is a powerful Indian inheritance. The excavations at the Harappan site in Kalibangan in Rajasthan led to the discovery of tools and utensils that point to the existence of a thali as early as 3500–2500 BC. During our visit to Hampi, we saw in the ruins rows of 'plates' and 'bowls' carved into the rocky surface, to feed the armies the traditional thali. When I was at university in the US, I would be told by friends whenever we cooked together, 'You can just make one dish.' I never knew how to do that. I mean, surely a dal would need to be accompanied by rice or roti, and vegetables? Unless it was a snack or a dessert, most Indian dishes would need to be served in combination with other preparations. I soon realized that my inherent expectations in the diversity of the food plate were part of my cultural conditioning.

We all grow up eating different food of different communities at school, college or at the workplace. These experiences bring India's culinary vastness to young boys and girls who remember the idli, the parantha or the dhokla cooked in their friends' homes as having been the best ever. Food is central to the Indian way of life. We have dishes for different seasons and occasions. We mark celebration or mourning with food. Food is part of our rituals and traditions; finding its rightful place in our worship of the divine and in warding off evil in equal measure. In fact, we have rituals for preparing food, serving food, and eating food. We have special prayers for ploughing

the agriculture fields and festivals that celebrate the harvest season—
Onam, Ugadi, Padwa, Baisakhi, Bihu, Pongal, Sankranti, and Aoleang
being some of them. Every state or region has its own sowing and
harvest festivals, its own cuisine, its own varieties of grains, lentils,
legumes, millets and spices, its own pickles and savouries and its
own sweet dishes. We have special foods for the worship of different
gods and goddesses. We also have our own goddess of food—Mata
Annapurna.

Annapurna and Annadaata

Annapurna literally means 'the one who fulfils the need for food'—
anna means food and *purna* means to fulfil. Goddess Annapurna is
depicted holding a ladle and a pot. Legend has it that she is actually
Lord Shiva's consort and that she decided to make her husband
understand that food is essential for sustaining life on earth and that
meditation alone cannot sustain life. There are different versions of
this legend, depending on which ancient text you refer to, but the
legend survives to this day. People still revere Annapurna as the giver
of food and nourishment. I know that there are Greek, Roman and
Egyptian deities associated with the harvest or with nourishment,
but none of the cultures they belong to celebrate them as widely
today as India does Goddess Annapurna.

Annapurna is a well-known deity. There is a famous temple
dedicated to her at Varanasi on the banks of the Ganga. But across
India, in villages and cities, people make an offering of food to
their gods with their daily prayers, at temples or in their own puja
rooms, and then distribute this food as prasad—blessings. It is
considered not just rude and improper but a sin to refuse prasad.
Large temples have dedicated kitchens to make prasad for devotees.
Food, therefore, is not just meant for survival and nourishment of
the body but is regarded as a boon and a blessing from the divine.

Outside Hindu temples one will find long queues of poor people, who are fed by the devotees. We have rituals for serving food to young girls, the elderly, priests, teachers, the poor and the needy, and even cows and crows. Such is the importance of annadaan—donation of food—in our culture. The practice of annadaan is not limited to the Hindus alone. Sikh gurudwaras have the tradition of langar, where people sit in rows and are served the food cooked by devotees at the gurudwara. At the dargah of the Muslim Sufi saint Khwaja Moinuddin Chishti at Ajmer in Rajasthan, one can donate money to serve a badi (big) or choti (small) deg (a cooking pot that allows a large amount of food to be cooked) of food to the needy or the faithful. Thus, to cook, serve, and eat are all acts of faith for a large number of Indians. And India's relationship with food is one of reverence and regard.

It is probably this regard for food that ensures that 'culture' remains an integral part of agriculture in India. It is not simply a production activity of generating food but an integral part of life and livelihood in India. People were traditionally encouraged to bring human enterprise and ingenuity to partner with nature and cultivate a vast variety of produce. Conventionally, because of the divine status of food, the farmer was regarded as an annadaata (giver of food). He was, therefore, accorded much importance. Stories in the ancient texts allude to the gods, kings and others in powerful positions ploughing the fields to bring good fortune to the people. To be a farmer was a divine privilege of sorts.

As time progressed, the role of cultivating the lands was assigned to a specific class and community and the status of the farmer started losing its sheen. As invaders and colonists conquered and enslaved India, the farmer became nothing but a tool to produce goods that could be taken away at low prices to foreign shores for bigger profits. The British also introduced a land revenue system to allow them to earn large amounts of money in the form of land rent or tax. Later they introduced land settlements and revenue collectors became private landlords called zamindars. This meant that land revenue was fixed for perpetuity and even though the farmers still tilled their own lands, the ownership of their farms remained but in name.[2] The annadaata became impoverished, and the zamindars started extracting cheap labour from poor farmers while denying them the right to their lands or fair compensation. A system of oppression developed, and the annadaata was reduced to a beggar, begging for a share of harvest from his own land and his own hard work. The 'culture' in agriculture survived through festivals and the worship of Annapurna and other deities continued, but the annadaata was forgotten, vulnerable and reduced to poverty.

As regard for the annadaata diminished, so did the value of what he or she did. Even though a large number of people in India continue to be engaged in agriculture, it has become common practice to say that many of these people need to be steered away from agriculture and into manufacturing and services. Over the decades, post-Independence, agriculture became an economic activity that was necessary to feed our large population. It became an economic burden on the government finances as it needed to be supported by massive subsidies. In the 1960s, when India faced drought and famine, the Indian prime minister of the time, Lal Bahadur Shastri, equated the farmer with the soldier who fights wars for the country with the slogan '*Jai Jawan Jai Kisan* (Glory to the Soldier, Glory to the Farmer)'. This was followed by the era of the Green Revolution, when irrigation techniques, high-yield inputs, and seeds and water and power subsidies were made available to farmers to encourage them to continue to pursue agriculture and achieve food security for the nation. But this also meant loss of crop diversity.

Today, almost 70 per cent of the rice fields and 90 per cent of the wheat fields in India grow only a few high-yield varieties.[3] Traditionally, India has grown over 1,00,000 different varieties of rice alone.[4] This means that our traditional science of nutrition, which promoted diversity of plate, and the agricultural practices that helped sustain those food habits has been shunned in favour of a few high-yield varieties. Of course, this provided food security and we were liberated from our dependence on other nations for food but it also led to the disappearance of the indigenous varieties of crops, some of which were, drought or flood resistant. With this, the farmer and the nutrition on our plates both began to suffer. A vicious cycle developed, and India became a country with a large number of hungry and malnourished people.[5]

Annapurna's Hungry

In 2021, India—the largest producer of milk and the second largest producer of grains, fruits and vegetables in the world—was ranked at 101 among 116 nations in the Global Hunger Index.[6] We can argue about the methodology used for this index, but it is amply clear from the various reports of the government of India itself and of multilateral institutions and civil society organizations that there is significant hunger and malnourishment in India. As of 2020, as per the Food and Agriculture Organization (FAO), 189.2 million Indians—14 per cent of our population—were undernourished.[7] According to UNICEF, hunger is a direct or indirect cause of over 1,500 child deaths every day in India.[8] How can this bode well for a nation whose biggest superpower are its people? All the advantages of a large young population and a massive market will remain under-realized if we don't address this issue with the urgency it warrants.

How does a country that is in the top-five producer lists for 80 per cent of the crops in the world remain incapable of feeding its own people nutritious food? Many blame the food distribution system, but quite a few point to the large number of small farms that are unable to connect to the markets as the reason for our farm to market supply chain inefficiency. The reasons are plenty, but the truth is that our power of food is now only limited to the variety in our cuisine and in the festivals we celebrate and the gods and goddesses we worship. We have forgotten those annadaatas who toil in the sun, rain, hail and storm to put our food on our table. We have also chosen to turn a blind eye to our malnourished. Moreover, we have done little to take a fresh drawing board and redefine the food ecosystem—from farm to plate—for the nation. We have not done much to arrest the criminal waste in our food supply chain. India loses on average 38 per cent of its agricultural produce in post-harvest distribution.

We have become a nation that produces a large amount of food, but with a drastically reduced diversity of crops, and are inept at arresting losses in our farm-to-market distribution. We have kept a large number of our farmers—big and small—dependent on state subsidies for inputs, water, electricity and market access. We are raising a stunted population, with many dying of hunger and malnourishment. What we need is a complete rethink on how we grow, distribute and eat our food. We not only have much help available from our traditional sciences, but also from new-age technology. We only have to be willing to re-examine our food ecosystem from a fresh perspective and with renewed commitment.

Diversity of Farm

As per the last census of India (2011), 263.1 million Indians were engaged in agriculture—a whopping 54.6 per cent of the total Indian workforce.[9] India ranks second in the world in agricultural production. India's arable land area of 156.4 million hectares is the second largest in the world.[10] With 2.4 per cent of the earth's surface, which is home to 1.38 billion people, what land use and agricultural practices India and Indians will adopt can shift the needle on eradicating hunger, reducing malnourishment, arresting food losses, increasing farmer incomes, reducing poverty, and last but not least, mitigating climate change through responsible, sustainable and regenerative agriculture.

According to FAO, 75 per cent of the world's food is generated from only twelve plant and five animal species currently, and more than 90 per cent of crop variety has disappeared from farms.[11] Imagine how difficult it would become for someone like Alezo Kense to source the 200-plus ingredients for the Naga Chef competition without the diversity of Naga farms. Fortunately for him, Nagaland is now going back to farming traditional crop varieties. In fact, an astounding 867 traditional varieties of rice have been catalogued already in the state.[12]

The traditional Indian farms were diverse in the crops they grew, and many had as many as three harvest cycles, with multiple crops per cycle even on a small family farm. This was mainly because the diversity of plate, where carbohydrates, proteins, vitamins and minerals had to be had in a balanced meal, expected diversity in agriculture, where grains, millets, legumes, pulses, vegetables and fruits were grown even on a small farm for self-consumption. The farmers grew food sustainably and benefited from the great range of nutrition it provided. Their crop rotation process regenerated the soil, sustaining its fertility and keeping the water tables balanced—a virtuous production and consumption cycle indeed. The power of food was considered intrinsic to the well-being of the individual and society, and much effort went into maintaining the balance for it. This spurred a rich culinary science and tradition that is thriving till date. In this way, Indian cuisine—a general combination of grains, pulses, vegetables at the very least, became one of the most nutritious meals to have. For traditional Indians, a diverse plate and a diverse farm were more of a rule rather than the exception. It is time that this powerful idea of crop diversity and plate diversity is brought back from oblivion.

The government's National Bureau of Soil Survey and Land Use Planning recognizes twenty broad agro-ecological zones across India, distinguished by their natural features and crop-growing periods.[13] Each of these agro-ecological zones is further composed of large numbers of micro-habitats. Over several millennia, endemic biodiverse conditions have spurred an amazing diversity of crops and livestock on the Indian farm. This is truly our superpower. But bringing back this biodiverse farming concept into large-scale practice will need training, skilling, knowledge transfer, technology, supply chain and market access. More importantly, it will need to challenge the wrong notion that biodiverse, sustainable agriculture can only be practised on large farms. In fact, small farms may be the key to bringing farm biodiversity back into vogue.

Small Is Beautiful

There is no denying that it is the large-scale farming using modern tools and inputs that led to India achieving food security through the Green Revolution. But there is also enough evidence that hybrid seeds that led to higher yields were poorer in nutritional content and climate adaptability compared to the indigenous varieties. Lack of crop rotation affected water tables as well as nitrogen content in our soil and consistent use of fertilizers led to decrease in soil fertility. Therefore, when it comes to deciding what agriculture reforms we must usher in, we are at crossroads now. On the one hand, we have a large population to feed and know that large scale farming supported by use of chemical fertilizers will allow us to do that. And on the other, we know that this large-scale farming leads to soil degradation and chemical fertilizers pollute the soil and water bodies. Then, there is the argument that small farms are commercially unviable.

Advocates of industrialization of agriculture believe that it is the small farm holdings in India that keep India's farmers poor and their farm productivity low. But studies and projects undertaken by the International Fund for Agriculture Development (IFAD) show that small-scale farms tend to be more productive and sustainable when given the same access to inputs and markets as for their larger counterparts.[14] This is indeed welcome news for the 86 per cent of farmland owners in India whose farms are of less than 2 hectares.[15] For small farms to commercially succeed in India, we need to pay close attention to the ecosystem they will need for it. Through training, inputs, tools, research and advisories, we can equip small farmers to use their land more sustainably. Many small farms were traditionally diverse farms but shifted to cultivating a single crop or two crops at best annually due to market pressures.

An important factor impeding growth in small-farm incomes is the vicious system of moneylenders and local middlemen who keep farmers away from exploring market channels outside their system. Therefore, when we think of agriculture reforms, we need to make sure that small farmers are set up for success and are given the tools and skills that empower them to deal with free market fluctuations, digital platforms, financial instruments and use of technology for improving farm yields. We should support them with viable credit options that leave them the option to choose their market linkages with more freedom. We can also reimagine the role of the middlemen and repurpose their activities in post-harvest supply chains with village-level pack-houses and cold-chain solutions. We can do away with state-supported mandis (markets) only after our farmers are knowledgeable about market competition and free market operations, leaving the choice to them as to whether they want to avail of the mandis or not. We must bring about these changes in a gradual manner. If we introduce reforms that simply eliminate middlemen or state markets or subsidies but do not put in the hard work to equip farmers with the necessary tools, infrastructure, processes, tech and skills, the changes will backfire, as the farmers themselves will reject such reforms. As that would be akin to telling a thirsty man that he is no longer able to use the dependable and easily accessible community well for water and has to look for his own sources of water. Which thirsty man would like that?

Reimagining the Food System

To understand what changes we need to bring about and at what stage in our food system, we first and foremost need to think of it as a whole system and not address agriculture productivity, markets, climate, nutrition and economic growth of farmers as separate functions. Here we may need to take the approach of 'systems thinking'.

Systems thinking envisages an approach to understanding and working with a system holistically; we analyse and comprehend how different parts of the system relate to each other and impact the functioning of the entire system. 'Thinking' as such is different from 'information gathering'. Thinking allows us to organize information in our own distinctive ways. Thinking allows us to bring purpose and causality to the information we have. Becoming aware of how we think and how we apply that to the world around us gives us the ability to be a 'systems thinker'. It is time we become systems thinkers if we want to address the perils of our food system.

The way we think stems from the mental models we have developed. We build our mental models using four different tools concurrently: 'distinctions', 'systems', 'relationships' and 'perspectives'. Our ability to comprehend the state of our agriculture, nutritional well-being and farmer incomes as a system will come from our mental models of how we think and feel about each of these subjects. This entails looking at how we comprehend the role of different pieces of the food system, how we understand the relationship between those components and ourselves and our perspective of food as a whole. This is where our superpower of food can come to our rescue.

Our reverence for food as a boon of the divine can help us immensely in building a mental model that is both unique and useful. This means that deep down in our psyche, food is our holy grail. Indians are food-obsessed. Illustrations of this obsession range from the restaurant serving Indian food atop the Swiss mountain Jungfraujoch and the packets of food that Indians travel with or those who live abroad call for from India. I call food our obsession because it is our primary expression of love. Indian mothers shower love on their children, family and even strangers through food. No visit to a home is complete without the guest being fed the best savouries from the kitchen. Such an intimate, obsessive and reverential relationship with food can help us make sure that we don't discount food as simply a means to survival and that we don't demean the farmer who grows this food by seeing him as a labourer who produces commodities. This approach can aid us in building a mental model of food as divine, nourishing, enjoyable and aspirational.

Our traditional science of diversity of plate is still not completely lost. Many nutritionists and chefs are now working hard to bring it back into fashion, if you will. Decoding our age-old food habits using modern-day nutritional science is making many young urban Indians return to traditional millets, pulses, spices and herbs. The concept of fresh and local, being popularized by new-age diets, is making local vegetables and fruits more and more attractive. India recently sponsored a resolution at the United Nations to adopt 2023 as the Year of Millets. This resolution was supported by seventy other nations. These are very good signs indeed. They indicate that the market is getting ready to welcome back diversity on the Indian food plate. But how equipped are our farmers to both understand this phenomenon and profit from it?

It seems that before we are able to nourish our plate, we may need to nourish our annadaatas. The key to achieving this lies in their education and skilling. Farmers in the twenty-first century are faced with a wide variety of challenges and opportunities. Discerning how and when these challenges/opportunities impact them, is a critical aspect to ensuring that farmers both survive and succeed. Take climate change, for example. Every farmer is or will be impacted adversely by global warming. But how many of them understand that agriculture contributes to global warming by as much as 20–25 per cent? Indeed, Indian agriculture contributes to 16 per cent of the country's greenhouse emissions, and this doesn't even include land-use changes of forest lands converted to farm land.[16] The large-scale cultivation of rice and oil palms is an example of how agriculture adds to climate risk. A case in point are the vast paddy fields of Punjab, Haryana and Uttar Pradesh, where stubble burning contributes to air pollution in New Delhi and the National Capital Region during October and November every year. The clearing of forests for agriculture is another example of how agriculture is adding to climate change. The rearing of livestock is also a major contributor. As a country with the largest number of livestock on the planet, India has a lot to work on as global warming knocks on our doors.

It is not that our farmers have no knowledge of climate risk. But many are not trained to understand how their own actions can help mitigate this risk to their own micro-habitats or agro-ecological zones. Do they understand, for instance, that their farming methods can either enrich or deplete the quality of their soil and its ability to produce nutritious food? Do they comprehend that they may need to change their crop-selection and crop patterns to adapt to the changing climatic conditions? We need to address this immediately. Nature is a farmer's best ally. Since our planet is going through accelerated changes in its natural world, we must prepare our farmers to be not just ready for its collateral effects but also to understand that they can be climate warriors too, if they adopted methods of climate-smart, biodiverse, sustainable and regenerative agriculture. But will this transition support our objectives of food security? Brazen changes to farming methods that do away with chemical fertilizers instantaneously on a large scale can bring shocks to the entire food system. Output from the farm and earnings of the farmer could both decrease suddenly. Therefore, how, where and for what crops regenerative practices should be introduced, needs to be a plan guided by both science and economics. We need to make informed decisions in a gradual manner so as to ensure food security, climate mitigation, farmers' incomes and soil rejuvenation are addressed in a holistic manner. For this to work, we need the farmers to be part of these decisions. Therefore, we also have to educate and empower farmers with knowledge and skills that aid them to participate in such decisions.

Most farmers are not formally educated in agriculture. Many have not even passed school. Therefore, we must think of a system where village-level programmes are conducted for upgrading their skills. Over the years, governments at the Union and state levels have conducted many training programmes in agriculture, apiculture and horticulture in rural India, but they have helped farmers only marginally. Why? Because, along with specific-produce training, financial and digital literacy must also be taught to farmers. This will enable them to understand market forces and financial products like crop insurance better. If we want to wean them away from the middlemen who are their moneylenders too, then we will need to train them to understand new financial products, systems and technologies.

In 2013, I visited the Dutch Flower Exchange in Amsterdam. I was taken aback to see farmers placing bids and using technology. We visited companies, universities and farms where cutting-edge research was being conducted in food and agriculture. The Dutch system of farmer cooperatives was quite interesting. I think we can have an Indian version of it. Recently, the government of India has given much impetus to the formation of Farmer Producer Organizations (FPO) and investment in farm and food processing equipment through interest subvention schemes. But how many of our farmers are capable of understanding these schemes, let alone benefiting from them? Education and skills will empower our farmers to benefit from these interventions.

We can establish farmer facilitation centres across the country at village-cluster levels. These centres can help farmers with inputs like seeds and crop medicines, and also allow companies to sell farm equipment and crop nutrition products. They can also house labs for testing the quality and nutrition of produce and provide advisories to farmers to help them become more climate friendly and climate prepared. The centres can help them participate in online auctions and also provide them access to financial products such as loans, credit, encashment of warehouse receipts and insurance. The centres can also actively engage in training the farmers to upgrade their knowledge and skills to comprehend the complex food system they are part of so that they may be able to take advantage of new market trends and protect themselves against financial risks. It can be pointed out that state horticulture departments are designed to do all this. But the farmer facilitation centres I am suggesting need to be equipped with state-of-the-art technology, equipment and trained manpower, all of whom must be skilled and educated in agriculture and food science.

At the heart of these changes must lie the voice of leadership that looks at farmers not as poor vote banks to be swayed at the time of elections through farm loan waivers and new subsidies. Instead, the political leadership must see farmers as partners in the growth of the nation and its fundamental well-being. When we manage to restore our mental model of our farmers as annadaata in the truest spirit, we will stop treating them as a burden on the commons and will respect them as our fellow citizens who sustain and nourish our commons.

When Alok and I first moved to Munsyari, we were taken aback to see that the local horticulture department disbursed seeds based on the caste of the recipient. If you were a person from a scheduled tribe—the largest vote bank locally—then you would get seeds of higher-yield crops. This is the kind of apathy, inequality and injustice that holds back our small farmers from realizing their full potential. This must change.

While we build capacity at the farmer end and augment market conditions to achieve a more diverse food plate, we need to also fix the massive losses in India's post-harvest supply chain. In 2017, in collaboration with Wageningen University, Netherlands, one of Europe's top-ranking universities for agriculture, we undertook a project for the World Bank at our SCA Research and Development Institute. The intention was to explore how India's post-harvest losses could be reduced by using India's coastal logistics. We looked at several crops and focused on a few to examine what benefits could be had by moving produce through coastal logistics instead of by truck. The results were thrilling. There was clearly a saving in time and costs, and the post-harvest losses reduced significantly. We all felt that the losses could be further reduced if there was an end-to-end farm supply chain for perishable goods, right from the farm to the market. Temperature-controlled storage immediately after harvest significantly reduces the chances of damage of fresh produce.

In fact, smaller pack-houses located near farms that can store farm produce at the requisite temperatures and humidity levels are very few in the country. There is a 97 per cent deficit in availability of pack-houses in India, in view of the demand. This is the first immobile infrastructure that needs to be established near the farm. India, unlike the US and EU, can grow its produce almost throughout the year. Therefore, its storage requirements are different from those of the US and EU. The variety of farm produce that grows throughout the year gives us the opportunity to create compartmentalized pack-houses and a refer vehicle system not tried in many developed economies. Therefore, there is room for homegrown innovation. The much-dreaded middleman can be transformed into a logistics entrepreneur and can earn much more through cold chain logistics ventures. A vast number of skilled jobs can be created closer to the farm via pack-houses and local refer-pool transport services in rural India.

There are some systemic challenges, though, and one of them is the cost of the energy and fuel that would be required to run pack-houses and refer vehicles. Energy costs in India constitute around 30 per cent of operating expenses in the cold storage industry, against 10 per cent in the West. Further, cold storages are dependent on steady supply of power. But most Indian regions in the hinterland face power cuts. Hence, companies have to invest in power back-ups, which pushes up the capital investment. When the government mulls reforms, it must not only look at corporate access to farm produce or free market access for farmers, but also look at enabling the post-harvest supply chain. Otherwise, its reforms will be perfunctory in nature.

It is only when we reimagine our food systems will we be able to see the distinct relationships between its components—farmers, climate, markets, nutrition, supply chain and economic growth. Only then can we put our reverential and obsessive regard for food to use in order to give it the importance it deserves in our policies and public debates. The end result of this is tied to the overall well-being of the nation. It is futile to think that we can tackle the challenges of malnourishment and hunger without focusing on the homegrown foods that constitute our nutritious and diverse plate. Such a plate is not possible without a biodiverse, sustainable farm. Moreover, such a farm will not survive the accelerated pace of climate change if it is not tended using regenerative agricultural practices in a gradual manner. Such practices, in turn, will not be possible without equipping the farmer with information, knowledge, skills, technology, finance and market access. What the farmer grows will not reach the market if robust and affordable supply chains are not deployed at scale.

For generations, the Indian farmer has been subjected to poverty, unfair trade practices and price laws that create artificial security. Our naturally regenerative practices have been junked for pesticide and chemical-based farming for greater yields, which constantly harms soil quality. When the British first came to India, they were surprised at the ability of the Indian farmer to manage three harvest cycles a year. They created artificial pricing laws that purchased the produce grown by the toiling farmer at very low prices and kept the Indian farmer poor. The multi-layered system that they created, with its middlemen, continues till date. Farmers are the most underserved group in our society, and yet they perform one of the nation's most important tasks—producing food for all of India. They ensure our sustenance, and yet we keep them in poverty.

There are models of success in small pockets of organic farming, like in Sikkim, or of market-driven agriculture and allied produce being implemented in Meghalaya and Himachal Pradesh. But a national-level vision and plan for India's farming and related sectors is imperative. Here, being hasty won't do. We will need to gradually fortify the different components of our food system and facilitate innovation and change so that the annadaatas of India can ensure that no Indian ever goes hungry and no child is left malnourished. Our ancestral power of food is useless if we don't call it to action to uplift our farmers from poverty and make sure that every Indian has an easy and affordable access to a nutritionally balanced meal.

Gau

I met Aman Preet Singh at an entrepreneurship masterclass I was conducting for our IEF Entrepreneurship Foundation in Kota in Rajasthan a few years ago. He introduced himself as the founder and marketing director of PEI Organic Foods. I was intrigued to meet a young, educated man who was involved in agriculture. As we got talking, I discovered that he ran an organic farm on the outskirts of Kota.[17] He sold produce from the farm under the brand name 'Gau', which is a colloquial Hindi name for a cow.

Gau Organics produces dairy products, wood-pressed cooking oil, natural jaggery, bee honey, organic flour, organic spices, organic manure, and more. After the class, when I went back at the hotel, I Googled the brand and what came up was an item called 'cow dung cakes' on an e-tail platform. This made me even more curious about Gau. On my next visit to Kota, I was invited by Aman to visit his farm, and what I saw there completely blew my mind. Early in the morning, as we sat on the lawn looking over his products of ghee, milk and paneer, Aman told me the story about how he came to helm an organic fresh-produce revolution of sorts in India's most arid and water-scarce state.

Aman grew up in Kota where his family has a business in engineering services. He decided to study electrical engineering with the goal of joining the family business. But his regular visits to the family farm with his grandfather throughout his childhood had already quietly nurtured the farmer inside him. After his graduation, Aman dabbled in the family business but soon came to the conclusion that his heart's calling was in agriculture. He decided to pursue a master's degree in advanced dairy technology from National Dairy

Research Institute at Karnal in Haryana. He even went to Israel, where he trained in dairy and food automation in Tel Aviv. An early success in sun melon farming in 2013 gave him the confidence that he could pursue this field. Thus, a young man from a business family, an engineer by education, became a farmer by choice.

Aman explained to me that the values on which the Gau brand is built are what he holds close to his heart. Gau was founded on the values of ancient food science and ecological sustainability. Aman's intention is to bring to the market food that is wholesome, ethically produced, and traceable to its source. He proudly calls himself a seventh-generation farmer. As a fourth-generation entrepreneur myself, it made my heart swell to see the pride he took in his intergenerational occupational legacy. I intuitively understood what he was trying to do. He was taking the work of his forefathers forward, using their rich experience of the past and the new technologies of the present. I secretly wished that many of India's farmers could be farmers by choice and rejoice in their occupation.

Aman's education came in handy in the early days of Gau. He interned at several companies and even travelled across the country to visit farms and farmers before taking the plunge. He conducted market research and focused on brand development from the very start, but the core of Gau's business was the quality of the produce. Aman realized that there was a problem with Indian agriculture, and he wanted to take a shot at solving it in his own small way. He observed that much of the Indian genetic seed stock had been depleted through destruction of traditional cultivars (varieties of one species developed for certain features). This had diluted the resilience of the parent stock of various species of plants. And there were doubts regarding the compromised nutritive and other values of hybrid varieties of the same species being developed and sold by the industrial giants and corporations. The resultant degradation in nutritional value down the entire food system has had the side effect on our well-being as people. Farmers were never aware of this. They just knew how to grow food full of nutrition. 'In the past few decades, India's farmers have been exploited brutally,' says Aman. Therefore, he made sure that Gau's vision would be to provide raw produce from indigenous cultivars straight from the farmers to the consumers. He intends to fill the nutritional void in the modern Indian food plate.

Even though Aman's grandfather was into farming and the family had their own farm, convincing his parents about his career choice of becoming a full-time farmer was not easy. Aman told them that he saw huge potential in pursuing farming. Given the dependency of Indian farmers on state subsidies and the skewed market conditions, his parents were not wrong in trying to dissuade their son from his choice. Once the family was convinced, the next challenge for Aman was to work on the farm, build the brand and find customers for the produce in a tier-3 city like Kota. Aman was committed, and was up for challenging his comfort zones and pushing his limits.

In 2016, Gau was established as a premium organic FMCG brand in Kota. Gau won an award for best operational dairy farm at the Global Rajasthan Agri Meet. In 2018, Gau won the Amazon Sellers Award for best sales in the segment, and in 2019 Zomato recognized it for best customer experience and satisfaction. Aman has had support from Gagandeep Singh and Uttamjyot Singh, the other two directors of the company. At Aman's farm, I witnessed the scientific methods by which the cattle were fed and the milk collected and processed. I saw their systems for delivery and order management and, most importantly, I saw happy cows. In fact, I even told Aman that I had never seen so many happy cows in my life. The PEI farm was spread across 40 acres and had more than 120 cows at that point. A large part of the farm was used to grow the cattle feed and remaining for compost making and allied activities The livestock were tagged with radio-frequency identification (RFID), helping the farm managers to track the health of the cattle from anywhere across the world.

I could not help but ask Aman about the cow dung cakes for sale. He laughed and explained, 'The idea of reaching out to buyers online came because of the demand from tier-1 cities, where there is not much livestock. People basically want cow dung cakes for religious purposes in these cities, and we decided to seize the opportunity. These cakes are the size of a quarter plate and are priced at Rs 120 for a dozen.' It made me smile—nothing in this farm was going to waste. Everything was transformed into either an input on the farm itself or a market opportunity. As we walked by an open area, Aman pointed out that the waste from the dairy farm was also utilized to produce gas. Gau's is the first dairy farm in Rajasthan with a biogas plant that generates electricity. It is also the only source of electricity at the farm, producing 40 KW per day, saving the company Rs 24 lakh every year.

Gau is a fully organic, biodiverse farm where fodder for the cattle is grown without the use of chemicals and where the milk is processed scientifically into various dairy products and delivered through hyper-local delivery platforms. The waste is used for making and selling cow dung cakes, producing compost as fertilizer and for generating electricity from biomass. There is also bee-keeping on the farm to foster pollination, and the honey is harvested for selling. Moreover, everything is tracked using modern technology, and source purity and nutrition are ensured. Wow!

Aman calls himself an 'agripreneur'—an agriculture entrepreneur—and sees huge opportunity for farmers like himself. He feels that the same models that companies such as ITC are propagating through e-choupal and what Verghese Kurien has done for the dairy farmers at Amul need to be applied in the organic food sector too. He laments that in the past decades we have exploited the soil and water and have distanced ourselves from the original and raw essence of our food. But it is time to go back to the basics and bring back biodiverse, regenerative and sustainable agriculture to our farms on a large scale. Can such an activity make money? Of course. Gau is a fine example. But Aman's biggest disappointment till date concerns the government bodies and regulations in the sector. He believes government institutions need to be upgraded and the regulations enforced so that our food is nutritious and unadulterated.

When I asked him where he sees Gau in the next decade, Aman promptly replied, 'We want to grow with the fellow farmers of the country. For now, we are a few twenties in number, but in the next decade we should be on our way to a six-digit strong community.' He wishes that more and more Indian farmers would pursue an education in agriculture and allied sectors and equip themselves with technology and skills that they can bring to their farms. He strongly feels that if Indian farmers get such an education, then they would have the opportunity to become masters of their domain and have the ability to shape the food ecosystem of which they are an integral part. He hopes that the agriculture sector never gets monopolized by a few large farmers or companies and wishes that the sector becomes peopled with prosperous groups of small farmers who take the Vedic science of eating, cooking and growing diverse food to the world. He reminded me of Alezo and his drive to take Naga food to the world. Both these young men have chosen to give life to their own intrinsic understanding of the power of food. I hope many others do too.

When I asked Aman whether he found all of this too hard or had any regrets, he responded with a striking clarity of purpose, 'I don't see the difficulty factor in this stream—things what you love to do, you do out of passion, and passion doesn't account the ease or difficulty of the subject.' Truly, agriculture was his heart's calling. Sipping milky tea under the blue sky and listening to happy moos from the cows on the Gau farm, I felt that Aman Preet Singh was truly 'living his power of food', so to speak, and in doing so was shaping the food system of his micro-habitat. I sent a prayer to the powers in heaven—may all Indian farmers gain his kind of satisfaction from growing nutritious food, in an environmentally sustainable way, in farms that are biodiverse. May they enjoy prosperity and success while doing so.

8
Power of Beauty

Ajanta

The U-shaped gorge of the Waghur river in the Sahyadri mountains in India's western state of Maharashtra is an enchanted place. Here, for over 800 years, monks, priests, artisans, travellers, merchants, sculptors, painters and royals undertook an endeavour which is, to my mind, incomparable in human history. The thirty caves of Ajanta near Aurangabad were hewn out of the rock and painted and sculpted in two phases. Their audacious journey began in the second century BC. It was a time when the Theravada school (the school of the elders) of Buddhism was prominent and the Satvahana kings who ruled this area were committed to providing wandering Buddhist monks a place for prayer and refuge during the rain-drenched monsoon months.

The first time I heard of the caves at Ajanta was when I was in school. My mother is a doctor by profession, but she is passionate about painting and excels at it, even if I say so myself! She would usually paint in the afternoons, when her clinic was closed. One day when I returned from school, I saw her painting an ornate figure. The eyes were long and expressive and the head-dress of the woman was elaborate and glamorous. Having never seen a woman like that in my life, I asked my mother who she was. My mother said that perhaps she was an apsara, a beautiful, supernatural female being. I was curious and asked my mother where she had found this woman. Finally, looking up from her canvas, my mother explained that she was making a copy of a photograph of one of the murals painted on the walls of the caves at Ajanta. Looking at the photograph in her hand, I couldn't help but exclaim, 'There are such beautiful paintings inside a cave?'

Decades later, I got to visit the caves at Ajanta myself. It was a trip taken during the monsoons. A friend had advised that even though the caves became a bit damp in the rains, the best way to experience these erstwhile Buddhist monasteries was to go at a time when there were fewer tourists. As we walked up the now concrete pathway built to access the caves, the Waghur river roared nearby. Small waterfalls gushed out of the rocks and the tranquil atmosphere only added to the mysticism of the place. Our guide explained that just how we were climbing up the lush green valley now, Buddhist monks had come here more than a millennium ago, to craft out a sanctuary for themselves.

Simply put, the core message from the life and teachings of the Buddha is to overcome suffering and the cycles of rebirth through attainment of nirvana (salvation) or by walking the path of Buddhahood. Meditation, prayers, detachment from worldly desires and material things, monastic living, compassion for all living beings and non-violence are some prominent and prevalent teachings of Buddhism. Therefore, the requirements of the monks from their caves of refuge were simple. They needed a place to stay and a place to meditate, collectively and individually. Hence, most of the caves at Ajanta are either Chaitya Griha (meditation and prayer halls) or Vihara (monasteries for the monks to live and meditate).

Yet, these are not some barren caves that we imagine the ancients built, with basic elementary wall caricatures or carvings. In the world of art and architecture, the Ajanta cave paintings and sculptures are some of the most magnificent and celebrated of their time period. The walls, pillars, facades, and in some cases, every inch of the surface of the caves, is painted with ferocious commitment and spectacular imagination. Where there is no painting, there is mind-boggling sculpture. In every form, the beautiful art of the caves depicts details from the life of the Buddha, stories of his rebirth from the Jataka tales, and scenes from everyday life during those times. It is a rhapsody of art and beauty, as if those who painted and sculpted these caves took every drop of desire in their being and splashed it across these walls. Painted as they are with ornate, astonishing detail and dazzling beauty, there is nothing understated in these murals. I was left awestruck. I was overwhelmed by the exquisite and expansive beauty all around me, which simultaneously aroused and numbed the senses. I have never felt so satiated and austere at the same time. I looked for a name or a signature—a clue somewhere crediting the artists who had poured their deepest emotions into their work. But I found none. I was also struck by the fact that these artists had such scant resources at their disposal. A hammer, a chisel, a brush and some basic natural paints were all they had to work with; yet they had produced resplendent work of the kind that still awes the visitor, some 1,500 to 2,000 years later.

In fact, in the caves that came up in the later period of the Vakataka kings (fifth to sixth centuries CE), the influence of the evocative style of Gupta art is visible in both the paintings and sculptures. There is more iconography and the Buddha is represented with lavish attributes, in line with the more prevalent Mahayana (the greater vehicle) school of Buddhist practice of those times, which permitted worship of the Buddha as a divine figure.

But all this extraordinarily opulent display of belief and faith for a path that espouses detachment also left me a bit confused. It was hard to reconcile how monks who were on the path of renunciation were comfortable with paintings and sculptures of voluptuous figures of women bedecked in jewellery, market scenes, court proceedings and the panoramas of daily life that the monks had chosen to forgo. I asked our guide about the concept of beauty and art in the minds of these artists and monks that had inspired them to adorn the walls of their monastic sanctuary with such extravagant splendour. He had no clue, but he nudged me to remember that Ajanta was no artistic expedition. It was a monument of unwavering devotion to the Buddha and his teachings.

I must have looked thoroughly lost, because two female monks who were also in the same Vihara approached me with knowing smiles on their faces. They were from a Buddhist nunnery established in the Tibetan settlement of Bylekuppe in Karnataka. They explained that the power of Buddha's teachings and the dedication of those who lived by them were so intense that it inspired generations to carve out these caves, drench them in the colours of their imagination and illuminate them with the symbols of their faith. As much as the caves at Ajanta are about the invincible spirit of the monks and artists who worked with infinite patience to coax the rigid volcanic rock into an expression of beauty, they are also about the unconditional surrender of man to the path of the master and his teachings. They further expounded that just like the erotic figures on the walls of the Khajuraho temples in Madhya Pradesh were about humanity seeking union with the divine; the expression of beauty in these paintings and rocks were about seeking the ultimate beauty within ourselves. The nuns' explanation made complete sense to me.

In a way, the artists who worked on the caves at Ajanta were only continuing the tradition of the Indian artistic schools of marrying beauty with divinity. As most structural and artistic endeavours in ancient India were of a religious nature, the idea of dedicating expressive and ornate beauty to the glory of God must have been already well ingrained in the artisans and craftsmen. What was this powerful idea of divine beauty, both within and without, that permeated our ancient arts? How could the formless be reached through the artistic form? The answers can be found in the nine rasas of the classical Indian artistic traditions.

Sringara

It is believed that most of the later Ajanta paintings are a continuation of the artistic traditions from the Chitrasutra of the Vishnudharmottara Purana, a tradition passed on from father to son and from master to disciple. The Chitrasutra is one of the oldest treatises on painting in the world and includes guidelines on form, colour, line, expression, et al. It follows in the footsteps of the Natya Shastra, an earlier Sanskrit treatise on the performing arts.

I was introduced to the Natya Shastra as a six-year-old while learning Bharatanatyam at a neighbourhood dance school called Kalasadan in Mumbai. Guru Mani ran the school as traditionally as possible, and while we learnt the dance steps and the mudras, he also ensured that we learned about the principles and ideas behind our art. The Natya Shastra has thirty-six chapters and 6,000 verses that describe the performing arts. Apart from being an ancient encyclopaedia on the performing arts, it is also one of the earliest treatises on pursuit of the divine through artistic expression. In the sixth chapter of this exhaustive work, we find mention of the rasas. In essence, the rasa theory articulates that artistic performance is not simply about entertainment and physical sensory elevation, but also about transporting the performer and the spectator both to another reality. This was the core principle that our Guruji wanted us to imbibe fully when we danced.

Over the centuries, the concept of rasa has been fundamental to many forms of Indian art, whether dance, drama, music, literature, painting or sculpture. There is a total of nine rasas: sringara (beauty), hasya (laughter), raudra (fury), karunya (compassion), bibhatsa (disgust), bhayanaka (horror), veera (heroism), adbhuta (wonder) and the later-added santa (peace). Of these nine rasas, the most prominent one is sringara.

Sringara encompasses not just beauty, but also romance, attractiveness, erotic love and intimacy, and is wide in artistic scope. It is a powerful rasa, and many art schools call it the 'mother of all rasas'.

In expressing the sringara rasa, the performer or the artist transports their audience to experience the beauty and love of the divine. Similarly, the artists and monks who created the rock-cut monasteries and prayers halls of Ajanta allowed their sringara rasa to overpower the dwellers of the caves in such a manner that through these exotic paintings and sculptures, the seeker experienced beauty as a conduit to the divine. No wonder I had felt both aroused and numbed in equal measure at Ajanta. I can well imagine a monk meditating for months on end in these caves and reaching a certain oneness with the artistic beauty that surrounded him. At that point, the power of beauty would not merely be experienced in the artistic expression that was on the walls, but it would have been felt in the compassion of the master and his teachings. The beauty without would have lifted the veil from the beauty within, and an enormous experience of oneness and intimacy would have been experienced. As the female monks from Bylekuppe had tried to explain to me, the power of beauty in the art of these caves was not for the pleasures of the five physical senses but to unlock the potential of the seeker to go beyond those senses and unleash the beauty of their inner being.

The sringara rasa is deeply entrenched in the Indian arts, and therefore, in the Indian way of life. Expression and experience of beauty is fundamental to our existence. We draw strength and power from the beauty of the divine and that of the mundane in equal measure. We adorn images and idols of our gods and goddesses with beautiful clothes and jewellery and decorate our temples with all kinds of artistic forms. Therefore, the *Power of Beauty* is overwhelmingly influential on our ethos. In the caves at Ajanta, this power of beauty allows us to commune with the divine on a grand scale. But even in our daily lives, we indulge in our inherent need to revere and seek the power of beauty in myriad ways.

The Kolam

I was a student at Kalasadan in Mumbai from the ages of six to fourteen. In those eight years, I not only learnt the art of Bharatanatyam, a dance form from the southern state of Tamil Nadu, but I also learnt a lot about Tamil culture and traditions. Every evening, when my mother dropped me off to the dance class, I would see a design drawn with white powder on the floor, in front of the door. On special occasions like Dussehra or the Tamil New Year Puthandu, these designs would be more ornate and extravagant. One day, I asked our Guruji's daughter, who was also one of my teachers, about these white-powder designs. She told me they were called kolam and that they were almost like the north Indian Rangoli, but made with a fine paste of ground rice powder mixed with soapstone, white stone and limestone powder, and a type of red soil. The resultant mixture was called kola-podi. In fact, kolam is a Tamil word that also means gracefulness and beauty.[1]

My teacher explained that the women of Tamil Nadu wake up in the wee hours of the morning to perform the daily ritual of kolam. It is a ritualistic art form, drawn on the thresholds of temples and homes mainly. The ritual begins with women in the villages and towns cleaning the threshold of the house, as if preparing it for a prayer ceremony. Post that, in some homes, a cow dung paste is applied on the floor area where the kolam is to be drawn. Women would hold the kola-podi pinched between the first finger and thumb, and gently let it slip on the floor as their hands moved in the direction of the design of their kolam, at all times only an inch away from the floor. There is a variety of kolam designs, of different shapes and forms, and also ones for special occasions and festivals. Most have a pattern of dots, called pullis, which are encircled and then looped through using straight or curved lines. The nimble fingers of an expert kolam maker effortlessly move over the freshly prepared floor and designs of intricate beauty take shape.

As simple as it seems, kolam is a complex process. It needs a good measure of mathematics and aesthetics, not to mention mental concentration and dexterity of hand. But interestingly, this complex daily ritual art is not recorded in any treatise or documents. It is a tradition passed on from mother to daughter. Women learn it by observing the elder women in their family. For many, it is a matter of pride to be able to do the same kolam that their grandmothers made. It is a tradition of beauty and aesthetics and it is an integral part of daily life for the women of Tamil Nadu.

One of the key aspects of kolam is that it is transitory in nature. It is made every morning and then, over the course of the day, it disappears under the feet of people. It is either blown out of shape by the wind or is consumed by ants and other insects that feed on the rice powder. Depending on the design chosen, a kolam can take a few minutes or a few hours to make, but in both cases, it disappears before the day is over—as if the twin aspects of creation and dissolution are interwoven in the very idea of kolam. There is also a deeper meaning as to why kolam is done on the threshold of a house or building. Traditionally, thresholds are considered to be meeting points between the internal world of your home and the external world.

In the month of Margazhi in the Tamil calendar, which falls sometime around November-December, women in villages and towns across Tamil Nadu participate in kolam competitions, where streets and households compete for the best kolam awards in their localities. Kolam is a deeply personal experience, an offering of beauty for the community. Often, the women who do kolam daily share their emotions through this art. It is an expression of personal beauty that transforms a threshold into a doorway of auspicious beginnings. Transient though it may be, this long-standing tradition also constitutes a daily ritual of cleansing and beautification.

The beauty of the kolam is that it is not something done on a majestic scale that lasts for millennia like the Ajanta cave paintings, but is a humble submission to the divine so as to seek blessings for a bright new day, every day. The power of beauty of the Ajanta caves enabled the monks to unleash the beauty within, whereas the beauty within a woman's consciousness permeates the kolam, making it an expression of beauty without. In both cases, the power of beauty empowers the exchange between our inner core and the outside world. It acts as a bridge for our deepest ideas and imagination to take tangible form in the world and acts as a doorway for the beauty of an artistic endeavour to carry us into another reality so that we may connect with our inner consciousness.

Beauty and the Beast

Whether in the cave art of Ajanta or in the kolam of Tamil Nadu, we see ardent display of the sringara rasa and our power of beauty.

What is uncanny is that this power of beauty has been passed on for generations and has continuous lineage of expression and manifestation. What is incredible is that this expression of beauty is not limited to the caves of Ajanta and the home thresholds of Tamil Nadu, but is expressed in a plethora of aspects in the Indian way of life.

The humble kolam itself has cousins across the country. It is called rangoli in the north and west of India, where it is done with natural or artificial colours. During the annual harvest festival of Onam, people in the south Indian state of Kerala do Pookkalam, laying a carpet of flowers made in various designs on the floor of their homes or compounds. In Chhattisgarh in central India, rangoli is known as chaook, and in the eastern states of West Bengal and Odisha, it is called alpana and jhoti chita, respectively. In Andhra Pradesh and Telangana, it is called muggu and in the Himalayan state of Uttarakhand, aipan. All of these arts express beauty, and share the artist's inner joy with the outer world. Their power is as much in their spiritual connection as in their aesthetics. They are a manifestation of the inner power of beauty, deeply seeded through family traditions, social celebrations and personal passion in our collective ethos as people.

Beauty in India is both personal and public. It is expressed fully and freely. It is as if the entire country is steeped in sringara rasa. The Taj Mahal, for example, is a mausoleum for Begum Mumtaz Mahal, but is adorned with some of the most exquisite stone carving and inlay work seen in the world. From the palaces of Rajasthan to the temples of Odisha, the monument art of the country embodies beauty. In the intricately woven, colourful Manipuri shawls and in the hand-woven mirror-work fabrics of the Kutchis of Gujarat, there is expression of beauty. In the brocade work of the silk sarees of Banaras and the motif-work of the Paithanis of Maharashtra, one can sense the craftsman's inner need to convey beauty. We have rituals such

as the haldi and mehndi ceremonies during our weddings, which
are anchored in beauty. In the solah shringar (sixteen adornments)
of Indian brides, there is much attention paid to beauty.[2] In the
performing arts, from dance forms to theatrical performances and
even films, beauty is coveted zealously.

Whether it is the manner in which we dress up for a festival or
the way in which we adorn our gods, goddesses and shrines, Indians
have a bias towards beauty. We seek beauty in everything, and the
power of beauty reigns supreme in the Indian mind, sentiment and
way of life. But objectification of beauty is also rampant in India.
There is a misplaced obsession with fairness of skin and its linkage
to beauty. This can be seen in the classified advertisements for brides
and grooms and in fairness cream ads, where beauty is reduced to
the colour of one's skin. In a way, this understanding completely
contradicts the original idea of beauty as a doorway to the divine. It
limits our ability to experience beauty beyond its form. This is the
harmful side of the double-edged power of beauty that we nourish
and cherish as a society. This is our bane. But this is not our only
issue with beauty. As obsessed as we are with personal beauty, we
have, for the most part, become careless about the aesthetics and
cleanliness of our public places over time.

From the high mountain passes of the Himalaya to its sun-
kissed beaches, India suffers the poor behaviour of its public in the
matters of garbage and sanitation. Plastic bags, empty food packets,
drink cartons, cans, cigarette buds, beer bottles and plastic water
bottles richly 'adorn' our public places, whether they are natural
spaces or human settlements, whereas curated art pieces and objects
of beauty adorn our private spaces. From our big metros to small
towns and even villages, people are habituated to littering in public
places even as they keep their own homes super clean. This is a
trait prevalent across the country. The poor, the rich, the educated,
the illiterate, the working class, the jobless, the religious, the non-

believers, all dump garbage on the roads and urinate or defecate in the open. It can be quite confusing to grasp how a people so obsessed with beauty can be so callous when it comes to cleanliness. There is, of course, a small caveat here. As mentioned earlier, they are irresponsible about public cleanliness, but in their own homes, they are as committed to cleanliness as they are to beauty. In fact, because of being so pervasively dirty, Indian cities continue to suffer a low quality of life. Our villages are not far behind in this respect. This is our Beast!

Inherent in all applications of beauty is the basic need for cleanliness. No kolam is made on a dirty floor. The Ajanta caves were not full of garbage, but places of worship and meditation. A performer doesn't dance or act on a stage full of trash. A devotee bathes the gods before adorning them daily. We do not wear festive clothes on special occasions without taking a bath. Indians will clean their homes before festivals such as Diwali, and we even have rituals to throw out negative energies and unclean ideas, objects and emotions from our lives. There is no mistaking the fact that in our psyche, cleanliness is a prerequisite to beauty. We need no convincing that a pure and positive environment is a precursor to beauty and therefore, divinity. Then why not call upon our attraction towards beauty to bring more cleanliness and aesthetics to our public places?

In ancient times we expressed much beauty in our public spaces. Inherent in the concept of beauty are the important aspects of cleanliness and aesthetics. There is no reason why we cannot do the same now. But simply beautifying public places through the lens of objectification will not yield significant results. We have tried this, and failed. If we truly want to restore cleanliness and aesthetics in our country through exercising our power of beauty, we will need to walk the hard road to challenge our own misplaced biases. This will also need a deeper understanding of the reasons behind the lack of cleanliness in India's public places and what solutions have worked so far and what have not.

Moral Disengagement

Several systemic impediments, such as lack of garbage collection facilities, out-of-capacity waste processing, manual scavenging, lack of awareness about recyclable waste, etc., are cited when one raises the issue of filth in public places in India. But the most acute issue is the attitude of the citizen and the deep social biases that make cleanliness the job of certain classes or castes. In terms of awareness, there is no dearth of clarity that cleanliness is a virtue and a must-have for a good quality of life. Therefore, we cannot hide behind the curtains of information asymmetry here.

The truth of the matter is that despite being well informed and despite also practising cleanliness in our homes and private spaces, we continue to litter our public spaces. So we may conclude that public filth is a matter of conscious choice for most Indians. We *choose* to throw garbage on our roads or spit on walls and sidewalks and create dumpsters out of public squares. We avoid using dustbins and *choose* to keep our public places dirty. We have somehow persuaded ourselves to believe that to keep our personal self and spaces clean and concurrently keep our public places unclean is the 'right' thing to do. We have completely convinced ourselves that we hold no moral responsibility for the cleanliness of our public spaces. This is a disturbing aspect of our society, one that has been prevalent for a long time. It instigated the Mahatma, the father of our nation, Gandhiji, to write many essays on this subject in his publications and infuriated him enough to quip, 'Will the temples be clean once the British have left the country?'[3] What he was trying to say was that if we abdicated our own responsibility towards what is ours, then we would have no one else to blame but ourselves. He was pointing out that when we are morally disengaged from our conduct, we alone are the cause of our troubles and we alone bear the consequences.

Moral disengagement is the process by which individuals or a group of people distance themselves from ethical conduct. They do so by convincing themselves that unethical conduct is justified because of reasons beyond their control. Recent research has indicated that people will use moral disengagement effectively by either blaming others or reducing their own agency for action, or take refuge in excuses that cite herd behaviour, or refuse to see the consequences their action or inaction can cause.

In the context of cleanliness in public places, it seems Indians have become morally disengaged. They have shrugged off their responsibility for the cleanliness of shared spaces. In many cases, beautiful campuses of companies, academic institutions or residential complexes are surrounded by accumulated garbage just outside their enclosed spaces. When there is such acute moral disengagement when it comes to public places, simple nudge tactics will fail. Deep-seeded moral disengagement needs behavioural understanding, systemic thinking and reengineering. For that, we have to first tackle the elephant in the room: the age-old bias that any activity related to cleanliness and sanitation is the job of people born into a certain caste or class.

Apart from denouncing the idea that any human being's dignity could be below anyone else's, Gandhiji was clear in his rejection of the attitude that sweeping and cleaning is a 'polluting' activity. To exemplify his principles, he made it mandatory for himself and others who lived with him to clean toilets regularly. He would pick up a broom and clean his ashrams himself, whether in South Africa or India. He believed that cleanliness was akin to godliness and encouraged young people to engage in cleaning private and public places. With his actions, Gandhiji was trying to address two orthodox sentiments in our society. One was belief in untouchability, which he considered a social shame and worthy of eradication, and the second was societal apathy to the dirt and filth everywhere.

In his book *Moral Disengagement: How People Do Harm and Live with Themselves*, Albert Bandura[4] articulates four loci for moral disengagement: behavioural, agency, effects and victim. Expanding on the behavioural locus, he observes that people often cite moral grounds to engage in unethical conduct. The Hindu society that Gandhi was struggling to reform had convinced itself that untouchability was a religious act, and hence completely justified. Gandhi used Hindu scriptures and tales from famous epics such as the Ramayana to counter this notion and to prove that Hinduism did not justify untouchability. Gandhi was also acutely aware that untouchability was not just limited to the Hindu faith and that Indians from other faiths also practised it using the locus that it was the prevalent practice of the land.

Decades after Gandhi's passing and the framing of India's Constitution by a committee led by B.R. Ambedkar, which declared untouchability a crime, its practice goes on in villages in the hinterland. Its major impact continues in the lack of willingness among Indians to clean their own public places. The Bengaluru-based community group–The Ugly Indian (TUI)—is trying to change that.

The Ugly Indian and Delhi Street Art

When Alok and I moved to Bengaluru in 2015, we were struck by the amount of garbage piled up in the streets of this once pristine garden city of India. Its lakes were frothing from the garbage and pollutants being thrown into them on a daily basis. That was when we heard about The Ugly Indian (TUI). TUI is an anonymous group of volunteers who gather to clean and beautify streets and public places in Bengaluru. They call their cleaning activity 'spot fixing'.

You simply need to send an email to the group on Facebook to register as a volunteer. The group chooses small segments of sidewalks, subways, walls and street corners to 'spot fix', and calls for action. Volunteers turn up—they clean, sometimes paint the space, and then leave. The measure of their success lies in whether their intervention lasts for at least ninety days, whether it does so without continuous supervision, is low cost and scalable and creates minimal disruption for those concerned and, most importantly, changes the behaviour and attitude of everyone involved and impacted.

The Ugly Indian website has an interesting disclaimer for people who visit it. It says, 'This site contains a story of hope and optimism. Cynics are not welcome. By entering this site, you accept that: We Ugly Indians are part of the problem and only we can solve it. Explaining ourselves as "we are like that only" is cute. But does not help. You believe that change is possible in your lifetime.'[5] Gandhi would have smiled and taken some solace in the existence of such community groups, their self-assessment and self-commitment.

For many of the interventions that The Ugly Indian undertakes, there is an element of renovation, so to speak—of the street, wall or sidewalk. Cleaning is the start of the process, but it ends with beautification. One of the sidewalks the group had chosen to clean, had previously become a spot for urination and would stink through the day. The group not only cleaned it but also repainted the walls and beautified the sidewalk with a patch of flowers. The nearby Bishop Cotton Girls School adopted the mini-garden the group had planted. The group believes that if you leave a public place dirty, people will be further incentivized to add more filth to it.

The Ugly Indian is joined by crusaders like Yogesh Saini, who returned from the US to Delhi in 2013 and started the Delhi Street Art (DSA) initiative, which brings together artists and citizens to clean and paint parts of the city. An engineer and an MBA graduate, Saini worked in Fortune 500 companies overseas and is an entrepreneur now. In his own words, 'The idea occurred to me while on a jog in Lodhi Gardens, where I realized that people neglected their civic duty to keep the surroundings clean simply because the dustbins installed there, although new, failed to draw attention.'[6] He organized Street-Art-Saturdays in collaboration with the New Delhi Municipal Corporation, where artists gathered to paint dustbins. With Saini's initiative and DSA's efforts, Lodhi Colony in the heart of India's national capital is now referred to as 'Lodhi Art District'. We accidentally discovered its beautiful wall art while passing by a line of two-storeyed buildings there. New Cafes have come up and the area has an artisanal feel to it. For Alok, who grew up for some part of his childhood in Delhi, this has been a refreshing change.

What The Ugly Indians and Delhi Street Art are trying to do is to shift the agency and moral responsibility for cleanliness back to Indians. In essence, they have used the power of beauty and the subconscious emotive connect Indians have with sringara rasa to fight this social evil. Because when other emotions, such as raudra (fury) and bibhatsa (disgust) fell us, it is sringara and the power of beauty that can come to the rescue. These organizations have, intentionally or unintentionally, used the framework of moral disengagement and behavioural insight to help bring changes they want to see in society.

Khubsoorat Bharat

Behavioural insights are an outcome of behavioural science, which focuses on how human beings behave or make their choices and act. It traces its genesis to 'Nudge Theory', a concept popularized by two American academics from the University of Chicago, Richard Thaler and Cass Sunstein, in their book *Nudge: Improving Decisions About Health, Wealth and Happiness*.[7] In essence, Nudge Theory proposes that we can use positive reinforcement and indirect messaging to influence decision-making in groups and individuals. Over the years, many governments and public bodies have used this science to influence action and compliance among citizens. In 2010, the government of the United Kingdom set up the Behavioural Insight Team (BIT) within the cabinet office to apply Nudge Theory in the work of the British Government. Over the years, the unit has become a social organization and is now jointly owned by the UK Cabinet Office, the innovation charity Nesta and the organization's employees. It has done more than 700 randomized trials in over fifty countries.[8]

One of the key frameworks developed by the BIT team is the EAST framework.[9] EAST is an acronym for Easy, Attractive, Social and Timely. This framework suggests that if you want to encourage a behaviour in an individual or a group, then one has to make it Easy to engage in, Attractive to get and hold attention, Social so that people can nudge each other to do the work, and Timely so as to ensure maximum traction.

If we apply the EAST framework to our cleanliness beast, then we would be able to see the central role that the power of beauty can play in addressing one of our biggest civic issues. Because of their inherent bias towards beauty, Indians may find easy to beautify and keep public places beautiful. As in the ritual art of kolam, they will be forced to clean before they beautify. When we make mechanisms to achieve cleanliness easily accessible, as The Ugly Indian has done, attractive, like what Delhi Street Art has showcased, we attract wider social action, and with expediency. Beautiful wall caricatures and paintings and sidewalks with plants and flower patches ensure that beauty and aesthetics draw and sustain the attention of the public. The Delhi Street Art and The Ugly Indian both use this method to attract citizens and nudge them to keep the public areas beautified by them clean and aesthetically pleasing. Indians are a highly social race, and community plays an important role in our daily lives. Therefore, the use of beauty as a collective experience can be transformational.

The monks and artisans who painted the Ajanta caves harnessed the power of beauty by creating a beautiful space for communion with the divine. Similarly, our power of beauty can be an important ally in our cleanliness mission. We will still need to address the social evil of untouchability and the infrastructure gaps in garbage collection and processing, but we may manage to engage a larger section of our population and make cleanliness a shared aspiration and shared action.

When Prime Minister Narendra Modi announced it in 2014, the Swachh Bharat Abhiyaan had a massive challenge. More than 500 million Indians defecated in the open[10] at the time and there was acute shortage of public toilets in urban areas and household toilets in rural areas. Therefore, the first major goal of the campaign was to provide toilets to millions of Indians. The government of India subsidized the construction of more than 100 million toilets between 2014 and 2019.

Artists, sportspersons, media, corporations, business leaders, students and citizens from all walks of life were called upon to provide leadership and inspiration for the campaign. The prime minister, many of his cabinet ministers, and even chief ministers of several states, picked up a broom and cleaned the streets, persuading their fellow citizens to do the same. Social media was abuzz with posts on cleanliness drives and pictures of prominent citizens cleaning the streets and other public places. A mobile app was launched for this and millions of people downloaded it. PM Modi must be appreciated for lending his leadership to this acute issue faced by our country. He definitely looked at systemic interventions that could help reduce this horrendous state of our sanitation and public cleanliness. It is not that such campaigns and programmes did not exist earlier, but his personal push, his leadership and commitment, brought them to the forefront of public and political discourse.

The Swachh Bharat Mission has done significant work in providing toilets and in fighting open defecation, but it has met with limited success in cleaning up India's streets or changing the perception of public cleanliness among Indians. No doubt there is greater awareness today; for example, railway stations across the country do have a cleaner ambience than earlier, but the Mission's connection with the people is still not complete. Maybe, as Indians, we just don't understand cleanliness as much as we appreciate beauty.

Perhaps the Swachh Bharat Abhiyaan ought to be reengineered and renamed as 'Khubsoorat Bharat Abhiyaan'. If cleanliness is a necessity, then beauty is aspirational. People are motivated by aspirational messaging. They want to be connected to their higher selves, and we need to provide them a medium with which to do so. Beauty is a powerful conduit to achieve that. In the context of the EAST framework, Swachch Bharat Abhiyaan is Easy, Social and Timely, but it is not Attractive. Transforming it into a Khubsoorat Bharat Abhiyaan can be a game changer. Behavioural insight about our obsession and preoccupation with beauty can lead to better civic engagement for the cause of Swachchata.

India has seen much success when it has used beauty, divinity and aesthetics in mass communication. In campaigns such as Incredible India, attractive, evocative and beautiful images of India were used to convey what an incredible tourism destination the country was. It was further enhanced with programmes such as Athithi Devo Bhava (the guest is God) to sensitize the people at large about treating tourists with respect, fairness and courtesy. Taxi and auto drivers, tour guides, government officers, restaurant owners, hoteliers, street vendors and others who interface with tourists were trained in etiquette, hygiene and basic English language skills. The impact of the campaign was tangible. Tourist arrivals increased from 2.38 million in 2002 to 4.43 million in 2006 after implementation of Incredible India campaign (2005).[11]

We may not exactly know how and what will happen if we put the power of beauty to use on a mass scale to address our cleanliness issues. We have seen that it has worked in a few cases. We know it is an important emotive connect for us, but we don't have all the answers. We are fortunate in that modern technology gives us a helping hand here.

Today, we have the opportunity to marry the tools of artificial intelligence and data science with anthropology and behavioural science. Perhaps such tools can be used to gain a better understanding of the correlation between cleanliness and beauty. We can run randomized data trials to gather behavioural insights and engage organizations like the Behavioural Insight Team for this. Such insights can help policymaking, and when enhanced with the on-ground knowledge of organizations such as The Ugly Indian or the Delhi Street Art, a more nuanced policy that nudges more participative and responsible civic action for cleanliness is possible.

Indore

Swachh Survekshan 2021, the fifth annual countrywide cleanliness survey, reviewed cleanliness conditions in 4,320 cities in India. More than 40 million citizens participated in it.[12] The survey, administered by the Union government, involves both citizen inputs and views and expert reviews and checks. The city of Indore in the central Indian state of Madhya Pradesh has won the award for the cleanest city in the country for five years in a row. That may compel us to ask: What is so special about Indore?

Indore began its journey pretty much in the same circumstance as any other city in the country. It had a large population (3 million-plus); it had inadequate garbage collection facilities and processing infrastructure; public awareness about cleanliness was abysmal and there were high rates of open defecation. But the city took several steps under the Swachh Bharat Abhiyaan. It launched a city-wide campaign of 'Clean Indore–Green Indore–Beautiful Indore'.

Community-level programmes using street theatre, group discussions and music were used to make people aware of waste segregation. The gaps in door-to-door collection of garbage, especially in the poor areas, were bridged with the deployment of over 350 garbage collecting vehicles in eighty-five wards. The vehicles were specially designed to collect dry and wet garbage separately. They were tracked using GPS from a central control room.

Today, this has led to 100 per cent door-to-door garbage collection in the city and to 80 per cent of the garbage being segregated at source. The next step was to ensure that public places and streets were enabled for wet- and dry-waste collection. More than 2,000 dustbins for segregated dry- and wet-waste collection were installed in public places. Indore has a huge street food culture and is known for its street savouries. Hence, it was important to co-opt the street food vendors in carrying out dry- and wet-waste segregation at their shops and stalls.

The entire effort was supported by wet-garbage processing, which transforms the waste into compost, and dry waste processing, which is done through a Centralized Material Recovery Centre. The Centre engaged the city's ragpickers as government employees for sorting and processing of dry waste. The solution was unique in having achieved employment for the city's ragpickers and utilizing their skills for processing waste. The ragpickers were further skilled in the use of automation and other standardized waste processing techniques. One major challenge for the city was the 20 tons of organic waste generated daily at its chief vegetable market, Choithram Mandi. This waste would earlier get dumped at landfills. The city administration, under the Swachh Bharat Mission, implemented Asia's largest methanation plant, which processes the daily organic waste from the Choithram Mandi into biogas and CNG. It is an excellent example of generation of energy from waste. At the historical landfills, mechanization was put to use to process waste. Indore has now recovered 100 acres of land which was garbage ground earlier, and plans to grow a city forest on that land. The interesting fact is that for its overall waste management infrastructure, Indore has not utilized more than 10 acres of land and this entire initiative needed only six months of planning.

What is most heartening to see is how the citizens of Indore from all walks of life have embraced the 'Clean Indore–Green Indore–Beautiful Indore' idea. Cleanliness workers trained in modern waste collection skills clean the city twice a day; private organizations process their own waste, and hotels have set up their own on-site organic waste convertors. A cleanliness app linked to the national Swachh Bharat app, called Indore 311, helps citizens report any problems regarding cleanliness and sanitation. It has a decent record of addressing complaints and bringing awareness among the citizenry. Open defecation is being addressed with over 17,000 household toilets and 175 public toilets, which are cleaned and beautified so that people are encouraged to use them. Seventeen mobile toilet vans have been introduced in areas where public toilets are not available.

School and college students have taken the lead in using art, music and community festivals to spread awareness about cleanliness and its benefits. Jingles and radio music have built an emotional connect with the initiative among citizens. Wall paintings and beautiful art have been used to keep the people motivated. In Indore, we can see many aspects of sringara rasa and the power of beauty at play in a host of interventions designed to achieve cleanliness. Recognition of Indore's efforts followed, with the city consistently ranking at the top in national cleanliness surveys. Now, it has become a question of pride and tradition for Indore's people to keep striving for cleanliness. Indore has brought about systemic changes and scientific interventions, combining them with emotive connects and platforms for individual citizen action to surmount the public's moral disengagement with cleanliness. It has perhaps appealed to the collective psyche of its citizens to shake off their apathy towards cleanliness. Its city government has played the role of both facilitator and catalyst. The fact that the Madhya Pradesh state government has connected cleanliness with swasth (health), seva (service), haryali (greenery) and sundarta (beauty) may have helped. Campaigns such as '*Swachhta Mein Sundarta*' (beauty in cleanliness) have made cleanliness more aspirational among the people.

If Indore were observed as a case study for the EAST framework, we are bound to conclude that in making garbage collection and segregation available at the doorstep and in public places, and in providing for household and public toilets, Indore made it Easy for its citizens to participate in the cleanliness mission. By using art and beautification to build awareness and raise aspirations, Indore made cleanliness Attractive. By involving citizens through street-level messaging and creating tech tools such the 311-app service, they made cleanliness fervently Social. And by ensuring that systemic infrastructure changes were done in a Timely manner to match citizen participation, the local city administration ensured the success of the mission at hand.

Mawlynnong

The village of Mawlynnong in the north-eastern state of Meghalaya was selected by the *India Discovery* magazine in 2003 as Asia's cleanest village.[13] When I first visited it in 2013, I was amazed at the use of aesthetics and communication in this little village to achieve beauty and cleanliness. As we parked our car outside the village, a sign welcomed us with a list of instructions about what was permissible and what was not. It gave clear directions on what could be put into the dustbins and what garbage could not be left behind in the village. It also warned us about being fined if we littered. Being awarded as Asia's cleanest village has brought a lot of tourists to this small hamlet of ninety-odd homes. Therefore, the village has had to devise mechanisms to remain clean and maintain its coveted title.

As we walked down the small concrete pathways of the village, we were met with a paradise-like settlement. The small pathways that led from house to house were lined with flowers and fruit trees and even bamboo groves. Each house had a small kitchen garden and its own toilet. Mawlynnong became open-defecation-free way back in 2007. The idyllic pathways of the village are fitted with beautiful cone-shaped bamboo waste baskets.

In peak tourist season, a daily average of 200 tourists visits this village of 500-odd dwellers and its famous natural root bridge. The village reuses all its wet waste, but collects the dry waste separately. Every morning, children and community members gather to clean the areas in front of their homes and other public places in the village. Children have the responsibility of emptying the bamboo dustbins. Cleanliness as a habit is well ingrained from early childhood in this village. In fact, it is a tradition.

The village also takes great pains to maintain its aesthetics. Dedicated gardeners are entrusted with the duty of ensuring that walkways remain pleasant to walk on and that the street furniture such as the bamboo dustbins are properly installed. The manner in which the natural beauty of the village has been preserved also makes a visit to this village an enchanting experience. As misty clouds float through the hills, the residents of Mawlynnong go about their daily routines. Children walk to school, on the way picking up the odd pieces of trash left behind by tourists, while elderly women tend to kitchen gardens, and gardeners work on the trees along the pathways. Life in Asia's cleanest village is as one would find in any other village. But there is a universal expression of cleanliness through beauty and aesthetics. The village looks well looked after. Even its humble huts add to the picturesque landscape.

Mawlynnong is not a rich community and most of the people here depend on agriculture for their livelihood. It does not have vast resources. It relies on each of its residents to do their bit. It nudges them to be in charge of their own living conditions. It does not rely on outside support. It is morally engaged, and how! It uses beauty to enhance cleanliness. The people here are proud of their village and benefit from the resultant higher quality of living.

Examples like Indore and Mawlynnong tell us that when the citizen in engaged, anything is possible. The success of The Ugly Indian in Bengaluru or Delhi Street Art tells us that people respond to beauty, and that if attractive means are used to persuade the people to support the cause, then collective action for cleanliness is possible. Frameworks like EAST can be a guiding tool, but in the end, we have to build on our inherent strengths as a society. Our power of beauty is one of them. We can begin by raising the people's aspiration for beauty to achieve cleanliness. Our power of beauty has many applications, some beyond our comprehension— but if we can at a bare minimum summon it to improve our living conditions, that would do for now.

For the creators of the Ajanta cave paintings and sculptures, sringara rasa was a means by which to reach the divine and comprehend the ultimate truth. For the women of Tamil Nadu, the beauty of kolam is a symbol of auspicious tidings and an expression of tradition. A clear bridge between beauty and divinity is therefore established. But it was Gandhiji who connected cleanliness to divinity in the modern era by calling those who worked as sanitation workers as 'harijans', literally 'god's own people'.

If we can manage to make cleanliness a virtue, by making it an integral part of beauty, and use the power of beauty to engage Indians from all walks of life to fight the filth in our public places, we will address one of the largest gaps in our mission for sanitation and hygiene; and in doing so improve our societal well-being too.

Enhancing Swachh Bharat to Khubsoorat Bharat will create avenues for creative expression across different stakeholder groups, both in urban and rural India. When Indians are called forward to compete in making their neighbourhood, village, town or city beautiful, there could be an outpouring of a certain personal expression of beauty in public spaces, as we have seen in the case of Indore and Mawlynnong. In an era of personal fandoms and social media, slogans like 'My Village, the most beautiful', or 'My city, the most beautiful' can act as real incentives. We can use our inherent appreciation of beauty to bring cleanliness and aesthetics back in vogue. The power of beauty can be called upon to bring back the intimate bond Indians once felt with their public spaces.

9

Power of Wellness

Tere Mere Sapne

In 1937, Dr A.J. Cronin published his book, *The Citadel*. The book was a path-breaking novel that addressed the issue of medical malpractice and is sometimes credited with laying the foundation for Britain's National Health Service. Its story revolves around an idealistic young doctor who gets posted to a mining town and earns the love and respect of his patients and is focused on his research on lung disease. But later, he falls prey to medical money-making rackets, only to revert to his ideals in the end.[1] The book captured the imagination of readers across the world. A Hindi movie based on this story was made in 1971, titled *Tere Mere Sapne* (Your Dreams, and Mine).

My maternal grandparents, both practising doctors, would always get very excited whenever *Tere Mere Sapne* aired on national television. My grandfather, who hailed from a modest farming family, grew up in a small village on the outskirts of Surat in southern Gujarat. He ran away from home in his teens to pursue higher education in Mumbai. He told me that he earned his licence to practice while sleeping on the footpaths of Mumbai. In the mid-1940s, he met my grandmother, the daughter of a wealthy lawyer in Mumbai. She was a graduate from the premier KEM hospital and medical college, and when he met her, she was pursuing her Masters in Burns Surgery at Mumbai's Harkisan Das hospital. They both fell in love.

But she was from a rich family, the kind that didn't allow its children to even walk on the roads. As for my grandfather, he slept on those very roads every night. He was from a village and she had grown up in a metropolis. He had learnt to swim in the village ponds and she had taken swimming lessons at the prestigious clubs of Mumbai. She was older than he; he was from a caste inferior to hers. He was working hard to get his licence to practice and she was a brilliant student at one of India's premier medical institutes. It seemed they didn't have much hope of getting married as her family would not agree to the alliance. They spent a few years waiting, the local milkman acting as their postman, carrying their love letters to each other. After much tamasha, in the immediate years post India's Independence, Dr Sudha Gandhi and Dr Girdharlal Patel finally got married in a civil ceremony. My grandmother would often remark, with glittering pride in her eyes, 'You know at that time I didn't take even a penny from my family. I wore a cotton saree, two bangles and a mangal sutra—all bought by him and off we went.'

As struggling young doctors, they had to start from scratch. Neither was in any government service, and so they had to establish their own little clinic in a Mumbai suburb. They worked very hard for many years, from 9 a.m. to 9 p.m., with just a small afternoon break for rest. My grandfather would tell us that there were many opportunities for them to make money easily and quickly—people would want fake medical certificates, medical colleagues would ask them to give referrals for a commission, or a pharma company would coax them with gifts and money so that they would recommend their drugs. They did not fall for any of these tricks. He would often proudly say, 'You know, young lady, we doctors are made to take an oath. Your grandmother and I were never going to compromise on it—no matter what.'

Once I asked my grandmother about the oath she had taken as a doctor and whether she really believed in it. With a solemn expression, she replied, 'I believe in it more than I believe in the breath in my chest.' The doctor's oath my grandparents took reads as follows, (it has been revised recently to include a declaration to abide by the 2002 regulation):

'I solemnly pledge myself to consecrate my life to service of humanity. Even under threat, I will not use my medical knowledge contrary to the laws of Humanity. I will maintain the utmost respect for human life from the time of conception. I will not permit considerations of religion, nationality, race, party politics or social standing to intervene between my duty and my patient. I will practice my profession with conscience and dignity. The health of my patient will be my first consideration. I will respect the secrets which are confined in me. I will give to my teachers the respect and gratitude which is their due. I will maintain by all means in my power, the honour and noble traditions of medical profession. I will treat my colleagues with all respect and dignity. I shall abide by the code of medical ethics as enunciated in the Indian Medical Council (Professional Conduct, Etiquette and Ethics) Regulation 2002. I make these promises solemnly, freely and upon my honour.'[2]

My grandparents served their patients in accordance to the oath they took, in letter and spirit. In my early twenties, when I watched *Tere Mere Sapne* again, I realized why my grandparents loved to watch it so much. The movie brought the issues they saw as poisoning their profession into the open—malpractice, fake surgeries and prescription of wrong drugs, to name a few. Perhaps they looked at the hero of the movie and reflected that they would never want to lose their way as he did. After all, they were in this profession to serve humanity with dignity and honour.

My mother, Dr Anjani Jani, joined her parents in their practice after she graduated, though she chose to study homeopathy. She was a working mother who could not take time off work because her patients' health came first. So, as a child, I spent my weekdays after school in the small suburban Mumbai clinic where my grandparents and my mother practised medicine. My grandparents never held any biases against any school of medicine. They believed that any science that gave patient's health primacy and was able to cure disease should be used. Therefore, unlike many allopathic doctors of their times, they did not oppose my mother's pursuit of homeopathy. They were also very aware of the role they played in people's lives and society, even though they never let it get to their heads. They remained affable and accessible to patients from all strata of society. I would see patients of all hues come to the clinic; some were very poor and my grandmother would not take any money from them. Some were very rich and my grandfather would spend a lot of time convincing them that they didn't need expensive tests or medicines. If they only looked after their health and lived a balanced lifestyle, that would do, he'd tell them.

Sometimes I would be taken aback to see people coming and touching my grandparents' feet in gratitude, saying, '*Doctor saab, aap to hamare bhagwan ho* (Doctor, you are our God).' Once I asked my grandfather, 'Dada, you will never be out of work, right? I mean people will always need you.' He smiled at me and said, 'I wish I was not needed. There is nothing more depressing than to see a perfectly healthy person fall sick. And you know what is most frustrating? Apart from a few exceptions, most people encounter diseases because they have compromised on their nutrition, lifestyle and wellness.'

Wellness and Health

The ancient Indian system of Ayurveda is established on the principle of wellness, not just of body but of mind and soul too. It professes that wellness is about purification, whether for a healthy or sick person. It believes that everybody should be free of toxins, in both body and mind. Its core philosophy is that the human body is itself a micro cosmos, made up of the same elements found on the planet and in the universe—earth, fire, water, air and space. Ayurveda has created an entire system in which every human being's body type is identified for understanding that person's physiology, based on his or her own unique composition of these five elements. This is referred to as determining a person's prakriti, and it is intricately tied to the concept of doshas.

Doshas are of mainly three types—vata, of the air and space elements; kapha, of the earth and water elements; and pitta, of the fire and water elements. Every human being has all three doshas, but in most, there will be one or a combination of two doshas that are more prominent. In rare cases, the three doshas are present in equal measure.

In his much-acclaimed book *Perfect Health - The Complete Mind and Body Guide*, Deepak Chopra[3] gives insightful examples of how modern medical research and science have now proved some of the principles of Ayurveda. For his inspiring work in the field of healing and wellness, *TIME* magazine recognized Chopra as the 'poet-prophet of alternative medicine'.[4] In the book, Chopra explains that Ayurveda gives us the tools to understand our bodies at the quantum level. The book explains each of the doshas and also has a quiz for people to determine their own body type. But if one were to simply visit an Ayurvedic practitioner—vaidya—then he/she would hold your hand, study your pulse, ask you a few questions about your lifestyle, and immediately determine your dosha composition.

Ayurveda holds that when we live a life that is not in balance with our doshas, we invite disease. For example, if one has a prominent pitta dosha and continues to eat spicy and oily food, then one will experience acidity or bile disease more frequently. This is a very simplistic explanation, of course, the science of Ayurveda being very deep and precise. It originated more than 3,000 years ago, though many credit the ancient Indian surgeon Sushruta's treatise, *Sushruta Samhita*, as the foundation of modern-day Ayurvedic knowledge. Ayurveda literally means 'knowledge of life and longevity'. It is a science that is still being used largely in India. But of late, thanks to the focus on alternative medicine even in developed nations, it has come into practice across the globe. Yet, many allopathic doctors are not supportive of Ayurveda and some go to the extent of calling Ayurvedic practitioners quacks.

I remember asking my grandfather about it once. This was when I was doing my undergraduate programme in the US. I had been asked by a fellow student about the use of Ayurveda. My grandfather took a slightly different view from many in his fraternity. He told me that the principles of wellness that Ayurveda follows are sound. There is merit in treating the body as a whole rather than in compartments. The holistic wellness that Ayurveda speaks of has modern medical justifications too. Perhaps the medicines used in Ayurveda may not be useful to treat some new disease or it might take longer to cure people than the allopathic medication and treatment for the same condition. But when it came to preventive health principles, Ayurveda is not to be dismissed as quackery. My grandfather particularly liked the Ayurvedic ideas of keeping life in balance, eating right, and focusing on energy, endurance and detoxification. But he felt that Ayurveda alone cannot achieve complete health for human beings. Other practices such as yoga and meditation were also needed for complete wellness. When I asked him about what his idea of wellness was, he said, 'It is the art of listening to your body.'

As I discovered much later, it was an idea rooted in the Ayurvedic ethos of wellness.

Traditionally and culturally, India's approach to health is intrinsically linked to India's idea of wellness. To be healthy may be necessary, but to be well is what is desired. Health and wellness, although intricately linked, are different states of being. Health is a disease-free state of the physical body, whereas wellness is the holistic state of a person's physical, emotional, intellectual, social and even occupational wellbeing. It is not possible to achieve wellness without good health, but it is also not possible to have good health without focusing on wellness. This inter-linkage between the physical body, mind and soul was well understood by Ayurveda and other ancient Indian sciences, and perhaps this is the reason that, traditionally, holistic practices such as yoga were pursued by Indians. Our ancient science and philosophy about the body is also tied to our eating habits and the use of specific herbs or spices in our cooking, diversity of plate being an important aspect of it. In essence, the focus was always on physical vitality and endurance rather than on disease.

Wellness has a greater and more far-reaching impact than healthcare. From yoga to ayurveda to hakims and other traditional healers and even shamans, the approach of Indian healers and healing practices to personal health goes beyond the physical. In remote Himalayan villages, practising shamans are visited by one and all. They are sometimes the first and last stop for any ailment. Varied forms of yoga are important workout routines for the urban young and old alike. The household remedies that we have come to know as grandmother's medicine continue to be used in Indian homes. Chewing roasted jeera (cumin), inhaling steam with ajwain (bishop's weed), drinking haldi (turmeric) milk … are all household remedies for the common cold and cough. Every region of India has its own home remedies for common ailments, but more importantly, many have detailed cooking guidelines, eating times and lifestyle suggestions that ensure disease prevention. As the old proverb goes, prevention is better than cure. The Indian indigenous systems and home remedies are focused on wellness, where health, nutrition, prevention of disease and the right balance of work and life are all included.

In the decades post-Independence, India has focused much more on the health aspect of public health delivery than on wellness. Only recently, with the establishment of the ministry of AYUSH (Ayurveda, Yoga and Naturopathy, Unani, Siddha and Homeopathy), is there now a public sector impetus for these approaches to health and wellbeing. But in the rural context, perhaps because of the lack of access to modern medicine or lack of faith in it, the use of natural, Ayurvedic and Unani medicines has continued. In fact, the villager is always very sceptical of approaching the local health centre; it is always his/her last resort. They tend to first reach out to the community vaidyas, hakeems or shamans. Whenever I have asked our rural folks why they trust a local medicine man more than they do a modern doctor, their response is 'the doctor never really cures us, we feel our expenses keep going up even after initial treatment and most of the treatment is not available at the village level'. On the other hand, they feel the natural local medicines bring them some relief, save them money and are easily accessible. These views may stem from long-held biases, but they form the mental model of modern healthcare for a vast number of rural Indians.

Despite being a large hub for pharmaceutical manufacturing, being world renowned in biotechnology and having some of the brightest doctors and nursing staff in the world, India has a healthcare delivery system that is inequitable. As of 2016, India ranked 145th among 195 countries in a global healthcare access and quality (HAQ) ranking.[5] This ranking should worry us, as it is a clear indication that public and private healthcare access interventions have largely failed in India. Healthcare access disparities are stark in our country, and small towns and villages have poor-to-absent health infrastructure and a paucity of doctors. A recent report published by the NITI Aayog, 'Healthcare in India through Blended Finance', revealed that only 50 per cent of our population, that too from a few states, has access to 65 per cent of hospital beds, whereas the remaining 50 per cent have access to only 35 per cent of the bed capacity. We are in dire need of increase in our bed capacity by at least 30 per cent.[6] Despite their significant success in urban areas, Indian private healthcare players are hesitant to open hospitals in rural areas. We are struggling to increase the number of beds and hospitals to match the size of our population. India spends just over 1 per cent of its GDP on public healthcare (with the exception of the pandemic years, when this went up to 2.1 per cent).[7] The private hospitals charge very high rates in return for good facilities and qualified doctors, and a vast number of patients who get treated there have to borrow money for it.

My father's sister Dr Charu Jani is a renowned doctor and practices critical care medicine. Through her career spanning five decades she has worked in some of the best hospitals of Mumbai. Whenever, I visit her at the hospital to go through a medical test, I see poor patients waiting near the admissions desk. The helplessness on their faces saddens me. There is a struggle for paying the deposit to get an admission. Sometimes, they are waiting for a relative or friend to rush with money so that their loved one can be admitted. I would ask my aunt why is the hospital not setting up a charitable fund to help poor patients. She would reply with a tinge of exasperation that many do but the demand is so high that it is just not possible to help every needy patient. Our family runs a charitable healthcare centre where my aunt gives her time pro-bono post her working hours at the hospital. She once told me that even that centre needs scaling up as the demand is just overwhelming.

It is clear that our current approach to providing healthcare may not yield the necessary results and not help us meet the demand. Most of the existing health delivery mechanisms don't even address mental health or lifestyle issues. According to the World Health Organization, India has one of the largest populations in the world suffering from mental illness.[8] Despite this, mental health continues to be stigmatized, both in rural and urban India. Moreover, lifestyle- and poverty-induced diseases are increasing in the country. Ninety-eight million Indians are predicted to develop type-2 diabetes by 2030.[9] While middle-class and upper-middle-class urban Indians are dealing with obesity, the urban poor and rural folk are suffering from malnutrition. This means that our people are moving towards a reality where both health and wellness will be beyond their reach.

Experts say that India's healthcare challenge needs a more holistic approach, involving an amalgamation of modern medicine and diagnostic technology and the traditional sciences of well-being, alternative medicine when applicable, and greater investment by both the public and private sector in infrastructure. India has a public healthcare network of primary healthcare centres (PHC) at the village level, community healthcare centres (CHC) at the cluster/block level, district and state hospitals, and a few national institutions such as the AIIMS. In theory, this looks like a good set-up, except that most of the centres and hospitals, especially at village and district levels, do not have an adequate number of doctors, technicians, nurses, ward staff, not to mention their shortage of beds, diagnostic labs and intensive care support. For decades, the Indian healthcare system, both in the public and private sectors, has been under-resourced and has operated under immense pressure. Stories of doctors in large state government hospitals complaining of shortage of beds or of delivering babies in hospital corridors are a-plenty. The wide gap between urban and rural health delivery has plagued our entire public health system for a long time. With the advent of Covid-19, these disparities became more pronounced and the health system simply collapsed. I had the misfortune of experiencing this collapse first-hand.

A Pandora's Box

In March 2020, as the first coronavirus cases from across the world began to get reported, Alok, my mother and I left for our home in Munsyari. We hoped that the situation would come under control in a few weeks and we would be able to return to our urban homes in Gurugram and Mumbai soon. But a national lockdown was announced in the third week of March. The entire world seemed to come to a standstill. The WHO confirmed that after more than a century, and since the last outbreak of the Spanish flu, the world was witnessing a pandemic again.

We decided to ride it out by staying put in our small Himalayan village. But soon enough, the challenges started mounting. After a few weeks of the lockdown, we received frantic calls from the local designated Covid Care and Isolation Centre. They did not have enough personal protection equipment (PPEs) and they also didn't have enough oximeters to measure the SpO2 levels of patients if a crisis arose. Luckily, due to the sudden lockdown and the pragmatism of the village elders, our cluster of villages had very few people returning home from their urban centres of work. Thus, we didn't record more than a few cases, in the first wave of the pandemic. But still, the panic was palpable in the local team of doctors and caregivers. We managed to arrange for some PPE suits and started looking into the other items they needed. I also started seeing requests pouring in at our foundation from across the country, especially from rural areas, for sanitizers and PPEs. In May 2020, with the entire truck system in the country still paralysed due to the unavailability of drivers and trucks, it was hard to get things from one place to another. I could see that the villages across the country were not prepared at all for the pandemic.

As 2020 progressed, it seemed India had managed to somehow scamper through, with fewer fatalities than in many other countries of the world. Everyone brought their guard down. In early 2021, ignoring all signs of a more infectious variant on the rise, political rallies, travel, markets, sports events, and religious congregations such as the Kumbh Mela started taking place. This led to the new Delta variant spreading like wildfire. Suddenly, hospitals in the cities started running out of beds and oxygen, with the national capital Delhi being one of the worst affected. It felt like Dante's hell had been unleashed on the Indian people. Aid started flowing in from across the world. I got involved with the voluntary work that several organizations were doing at that time to bring oxygen concentrators, oxygen cylinders, beds, oximeters, mobile ICU units and even full-fledged oxygen plants from across the world to India. I will never forget the incredible generosity that people from across the world showered on Indians at that time.

Throughout the first wave of the pandemic in 2020, we only had to focus on helping the local CHC and Covid isolation facilities get PPEs, oximeters, etc. But in the second wave of the pandemic, the problem was much bigger. Initially, there were only a few oxygen cylinders at the local CHC and the nearest filling facility for oxygen was ten hours away. Out of fear or bad guidance, wrong or excessive medication started happening across villages on a massive scale in the Himalaya. I was told the same was true across the country. A type of malpractice developed in the cities where people profiteered from selling injections, medicines, oxygen concentrators and cylinders at sky-high prices. Outside hospitals, there were long queues of people waiting for beds. Hospitals in turn waited endlessly for oxygen and medicines. There were long lines outside cremetoriums and cemeteries. No one was left unscathed by this horrific experience.

It seemed that India's healthcare system had succumbed to the Covid-19 onslaught. The pandemic had opened a Pandora's box, unleashing and laying bare all the problems of our healthcare system.

When I visited the local CHC, I realized they didn't have even basic testing facilities. They had rapid antigen test kits, but for the more reliable RT-PCR tests, the samples would be collected at the CHC, to be taken to the district hospital six hours away, in Pithoragarh. From there it would go to the testing lab in Haldwani, nine hours away. The results would often come only ten days later. This left the local doctors no choice but to start treating patients who showed the slightest symptoms of Covid with medication that was not even needed. My friends from across the major metros later confirmed to me that this was the scenario in their cities too.

The protocols developed for isolation at home could not be applied in our rural settings. Rural households don't have separate toilet and bathing facilities. Everyone in the house uses a common toilet, which is installed or built in the front or backyard of the house. There was no way that patients who had tested positive for Covid-19 could isolate at home in our village. The common facilities set up at the village cluster level were only for critical patients who needed oxygen support. This not only allowed the virus a free run, but it also made the villagers afraid to report symptoms. Their years of distrust of the public healthcare system added additional fuel to a raging fire. Therefore, only after a patient's condition worsened would the CHC team come to know and the patient would be brought to the Covid care centre. If their condition worsened further, they were sent to the district hospital six hours away in an ambulance. Looking at these arrangements, I was glad that both my husband and my mother had already taken two shots of the vaccine. I had had my first shot, and so had all our staff.

But within a week of my first dose, I came down with a cold and cough. At first, we thought that since I had had my first shot, this couldn't possibly be Covid. But as the days progressed, I developed a high fever. We did a rapid test at the CHC, which returned negative. Then, suddenly, my SpO2 level started to drop—first from 96–94 to 92–90 and then to 90–88. The doctors from Mumbai I was in touch with advised that I start myself on steroids, and that brought the temperature down for a day. But my health was deteriorating. We called the CHC team and they took my sample again for an RT-PCR test, but we knew that by the time the result came it would be more than a week. My husband decided that we must leave immediately for Delhi or Mumbai. An air ambulance was arranged to fly me to Haldwani, where the state hospital was located.

When the CHC doctor wheeled me into the ambulance which took me to the helipad, he took my SpO2 one more time—it was 78. The weather gods were kind that day, permitting us to cover a distance that would normally have taken ten or twelve hours by road in forty-five minutes by air. An ambulance in Haldwani rushed me to the Sushila Tiwari Hospital, the largest hospital in the entire Kumaon region of Uttarakhand. As I was taken to the out-patient department for a check-up, I saw people lying next to me on stretchers to the left and right. Some were dead and some were trying to stay alive. I looked at my mother and my husband who were standing a few feet away, in full PPE suits. Their quiet resolve made me promise myself that I was going to live, no matter what.

I was soon transferred on a rickety metal stretcher, whose wheels screeched as it was moved around, for an X-ray and a CT scan. Both these tests being unavailable at the CHC in Munsyari, we hadn't known how bad my condition was up until that moment. I was then moved to a Covid ICU. I bid goodbye to my family from afar. Lying on the stretcher, I could only look at the worn-out ceiling of the hospital corridors. I have to admit I have never felt so frightened in my life. Inside the Covid ICU, I was started on medication through an IV. A team of doctors and nurses came to examine me. When I saw them, I was shocked; none of them had a full PPE suit on. What they had was a mask each, and the nurses had gloves in addition. That is all! What happened to all the PPEs we were moving across the country for medical staff? How were these folks safe without PPEs in a Covid ICU? My mind went numb. Later, the head-nurse informed me that they were constantly running short of PPEs as the patient load was very high, this being the only public hospital in the region of its calibre.

As I lay in the ICU bed, I thought about how fortunate I was to be able to chopper my way there. But what about my fellow villagers? They had no way of reaching this hospital at this speed! I thought about how my husband and I had steadily prepared for an eventuality like this at our home in the mountains. Knowing full well the oxygen situation at the local CHC, we had got ourselves an oxygen concentrator from my office in Delhi. But it could only reach as far as Haldwani. Then, in early May, even though there were no private transport vehicles plying their regular routes, my husband spoke to the medical store in Haldwani and we arranged for some medicines and the oxygen concentrator to come in a vegetable truck that travelled up and down the mountains twice a week. Had we not had the oxygen concentrator or the medicines, I would have never made it. But what about the other villagers? They could only rely on the public health system, which was collapsing like a pack of cards everywhere in the country.

As night approached, I had a hard time falling asleep in the ICU. It was the peak of summer, and I kept sweating as my fever broke. Cockroaches kept scuttling across the window panes of the room. I thought of my grandparents who had both long since departed our mortal realm. I thought of how much they cared for the well-being of their patients. I thought of my aunt and how dedicated she was to the care of her patients. I looked at the doctors and nurses on duty that night, and I felt sorry for them. They were human too. Most medical professionals across the country had been under tremendous stress throughout the first and second waves of the pandemic. I thought of the young men who worked in our companies, who loaded the aircraft with vaccines under the Vaccine Maitri programme of the government and yet died in the second wave of the pandemic—without a vaccine. The injustice of it all made me feel helpless and furious at the same time. Lying on my bed, hooked up to an IV drip on one arm, with an oximeter attached to a finger of my other hand and an oxygen mask on my face, I broke down and cried for a long time. In due course, either out of exhaustion or the strong effect of the medicines, my body gave in to it all and, finally, I slept.

The next morning, my husband called me and said that arrangements had been made for me to be flown in a Covid-pod chartered flight to Mumbai. Again, I was wheeled into an ambulance. At the airport in Pantnagar, I was packed like a mummy into a plastic pod and put on a stretcher inside an aircraft specially equipped to carry Covid patients. My mother and my husband took another chartered flight at the same time. Even though all of it seemed like an ordeal to me as I was feeling quite unwell, I kept thinking of the thousands of others in our country who had no timely access to hospital, oxygen and medicines and had died. I was aware of so many people who could not say a proper goodbye to their loved ones or could not perform the last rites of their family members properly. I felt so privileged and yet so angry at the disparities in our country. Access to quality healthcare must not be a privilege; it must be a basic social security all Indians should have.

When we landed in Mumbai and I was wheeled into one more ambulance that darted off to the private Lilavati Hospital, we all felt a bit relieved. At least I would now have access to quality healthcare. Alok and my mother stood at the Covid admissions area at Lilavati in full PPE. Everyone around me, from the doctors to the nurses to the ward boys and even the admin staff, were all in full PPE suits.

I was put in a wheelchair and taken to the Covid ICU, where there was nobody without a PPE suit. It made me think of the doctors and medical personnel at the Sushila Tiwari Hospital who only had masks and gloves. The difference in the quality of healthcare infrastructure and facilities between Uttarakhand and Mumbai hit me. In the ICU, I was quickly made to change and several different tubes and wires were plugged into me. A nurse came and took my blood and cardiogram (ECG). Another set of technicians came and took my X-ray. I thought of the CHC at Munsyari. There was no X-ray facility and a primitive blood check was the only diagnostic test available. Even RT-PCR tests could not be processed at our CHC, which served over 1,00,000 people. I knew that none of my fellow villagers would be able to avail of what I had access to at Lilavati. While it made me feel immensely grateful for my privilege, the unjust inequality of it all sent shivers down my spine.

I realized that an already stressed and under-equipped public health system was not going to be able to deal with a pandemic. Even though it had committed medical professionals, they were limited by the lack of diagnostics, medicines, medical devices and infrastructure. In that one week, I was able to witness and understand the gaps in our public healthcare delivery through my own personal experience. I finally understood the injustice we meted out to our rural and poor people because of our lack of intent and commitment towards their well-being. It made my blood boil. The right to health and well-being should not be denied to any citizen of India. I surmised that we had erred grossly in not investing in a robust, holistic and advanced public healthcare system.

Five days later, I was discharged and sent home. As I was still Covid-positive, my mother prepared a separate bedroom for my isolation at home. The Municipal Corporation of Mumbai came and sanitized our home. My mother and husband equipped my room with medicines, clothes and other items I might need during my isolation. All through I never forgot that all of this, including the private ICU bed, the antibody monoclonal treatment and the facilities at home for isolation, were a great privilege in my country. I took a shower in the attached bathroom of my bedroom and my cell phone rang. It was our doctor from the Munsyari CHC—my RT-PCR test result from the sample they took a week ago had finally come, and it was negative! The irony of it seeped into my bones and I felt deeply anguished. Not only did we not provide effective and timely testing, but we also gave the wrong test results to our people, taking away their right to even be sick! I am still reeling from that anger and exasperation. It tells me that something drastic needs to be done for a complete overhaul of our public health delivery. A paradigm shift is warranted.

Right to Well-being

In the past few months, whenever I have thought of our broken healthcare system, I have been confounded by the fact that this is the same country that propagated a science of wellness—Ayurveda—for thousands of years. The Constitution of India gives every Indian the right to health. Yet, we have no political will or leadership to do what is most necessary as our public duty. Is our huge population the impediment? Partly, yes. We will never have enough doctors for 1.38 billion people. But can we not look at this issue holistically? Maybe we need to break the problem into smaller components in order to be able to address it. Irrespective of our approach, if we are to completely overhaul our healthcare delivery anew, then maybe we ought to look at it more as a wellness delivery system instead of just focusing on health. Doing so will aid us in bringing the issues of nutrition, lifestyle diseases, mental health problems, etc., into consideration, along with medical care.

To bring this wider view into focus, we will need to understand that both preventive care and curative care are essential components of public wellness delivery. Preventive medicine is that branch of medical science that aims to improve and maintain health by ensuring that people do not fall ill in the first place. On the contrary, curative medicine restores and maintains health by treating people after they fall ill. For preventive care, we do not just have our modern-day medical advancements, such as vaccines, but also have support from the age-old science of Ayurveda for nutrition and balance. We can explore the holistic alternative approach of homeopathy and the vitalizing science of yoga for building energy and endurance in our people. We also have techniques for addressing mental health problems and traditional medicines that address lifestyle diseases. For curative care, we not only have the new-age healthcare science of medicine but we also have alternative medicines and care available. For diagnostics, we have devices today that can help us perform tests and analyse results on a large scale. The advances in genetic science and biotechnology have given further impetus to our understanding of the human body and has led to several breakthroughs in immunization and disease control. Even diseases like cancer have a trajectory of treatment today.

But what is most important is for us to remember that if we want to claim our right to well-being, then we must also shoulder the responsibility for well-being at the individual and community levels. If the community takes ownership of its own health, then wellness delivery becomes possible and even a pandemic can be mitigated. During the Covid-19 pandemic, we were brought countless stories of inspiration from across the world, of societies acting together and individuals taking responsibility for their own and societal well-being. Our continued recklessness in not even wearing a mask in public places despite suffering so much just over a year ago, points to the fact that we need to take better ownership of our own health and well-being. We could, for example, eat right by ensuring diversity on our food plate and focusing on community sanitation by addressing the issues of poor hygiene and open defecation.

We are quick to blame the government for the lack of sanitation in the country, but we too litter and dump garbage in public places, which leads to disease. We do not boil our water, knowing well that it may contain bacteria. Preventive care is more of a personal- and community-level responsibility. If we don't take the initiative to eat healthy and live a balanced life, especially if we can afford to, then only we are to be blamed for any ill-health that may result. Here, the privileged classes have a bigger responsibility, because they have access to nutritious food and can definitely avoid lifestyle diseases to a large extent. The underprivileged must also ensure they avail of the free immunizations for their children and not shy away from modern healthcare.

Many doctors nowadays complain that patients read about their condition on Google and come to them with ideas about what ails them. They appreciate that awareness helps a patient understand their illness, but sometimes it blocks a doctor from treating the patient using his or her knowledge and experience. Patients say that the information available online helps protect them from medical malpractice. Both are right in their own way, but we need to think of how we can restore the trust between doctor and patient in society

Applying a wellness lens to public health delivery, identifying preventive- and curative-care solutions and building a wholesome system of multiple approaches to health and well-being is imperative, but all this can only succeed when individuals themselves take charge of living in a society that is focused on wellness. A society that has intrinsic trust in its public wellness delivery system is bound to achieve its health targets. This would mean a wellness system co-owned by the citizens themselves, where they are not mere recipients.

Is this a utopia? No, a community of native Indians in the United States has not just done this but has succeeded at it with aplomb.

Nuka

In Anchorage, Alaska, the Southcentral Foundation has managed to deliver an innovation in public healthcare delivery that is truly outstanding. Alaska is close to the Arctic Circle with extreme cold climate. Its population lives dispersed across a wide area and its huge distance from mainland United States means that many public goods and services are delivered to the local population with difficulty. Health was no exception.

For many decades, the native people of south-central Alaska received their healthcare as 'beneficiaries' of the Indian Health Service's Native hospital. The employees here were not able to be creative or innovative because it was a large, bureaucratic system centrally controlled from Washington DC, 5,000 miles away. But in 1998, when Southcentral Foundation took over ownership of primary care in the region, things started to shift. They devised a system called 'Nuka', where patients are no longer beneficiaries but equal owners in healthcare delivery. Nuka is a native Alaskan Indian word for strong, giant structures. The system services 65,000 community members of the area with the approach of holistic wellness. Today, the 'Nuka System of Care' is a term that describes the healthcare system created, managed and owned by Alaska's native people to achieve physical, mental, emotional and spiritual wellness. It is inclusive of all parts of the organization—the behavioural, dental, medical and traditional streams—and all systems, processes and departments supporting health service delivery.

In the earlier system, patients waited for days on end to get an appointment with a doctor. Every visit, they were met by a different physician, resulting in a lack of continuity in their medical care. Often, the different departments acted in silos. The cost of healthcare was high, and efficacy of healthcare delivery dismal. It made many natives leave the system altogether. Then, the United States Congress passed a federal law in favour of self-determination, by which local tribes could take ownership of their own healthcare systems. This created an opportunity for the entire system to be redesigned under community ownership and leadership, bringing together native traditional healing practices and modern medical care.

The change that ensued allowed the community to transition from being mere recipients of healthcare services to determinants of it. They could make decisions about their own well-being. Most importantly, there was now a shared vision for the community's well-being. The goal of Southcentral Foundation is to ensure that every community member in south-central Alaska is able to experience multidimensional wellness. The vision, mission statements and the key pillars of the system are as follows:

Vision Statement: A native community that enjoys physical, mental, emotional and spiritual wellness.

Mission Statement: Working together with the native community to achieve wellness through health and related services.

Key Pillars:

Shared Responsibility: We value working together with the individual, the family, and the community. We strive to honour the dignity of every individual. We see the journey to wellness being travelled in shared responsibility and partnership with those for whom we provide services.

Commitment to Quality: We strive to provide the best services for the native community. We employ fully qualified staff in all positions and we commit ourselves to recruiting and training native staff to meet this need. We structure our organization to optimize the skills and contributions of our staff.

Family Wellness: We value the family as the heart of the native community. We work to promote wellness that goes beyond absence of illness and prevention of disease. We encourage physical, mental, social, spiritual and economic wellness in the individual, the family, the community and the world in which we live.[10]

In the Nuka system, every patient is given an integrated care team dedicated to their needs. The team consists of a primary care provider, a physician or a physician's assistant or nurse practitioner. This team works jointly with the patient and takes care of the entire agenda of his or her well-being. When a patient needs to visit the healthcare centre, the team ensures the visit is fully coordinated and is not in vain. When the patient needs to be referred to a speciality hospital, the integrated care team takes charge of the process and even ensures the patient's smooth recovery process post discharge.

The geographical area serviced by the Nuka system is vast. It stretches almost 3,218 km from east to west. Given such a vast area of service delivery in difficult terrain, Nuka focuses on building relationships with the patient, who is referred to as a 'customer-owner' in the system. The involvement of the native people in the design and delivery of their own healthcare system has had a direct impact on health outcomes in the area.

When I first came across the Nuka system, I was intrigued. Does such a system truly deliver quality healthcare at an affordable cost? But on seeing their data, they have been able to measure over the years, I could hardly argue. Since its inception, patients' overall hospital days are down by 40 per cent and the total ER and urgent care days at the hospital are also down more than 40 per cent, specialty care requirements are down by 60 per cent and primary care visits are down by 20 per cent. The services rendered by the system are 'pre-paid', based on legislative agreements and funding allocations for the 227 recognized Alaskan native tribes. The way I looked at it was that the capital infusion was brought in by the state and the management was done by means of collaboration between medical professionals and community members.

I think India could learn from the Nuka system to re-think our public wellness delivery system as a partnership between the state and the people—not a public–private venture but public–private–people one.

Sarve Santu Nirāmayāḥ

The phrase 'Sarve Santu Nirāmayāḥ' from a Sanskrit hymn literally means 'may no one suffer from illness'. If we want to achieve this state of health for our billion-plus citizens, then we will need to adopt the mission of wellness for all and take a leaf or two from Nuka's success and implement them in our context.

First and foremost, we need to create joint responsibilities for societal wellness at the village and block levels, where public sector healthcare employees collaborate with citizens who live in those areas. This idea is at the heart of Nuka's success. I also feel that there is nothing wrong in shareholders having a say in shareholder wealth. Let us imagine a block committee for wellness where the local village panchayat leaders, local PHC/CHC physicians, traditional medicine practitioners, block development officers and a few citizens are members. This committee is vested with the responsibility of overseeing the wellness agenda for the block. Their agenda can take into account the required infrastructure, human resources and, most importantly, the wellness needs of the people. The government's role is to provide capital and infrastructure here, just as an investor in a venture, and the committee's role would be that of a management team. I wonder how our rural folk would respond if they are given the power to decide the state of their health and wellness. It is time to bring the community into the workings of a community health centre and transform it into a community wellness centre.

What amazes me about India's healthcare delivery system is its over-generalization when it comes to disease and treatment identification. If we truly understand the power of wellness that systems like Ayurveda espouse, then we will also understand that we need to bring back the customized and individualized approach to wellness. Thankfully, with technology, this is far easier to do now. Today, many of our community health workers collect household-level information; more often than not, this information goes into some government file and then disappears. But if we want our approach to wellness to be individual-centric, then the data our health workers collect will need to be analysed further. Machine learning and AI-driven applications cannot only help block-level wellness committees collect more accurate data through community healthcare workers, but also help analyse it dynamically and thoroughly. Think about a data set that would tell us that in Z block, X number of households from Y number of villages have had at least one malaria case in the past one year. Or that joint pain among a certain age group of senior citizens has become common in the past three years. Or that children between ages X and Y are indicating early symptoms of mental health issues because of reasons A, B and C.

When empowered with information about the well-being of the community, the block wellness committee can then decide what health and wellness interventions are needed in their area. They don't have to go with a grand, generic plan developed by an officer in a government office in the state or national capital.

When we first moved to Munsyari, I would informally check with local women on what issues they faced during pregnancy. I wanted to identify the gaps in their healthcare. After talking to maybe 120 women, I concluded that one gap lay in the check-ups between the fifth and eighth month of their pregnancies, for which they had to travel to the district hospital, six hours away, on bumpy roads. That was a major pain point. These check-ups generally needed an ultrasound test, the machine for which was not available at the local CHC and nor a technician. When I spoke to people in the medical devices sector, they informed me that there now existed devices as small as a briefcase for ultrasound check-ups, and they could be transported even on two-wheelers. This would mean that a technician from the CHC could travel to the village of a pregnant lady and she would not even need to come to the CHC. I got pretty excited and asked how much such a machine would cost; the suppliers said between Rs 2 lakh and Rs 3 lakh.

But there was a glitch. As per the law, only a registered radiologist can perform an Ultrasound test. I was told this was so because unauthorized people might otherwise check the gender of the child, which may lead to female foeticide. That was a valid reason. I felt like banging my head against the wall. Now, where was I going to get a radiologist in these breath-taking boondocks? I went back to the devices companies with this problem. They said they can supply a machine that wouldn't allow the technicians to see the scan they have done. That scan would be sent via the cloud to a registered radiologist, who would then write out the scan report. I took the proposal to the local administration. They told me this wasn't possible because the law was clear on the matter. And so, the women of Munsyari continue to suffer the predicament of travelling six hours of hilly terrain, risking their pregnancies and lives at the same time. Many just skip the check-up altogether. If there was an empowered block wellness committee that could be more in tune with local needs, it would be able to look at more specific solutions. Since it would be a public–people–private body, it could at least try and seek authorization for such a solution. That is the merit in giving communities a say in their own wellness delivery systems.

An institution that I admire for its commitment to patient care is the Mayo Clinic in the United States. One of its founders, Dr William Mayo, told the graduating class of Rush Medical College in 1910 that 'the best interest of the patient is the only interest to be considered and in order that the sick may have the benefit of advancing knowledge, union of forces is necessary'.[11] My grandparents would wholeheartedly support this approach. I feel in the top-down approach to healthcare delivery in India we lose the benefit of local knowledge and traditions that have sustained the well-being of communities for generations. A block wellness committee would be able to ascertain what traditional medical practices have worked for the people of the area, something a person sitting in a ministry in the Union government can never do.

Currently, the doctors who get posted on duty at the local CHCs are under a government rotation system, so they don't have the ability to form lasting relationships with patients, as my grandparents could. This is an important factor in doctor–patient trust. Unfortunately, the way our system is designed today means that we don't have an immediate fix to this issue, but the hope is that at least the assistant staff that form the integrated patient care unit in a Nuka-like system can remain consistent for longer periods.

There is no reason why the Indian private healthcare delivery sector cannot invest in or partner with block-level wellness centres to bring best-in-class healthcare delivery standards to rural India. Digital platforms and data connectivity today offer a myriad ways in which such a collaboration can take place. This may free up resources from the primary health delivery system and lead to allocation of more finances for district-level hospitals that need overhauling too.

When I think of the ancient power of wellness we have inherited as a nation, and when I compare it with the pathetic state of healthcare delivery in the country, my heart bleeds. Before my Covid-19 experience, my understanding of the gaps in the public health system was purely academic and from a distance. But after I personally experienced these gaps as a patient, I feel that we need to fix them with greater urgency. Not doing so would impact our well-being as a nation. Holistic health and well-being for all its people should be a non-negotiable for the world's largest democratic republic.

10

Power of Assimilation

New Delhi Time

Much before digital watches and phone timers became ubiquitous, wall clocks were in common use across the world. On my travels abroad with my parents as a child, I found it fascinating to spot them. At airports and in major hotels, behind the front desks or in the lobby and reception areas, I would try to spot a series of four or five clocks, each displaying the time in different time zones in the world—New York, London, Tokyo, Hong Kong— as well as the local time. My eyes would eagerly search for a clock displaying the time in Mumbai or New Delhi, but I could never find one, except in India.

Observing my disappointment on one such occasion, my father tried to explain to me that the reason these clocks were displaying London, New York or Tokyo time was because these cities were global centres of trade and finance. He explained that travellers who

247

were travelling for business would need to know what time it was in these cities. Being a child and unaware of global trade mechanisms, I asked him, 'Why is it that our home town of Mumbai isn't a global centre of trade?' My father didn't have the heart to tell me that back then, in the late 1980s, India didn't matter in global trade. In fact, in 1988, India's global trade as a percentage of its GDP was barely 13.49.[1]

If you don't matter in global trade as a country, then why would a business traveller be interested in knowing what time it is in your country? But in 1991, a start was made to change this dreadfully low participation of India in global trade through much-needed economic reforms in the country. Throughout my teenage years, my father would make me read two newspaper stories aloud to him every morning—one from *The Times of India* and another from *The Economic Times*. I remember reading about the 1991 reforms on the front page of *The Economic Times*, which reported that India had opened up. My father explained to me that many export controls and import duties would be reduced now. That would mean Indian exporters could be more ambitious about their growth, and that lower customs duties in India would mean foreign products could get imported with ease. It meant that our family business of customs clearance and freight forwarding, started by my great-grandfather in 1896, would also drastically change. I recollect my father holding my hand and telling me with much excitement, 'Young lady, maybe now you will have the hope of finding a wall clock in a hotel or an office somewhere in the world displaying Mumbai or New Delhi time.'

Two decades later, on a visit to Silicon Valley in 2012 I spotted a set of five wall clocks behind an office reception desk. Four of those displayed the time zones of London, Tokyo, New York and San Francisco. The fifth displayed the Indian Standard Time with 'New Delhi' written below it. I have to admit, it made my eyes moist with tears of joy. It was a recognition that the Indian software industry mattered in the operations of the tech giants in Silicon Valley. In the two decades that had followed the liberalization of India's economy, the rise of call centres and Indian tech firms made the time in New Delhi matter. In fact, in 2012, India's global trade as a percentage of its GDP was 55.79.[2] India's increased participation in global trade had made its presence count. We mattered now. A nation home to one seventh of humanity finally mattered now. It was time for— New Delhi Time!

One of the reasons India has displayed reluctance in participating in global trade until recently is our irreconciliation with our colonial past. Until European colonizers came and monopolized our trade, skewing the balance of trade in their favour, India had always traded with the world openly and with trust. India had operated under the premise that trade was beneficial to its kingdoms and people. The country prospered with this 'open-to-trade' and 'everyone-is-welcome' approach. In fact, from the first century CE till the start of British colonization in India in the seventeenth century, India's GDP varied between 25 per cent and 35 per cent of the world's total GDP![3] While colonial conquests created more opportunities for cultural exchange and assimilation, the imbalance of economic benefits in India's disfavour made Indians lose their heart and courage for global trade.

This colonial hangover led to export pessimism and a view favouring import substitution in the planning of our economic and trade policies post-Independence. But traces of that bygone era when we fearlessly traded with the world still remain in our culture and traditions. During my travels and interactions across the country, I have observed this fearlessness in Indians. We engage with strangers openly and are also open to exploring opportunities abroad. But it was during a visit to Odisha that I came to understand how deeply entrenched trade was in ancient Indian society.

Bali Jatra

Kartik Poornima is a festival that falls on a full moon night and is one of the most auspicious times of the year in the Hindu lunar calendar. It arrives in the month of October or November, fifteen days after the night of Diwali, the festival of lights. For the people of Cuttack, a business city in the eastern state of Odisha, this day has a unique significance. Cuttack is an ancient city sprawled across and interspersed between the waters of the Mahanadi river and its tributaries Kathajodi, Kukhai and Birupa.

Until the turn of the sixteenth century, on the auspicious day of Kartik Poornima the 'Sadhabas' (traditional Odia mariners) would sail eastwards from the banks of the Mahanadi river in Cuttack to the distant lands of 'Yawadwipa' (known to us as Java), Sumatra and Bali in present-day Indonesia. The favourable winds at that time of year would facilitate a smooth sailing passage for the boitas, the large sailing boats that were built in the erstwhile kingdom of Kalinga, which included present-day Odisha. It is believed that women too sailed at times and were called 'Sadhbanis'. The Sadhabas would carry with them spices, rice, salt, earthenware, cloth, silk, precious stones, sandalwood, and even elephants on their journeys to the Far East. They would travel to the shores of South-east Asia to trade, but they also, carried with them India's culture, faiths, architecture and languages to those lands.

To celebrate this glorious marine past, the people of Cuttack observe a festival on Kartik Poornima called 'Bali Jatra', literally meaning 'Voyage to Bali'. This festival is organized on the Gadgadia Ghata (bank) of the Mahanadi river and lasts for eight days. The sheer size of the crowds and the scale of this festival make it one of Asia's largest open-air trade fairs. People from all walks of life come to the fair to relish the food here, to buy handicrafts and immerse themselves in the joy rides and other entertainment on offer. They slide paper or leaf boats into the Mahanadi as a prayerful offering. Women sing traditional songs with wishes for a safe and prosperous journey to the mariners. In fact, people across Odisha celebrate this festival as 'Boita Bandana' where boita stands for traditional Odia boats and bandana means worship by lighting a lamp.

When I first came to know of the Bali Jatra festival, I could hardly believe that it could exist—mainly because no mariners from Odisha sail to Bali anymore. After all, the last time the Sadhabas sailed to Bali was more than 500 years ago! A few years ago, when I visited Cuttack during the Bali Jatra festival, I was amazed at the passion and enthusiasm with which the people were celebrating it. When I asked a group of women why they were singing songs wishing for the safe voyage of their mariners when there were no more voyages happening, they replied almost in unison, 'Didi, this is our tradition. We sing in testimony to Odisha's prosperous voyages of yore which established our trade across the seas. We are proud that our ancestors crossed oceans and traded with the world. We know that one day, we will do so again.'

Their conviction in global trade, without having any idea about what it was really like in the twenty-first century, made me realize how deeply seeded this concept was in the community. It was clear to me that the people of Odisha were not afraid of the world or the unknown or the foreigner. They had a sense of openness about the world at large and were welcoming of it. I also knew that the Odia people are not unique in this respect in India. There is indeed a special place for trade and exploration in the collective psyche of the Indian society.

Chennamkary

Approximately 1,590 km south-west of Cuttack lies the island village of Chennamkary in the Alappuzha district of the Kuttanad region in the heart of Kerala's backwaters. The Kuttanad region is unique in its geography and is recognized as having the lowest altitude in India, at 2 m below sea level. Its vast canals, both natural and man-made, crisscross with the four rivers of Pamba, Meenachil, Achankovil and Manimala, creating farming conditions that have led to Kuttanad being christened 'Kerala's rice bowl'.

Thomas Zachariahs and his family run a homestay by the name of Green Palm Homes in this scenic backwater island. From the first European guests who came to stay more than three decades ago with Thomas and his family, their homestay has now seen people from more than thirty different countries. During our pan-India drive in 2014, Ejji, Mahesh, Venkat and I landed up at one of the backwater canals that separate Chennamkary from the mainland. Across the canal, we could see Thomas and his family preparing the traditional Kerala canoe boats to ferry us to his home. When we sat in the canoe, two at a time, Thomas told us that for centuries, traders and travellers from distant lands had crossed oceans in ships, arriving at the Malabar coast and then travelling in these very same canoes to the villages in the interiors of Kerala. Once we reached his home, his mother gave us a traditional Kerala welcome with fresh coconut water. As part of the homestay experience, Thomas took us for a walk around his village. As we walked past lush green home gardens under the thick canopy of coconut trees and wandered through the small pathways on the edges of rice fields that were submerged in water, Thomas shared with us the story of his people, the people of Kerala—the Malayalis.

An ancient people, the Malayalis are of mixed ethnic Indic origin. An amalgamation of various cultures, the people, their faiths, their beliefs and their way of life have been shaped by centuries of contact with civilizations, nations and kingdoms far and wide. The world came to trade with the Malayalis as far back as 3,000 BC. The Babylonians, Sumerians, Arabs and Egyptians were attracted to this kingdom of spices. It is believed that the first Jews to visit India came to Kerala as traders in the days of King Solomon. In the first and second centuries of the common era, the Romans would send as many as 120 ships a year from the ports of Egypt to the Malabar coast of Kerala[4] to trade in spices, especially black pepper. Kerala's interaction with people from different cultures and creeds shaped its own demography too. Narrating the story of how the early Syriac Christians arrived in Kerala with Thomas the Apostle (one of the twelve Apostles of Jesus) during the first century CE itself, Thomas mentioned that he and his family continue to be part of the Syriac Christian congregation first established in Chennamkary more than four centuries ago.

In 1498, the Portuguese explorer Vasco da Gama arrived in Kerala. In the years that followed, the Portuguese established their monopoly on trade here. They also brought the Roman Catholic faith to the Malabar coast. At this point, we were standing next to a church that was first established as a Syriac Christian church but had later been converted into a Roman Catholic one. To Ejji, I pointed out the tall brass pillar standing in the front yard of the church. The brass pillar was similar to the ones you could see in the Hindu temples of Kerala. Being an atheist, Ejji didn't think much of this at first. But he became curious when I pointed to the cross on top of the stambha, saying, 'Look, how well the Malayalis have assimilated.'

As we continued our walk through Chennamkary, I told Ejji that the brass pillar we had seen at the church was actually a dhwaja stambha (flag pillar), found mainly in the front yards of the Hindu temples of Kerala and other parts of south India. The dhwaja stambhas have a special connotation. They represent the cosmic connection that is believed to exist between those that dwell on earth with those in heaven. Traditionally, on top of these pillars, you would find three horizontal perches that point in the direction of the temple deity's sanctum. But in the case of the church, the dhwaja stambha had a cross on top instead of the three horizontal perches. It seemed to me that the Malayalis had taken a faith that came from another people and had assimilated their own traditions, rituals and symbols into it.

When we caught up with Thomas, Mahesh and Venkat, they were discussing how ethnically diverse present-day Kerala is. Thomas was explaining that over the years there have been so many different external influences on the Malayali people that today they are a distinctive culture that has emerged from the assimilation of many different cultures and ways of living. Ejji and I looked at each other and nodded in affirmation. The cross on top of the dhwaja stambha was a fine example of the assimilation Thomas was alluding to.

From the days of the early spice traders in 3,000 BC to the present day, when Malayalis like Thomas welcome tourists from all over the world in homestays across Kerala, the story of Kerala's economic and cultural exchange with the world continues. Significantly, while many foreign influences have mixed with what were once purely Indian Malayali practices, the original ways of life of the people of Kerala also continue. This unique interaction has led to the birth of a syncretic social milieu, where assimilation is the norm and not an exception.

In addition, as welcoming as the Malayalis have been of the world to their land, they have been equally excited about exploring new lands, very much like the Sadhabas of Odisha. As testimony to this, more than 1.5 million Malayalis are found in different parts of the world today. Their influence on their homeland remains so strong that for decades Kerala was known as a 'remittance economy' because of the money Malayalis working overseas sent home.

The Alchemist

The next day, as we drove down along the Kerala coast to reach Kanyakumari, Ejji and I kept spotting brass pillars with a cross on top standing firmly in the front courtyards of churches. We also spotted Hindu temples with their traditional dhwaja stambhas, often right next to the churches. Then there were mosques built in the traditional Kerala temple style of architecture. The assimilation of different cultures and varied traditions was on full display in present-day Kerala.

Ejji insisted that this was purely a Malayali phenomenon, citing that it was the 100 per cent literacy among the people of the state that had ensured this. I disagreed. I told him I had seen this assimilation at play across the country. I had seen it in the Chinese food dhabas and restaurants that serve the spicy Indian version of Chinese food which the Chinese themselves may not recognize as their own—a la Gobi Manchurian! The famous cheese dosa served in south Indian eateries across the country would be another example, not to mention the pizzas served with paneer toppings that might be found on any pizza menu across north India, from Domino's to Pizza Hut. But cultural assimilation in India is not limited to food alone. We can also spot assimilation at work in Bollywood film music and dance performances, and in the colloquial 'Hinglish', a combination of Hindi and English used by millennial and Gen X Indians. We find it in the Sufi dargahs adorned with flowers in the same manner the gods in Hindu temples are, and in the dhwaja stambhas with the cross atop them in the churches of Kerala.

Ejji finally agreed with my point of view, but he wanted to probe further: 'What is this unique ability we have, to constantly take different ideas and merge them with our own without losing our own identity?' I told him that I felt there was something distinctively Indian that catalysed the process of assimilating aspects of other cultures into our own. For, as long as we can remember, India has had the ability to take different threads and assimilate them into a unique fabric that is its own. It is akin to the power of an alchemist engaged in a magical transformation. This inherent power to assimilate stems from our civilizational values of trust, openness and exploration. It is our gift and our superpower. Our ability to venture out and explore new lands, welcome merchants and travellers from near and distant shores, trade in goods and exchange culture and beliefs, even as we make aspects of foreign cultures and beliefs our own, has been a part of our way of life for centuries. It is the alchemy India excels at and it is thus uniquely Indian.

This *Power of Assimilation* also empowers Indians to fearlessly interact with the world, stay open to new ideas while also being sure of their roots. No wonder, then, that the average Indian college graduate can learn new languages and accents and become part of a thriving back-office call-centre industry. People of Indian origin continue to migrate to nations across the world, and today 25 million people of Indian origin are found outside India. Many from the Indian diaspora continue to follow their traditions and openly share their culture with others, even as they embrace the values and ways of their new homelands. Examples of people of Indian origin rising to some of the highest public offices in different parts of the world are a-plenty. There are also shining examples of globally successful academics, business leaders, scientists, doctors and entrepreneurs of Indian origin. Some of these achievers grew up in India and later migrated out of the country for education or employment. Some are children of Indian immigrants. Thus, our power to assimilate from and into cultures is not limited to our shores; we take it with us wherever we go.

But despite these people-to-people interactions and the migration of a large number of Indians to other parts of the world for education or jobs, India, as a market, had remained largely insular since Independence in 1947, until it was forced by a balance-of-payments crisis to open up in 1991. Many large players in the Indian industry initially opposed liberalization of the economy and continued to bargain for protective subsidies while also wishing to benefit from international trade. Indians were initially slow to embrace the potential of this liberalization. In fact, until recently, Indian policy towards domestic business has been mostly protectionist, encouraging even more timid industry and creating very little incentive to build globally competitive businesses.

In the 1980s and 1990s, our neighbour China, with whom we like to keep comparing ourselves, grew massively, both economically and socially. It subdued its distrust of foreigners and developed a collective amnesia of its fear of outsiders, simply in order to transform its communist economic model into an export-driven trade behemoth. In just two decades since it made that decision, China began to heavily influence global trade. Today, it is an economic powerhouse. Global trade cannot be imagined without China playing a role in it. In comparison, India has, for the most part, remained a slow mover and an even slower influencer. During the last two decades, the world has changed both economically and geopolitically, yet we have not made any cascading changes (until recently) in the way in which we approach both trade and geopolitics.

In fact since 1991, the very idea of trade has undergone a metamorphosis. Today, designing in one nation, sourcing in another, manufacturing in three others, assembling in a fourth, has become a norm. The expansion of consumer products and brands to previously uncharted territories and markets has created consumption dynamics not seen since the colonial powers moved out of Europe to Asia and Africa five centuries ago. What constituted efficiency—with tools such as labour arbitrage, where availability of cheap labour allowed companies to outsource production to a country to gain cost advantage—has transformed into a much more intricate global value chain process. Services and their exports, especially in the fields of technology, business process outsourcing through call centres, and the advent of digital platforms and social networks have created a new reality for global trade. In this new world, how can India put its alchemy of assimilation to use? How can Indians use their unique ability to embrace the unknown and their own personal power of assimilation for their individual, national and global prosperity?

Globalization has permeated societies and economies across the world to such an extent that the role of internationally embedded value chains—whether in products, services or technology—is now irreversible. Yet, across the world, there is much disillusion with globalization. Financial meltdowns in the Asian economies in 1997 and in the aftermath of the housing crisis in the United States in 2008 brought home the risks of an unbalanced global system of finance and trade. In fact, it precipitated income inequality, with no protection for those most vulnerable to such crises. In countries hugely dependent on agriculture, climate change has brought production deficiencies. And the lack of governance in the matter of digital platforms and information flows has raised questions of privacy and data security. As communities in the mid-west in the United States lost auto jobs to workers in China, Japan and South Korea, and as migrants from north Africa and eastern Europe used the open borders of the European Union to flood the job markets in the United Kingdom, these two biggest proponents of free trade—United States and United Kingdom—began seeing opposition to the global trade narrative on their respective home fronts. As Thomas Freidman writes in his book *Thank You for Being Late: Succeeding in the Age of Acceleration*, 'Globalisation has always been everything and its opposite—it can be incredibly democratising and it can concentrate incredible power in giant multinationals; it can be incredibly particularising—the smallest voices can now be heard everywhere—and incredibly homogenising, with big brands now able to swamp everything anywhere. It can be incredibly empowering, as small companies and individuals can start global companies overnight, with global customers, suppliers and collaborators, and it can be incredibly disempowering—big forces can come out from nowhere and crush your business when you never even thought they were in your business. Which way it tips depends on the values and tools that we all bring to these flows.'[5]

Therefore, we must ask ourselves what values and tools India brings to the arena of globalization. Can it summon its power of assimilation and encourage more trust and openness in the world? Can India be the alchemist that transforms the current state of polarization and distrust in the global order into one that holds out new possibilities? How can we co-create a global framework that incorporates the values of mutual respect, reciprocal trust, equitable benefits and explorative openness, to name a few. What would that framework look like, and how can it benefit Indians and humanity at large?

The Corner Stone

Before we delve further into exploring the values and tools that India can bring to restore faith in globalization, we need to understand the changing landscape of globalization. The world interacts in a variety of ways today, other than through trade. Globalization in the twenty-first century is a complex phenomenon. It is a whole bunch of components with intricate webs of interdependence and tensions. Globalization today includes everything from climate change, trade and trade wars, border disputes, refugees, terrorism, pandemics, space exploration, digitization, hunger and poverty alleviation, education, inclusion, et al. We will only be able to aid its cause if we understand it well. Our ability to comprehend globalization will come from how we have personally experienced it and how we relate to it; from how we recognize and organize different components of the global system and how we understand the relationship between those parts and ourselves—for example, the connections we see between trade and tourism, agriculture and climate change or data and security. Finally, our ideas of globalization will be defined by our perspective of globalization as a whole. In other words, do we see it as a system that empowers us as a nation to bring a better quality of life for all Indians, or do we see it as a tool of inequality forced upon us?

If we are committed to using our power of assimilation to aid the cause of globalization as a nation, then we will need to help Indians on a large scale to upgrade their ideas about globalization— ideas that reflect its new reality. To upgrade this thought process, we will need to skill our people and provide them with opportunities to interact with the world. This can happen to some extent via tourism and trade, but it will not be on the scale that is required. What the world needs is not just a handful who understand and benefit from globalization, but a wider set of people everywhere who do so. Initially, many countries might find this hard to achieve, as they may be traditionally insular cultures, mistrustful of the world at large. But, as India's history and culture prove, this country is no stranger to such interactions, in scale or scope. Once this understanding is born, then there will be hope for fresh assimilation. Therefore, the next question that arises is: how do we equip ourselves with tools that can supplement our inherent power of assimilation?

The key may lie in people beginning early, at an age when the process of global exchange and assimilation can be transformative for the individual. I can vouch for this from my own personal experience. I did my undergraduate studies from Miami University in Ohio, USA. The university had only between 150 and 200 international students in a student body of over 16,000. Around 100 of us international students got to live in Clawson Hall, the designated dormitory/hostel for international students. There were a few American students who stayed there too, but only those who were studying international relations. It was not the best way to introduce foreign students to American culture, but for us international students, it was simply amazing to live with people from eighty different countries.

In my three years at Miami University, I don't recall ever sitting down for breakfast, lunch or dinner with the same group of nationalities more than once. This was in the late 1990s, when Google was just being brought to life. This incredible opportunity to interact with people from across the world, at such close proximity, was an education in itself! It has been one of the most life-changing experiences for me. The fact that I experienced this while I was still a young college student has, in fact, made all the difference in the way I look at and comprehend this world. It has served as a cornerstone for my own views of globalization.

Despite Indian students being either the largest or among the top three foreign student groups in many countries, a large number of young people living in our country do not get to experience foreign cultures, languages and people. One way to change this is to make our educational institutions attractive to foreign students. This may seem difficult, but it is not impossible. After all, a thousand or more years ago, students from a number of countries came to study at the famous campus of Nalanda. In the same way, in the twenty-first century, we have to focus on promoting campuses of academic excellence. I strongly believe that when students from across the world come to India to pursue their education, they will bring with them their ideas, beliefs and cultures for our youth to experience and learn from. In return, they will also take back our values, traditions and norms.

Another intervention we may think of is to teach foreign languages in schools and colleges. I am aware that there are urban schools that offer French, Spanish or German to students, but what I am referring to is not a limited introduction to foreign languages but a systemic change that makes learning a foreign language an option for everyone. I recollect a conversation I had with Thomas, an American student who lived in Clawson Hall. He was impressed that I spoke four languages fluently—namely, Hindi, Gujarati, Marathi, and English—and that I could understand and write Sanskrit and speak conversational Urdu to a decent degree. He was fascinated by this, but I didn't think much of it. Everyone in my school back in Mumbai spoke at least three languages fluently. In my junior college in Mumbai, based on where their families hailed from, people spoke Tamil or Malayalam or Assamese or Bengali in addition to Hindi, Marathi and, of course, English. But it was only when I interacted with people from across the world in my dorm that I realized that this multilingualism from early childhood was actually not as common across the world as I thought it might be, and that Indians were part of a very small group of societies that actually managed this.

As impressed as Thomas was with my linguistic skills, he was equally quick to point out that all the languages (with the exception of English) I spoke were of Indic origin. They were not the languages of another people. He asked me why it was so. I had no answer. In my first year at Clawson, I had a Japanese roommate. She would share stories of the Bunraku theatre (Japanese puppet theatre), but it was hard for me to fully understand them as I didn't know any Japanese. Language is the principle method of human communication, but over the years I have also realized that language is a window to the culture and society that speaks it. I wish I had known basic Japanese back then, because I would have been able to learn so much more from Ai Takayama and her ancient culture. In my second year, my roommate was from the south of France. Luce was at Miami for only one semester as an exchange student. But this time around, I decided to learn beginner-level French. As I began to speak basic French with her, she warmed up to me more. We started talking about our families, our cultures and our countries. Both these experiences showed me that language can open a door to other nations and societies. And it can do so in a way no other soft power or skills can.

The fact that our young people are born polyglots is our strength. Why not build on this strength and create a focused approach to teaching foreign languages to our young people? This has benefits at multiple levels. It can create large-scale awareness among Indians about people from different parts of the world, and it can also make it possible for us to deepen our trade and geopolitical ties. Look at it this way: If young people in India were taught Japanese, Korean, Khmer, Burmese, Malay, Vietnamese and Lao, what would that do for India's role in South-east and East Asia? More broadly, what it would do for India's Act East policy?

Learning about foreign cultures doesn't have to be limited to studying abroad or learning foreign languages. There are creative ways, especially in the digital age, to build learning bridges between children in India and their counterparts in other countries. There can be sister-schools, on the same lines as sister-cities in the world today. If Varanasi and Kyoto in Japan are partner cities, for instance, then why just limit the student exchange programmes to Kyoto University and Banaras Hindu University? Why can't the schools in these cities create bridge-learning programmes for their students? Why can't the schools of Varanasi offer Japanese as a foreign language? Maybe this will help people in the area to better serve the Japanese tourists who come to Bodh Gaya, Sarnath and Kushinagar.

To create deeper awareness about the different nations of the world, Clawson Hall ran what was called the 'Global Awareness Program—GAP'. As students, we would be assigned a passport from a country different from ours, and through the year we would be a national of both our own country and also of the GAP-assigned country. One year, I was assigned the nationality of Republic of Ghana. I had never been to Africa and had little clue about the vastness and diversity of the continent. I have to admit, I didn't even know where Ghana was on the map of the world. I can still recollect how ashamed I was of my ignorance. In the months that followed, I could, with the help of a friend from Senegal and another from Tanzania, develop a deeper understanding of my GAP nationality. As I mentioned before, this was in the late 1990s and the World Wide Web was a new phenomenon. Therefore, all the research one could do was from the university library or by talking to friends who knew about the country of your interest.

The GAP programme called for students to learn about their assigned country, its people, culture, history, economics, etc. At the end of the year, we had to present a thesis on our understanding of the country, complete with phrases in the local language and a local dish from its cuisine cooked by us for the others in the programme. Through the year, as I prepared for my presentation, I learnt a lot about Ghana, and also Africa. I came to learn, for instance, that Ghana is the world's second largest producer of cocoa beans and the second largest producer of gold in Africa. Its colourful national costume is made from a handwoven cloth called Kente. Its Lake Volta is the largest artificial lake in the world and can be seen even from space. I learned that in 1957, Ghana was the first sub-Saharan colony to become an independent nation. English is the official language of the country, but almost 50 per cent of the people speak the Akan language. By the end of the year, I had managed to learn and speak a few phrases in Akan. I also managed to cook a Ghanaian okra stew and imagined myself running a small eatery in Mumbai that would serve Kerala appams with Ghanaian okra stew.

What stops our schools and colleges from running programmes like the GAP? It doesn't have to be a subject to study, but something to explore and learn from. Would it not enable our youth to be more aware about the world? Becoming more aware about the world would, after all, upgrade our thinking. In turn, this would help us see the benefits of globalization for us and for others in the world.

Whether it is through language learning, exchange programmes, bridge and awareness modules or by any other intervention that promotes cross-cultural understanding, we need a global process for the coming generations to be more aware of their fellow global citizens. Not that other countries cannot or are not taking some of these steps, but in India we have the unique opportunity to do it on a large scale, purely because of our inherent ability to assimilate different cultures, languages and ideas from early childhood.

When we are able to understand people from other nations, our interest in interacting with them increases. Our capacity to collaborate in tackling the global challenges of climate and terrorism multiplies, enabling us to create an atmosphere of trust and openness. Interdependencies are deepened and the world becomes more peaceful and cooperative. This is something that the world badly needs today.

Assimilation helps us create possibilities where globalization is creating more inclusion rather than exclusion for our people. It paves the way for a new era of globalization, an era seeded with our values of trust and openness. In his thought-provoking piece for the *Print*, India's former permanent representative to the United Nation, Syed Akbaruddin, writes, 'Challenges that transcend borders are of cardinal importance to India's well-being. It is, therefore, time to conceptualise, in concrete terms, pathways to address them. This will need to include our envisaging the new (global) order and India's role in it as well as who our partners in this venture will be.'[6]

Globalization and Parochialism

As much as we have the potential to play the alchemist in transforming the world order, we still have a few ghosts in our own closet to deal with. One of those is parochialism. It is comforting to be a frog in the well. But does it serve our purpose as a nation? Will it allow us to participate in addressing challenges that transcend our borders, as Akbaruddin points out? Will it help us reimagine a new world order and our place in it? Does it lead us in a direction which is more in convergence with our inherent strengths and traits, or away from it? Should the raft of the republic sail in the opposite direction of the civilizational flow?

In the post-War era, as countries like the United States, Singapore, Germany, France, Italy and Japan took the lead in creating rule-based global trade mechanisms, India chose to remain a mere spectator. In doing so, we chose to become rule-takers and not rule-framers. In doing so, we acted in complete contradiction to what had historically been our natural and traditional approach to everything foreign. In short, we denied ourselves our own power of assimilation. The effects of this could be seen not just in our balance of trade, but on our collective psyche too. It hampered our ability as a people to play a constructive role in the new global order developing in the world at that point in time. We need to avoid making this mistake again.

We must acknowledge that the political hangover of the colonial era is hard to shrug off, given that many aspects of our Independence movement were rooted in the idea of Swadeshi. Any view of globalization that Indians can relate to will need to take that into account. Swadeshi is an adjective form of a conjunction of two Sanskrit words—*swa* (self) and *desh* (country)—and literally means 'of one's own country'.

The popular understanding is that the Swadeshi movement was started by Mahatma Gandhi, but in actual fact the movement had its genesis in the 1870s. Its originator was Baba Ram Singh Kuka, a Sikh guru of the Namdhari sect in Punjab. The movement reached its peak in 1871–72, when Baba Ram Singh asked people to wear clothes made locally and boycott foreign goods, British schools and courts.[7] In its more popular phase, the Swadeshi movement was taken forward by the early Independence leaders such as Lala Lajpat Rai,

Bipin Chandra Pal, Aurobindo Ghosh and Bal Gangadhar Tilak. It
received much national attention from 1905 to 1911, when the then
Viceroy of India, Lord Curzon, declared the Partition of Bengal.
After Gandhiji's return from South Africa and during his leadership
of the Independence movement, the concept of Swadeshi rose to
the centre of the very idea of everything Indian. But in essence, it
was a tool used by all these leaders for communicating distrust and
rejection of the imperial rule and as a negotiating tactic for deriving
greater political autonomy and eventually complete independence.

Swadeshi was, therefore, at its core a geopolitical instrument to
deliver self-rule for the Indian people. It began with demanding a
fair and equitable place for Indians in the trade that emerged from
their own land, labour and resources. And so, we must note and
accept that Swadeshi did *not* mean negation of the world and global
trade. Rather, it stood for the equitable interest of the Indian people
in global trade. Does the current government's Atmanirbhar Bharat
mission echo this sentiment? In spirit, yes, especially when Prime
Minister Narendra Modi has himself stated that a self-reliant India
does not mean an India closed to the world. But we have to see
how this mission unfolds. India's definition of global trade should
definitely be in opposition to the rules that she has rejected in the
past, such as those of the imperialist East India Company or the idea
of company-states like China, with their state-sponsored capitalism.

The Hindu dhwaja stambhas continue to exist in Kerala temples
in their original avatar and authentic glory, and yet there is an
assimilated version of it with a cross on top for the Christians of
Kerala. In China Town in Kolkata, you can eat a delicious authentic
Chinese meal, and yet just two streets away you can also eat its
Indian-Chinese version, a product of culinary assimilation. Our
openness to new ideas and our ability to merge them with our own
without either of the two losing its unique identity can be a great
strength for us in the current global state of affairs. For example, we

can apply our power of assimilation in co-creating trade frameworks that have local stakes in global value chains, where the assimilation of global and local trade is seamless—all the while giving each their due. We can become torchbearers of the idea that local and global are not antithesis to each other and that enhancing self-reliance is not ideologically opposite to being an active part of the global trade system.

Globalization 2.0

For India to deepen its global interactions and expand its global trade footprint, it is important to reimagine the organs of our government that drive these engagements and shape our global presence. India's geopolitical interaction with the world is anchored in its ministry of external affairs and its policy for global trade in the ministry of commerce and industry. Therein lies our fault line. If we honestly upgrade our understanding of globalization, we will be forced to question how two different ministries can deliver the larger global systems role that India needs to play. Of course, one can argue that the overall strategies are aligned at the Cabinet level but down the line the division causes much confusion and delays. A recent reorganization of the ministry of external affairs has ushered in some change that will facilitate the ministry's deeper involvement in development, commerce, technology and security issues, but this is not enough. The world is moving at an accelerated pace and we must press for systemic changes on the home front too.

We need to rethink and restructure the ways in which we function. We cannot think of globalization as one whole system and have different government organs dealing with it using a piece-meal approach. Trade is a geopolitical tool. Separating it from the rest of foreign policy is harmful to India's strategic interests. Some nations have been reorganizing the foreign policy and trade organs within their governments for some years now. Canada, for instance, has gone a step further by regrouping its foreign trade and policy, international development assistance and diplomatic missions into a single public identity: Global Affairs Canada.

As much as there is an urgent need to restructure, there are also some immediate considerations that can help increase India's share in global trade. This is important because trade and investment give us the power of capital and influence in geopolitics. In their pivotal article in *Mint*, Vijay Kelkar, R.A. Mashelkar and Niranjan Rajadhyaksha write:

> The world faces several profound challenges in the 21st century—public health, climate change, depletion of fossil fuels, a water crisis and protecting biodiversity, for example. The forces of techno-globalism should be used to create public goods that help humanity meet the emerging challenges. India can play an important role in this quest if it remains open to the flow of knowledge and ideas, partly by participating in multilateral institutions and partly by being a centre of trade and investments.[8]

The writers make the case that without trade, investment and participation in the global economic flows, India may not be able to fulfil its destiny to collaboratively shape the new world order.

For Globalization 2.0 to make sense to Indians then, there have to be equitable benefits coming their way. It must translate to more income, livelihoods and prosperity domestically. Our vast consumption market gives our foreign trade policy some teeth in negotiating for more mutually beneficial trade frameworks with other nations. Despite this, we have signed some free trade agreements in the past that allowed our advantages to slip away, with no major gains accruing at our end. This skewed approach to trade negotiations and agreements needs to change. The second area to focus on is that of local and global value chains and the debate of local versus global. This needs strategic thinking in terms of what sectors to nurture domestically, what activities to outsource, what leads to more competitiveness and what our value addition is going to be. It needs investment in skills, infrastructure and innovation. If we analyse this perspective in-depth, it will be clear how our neighbour China has been able to develop a comprehensive roadmap to economic prosperity and development in the past two decades. In India, we must learn from that.

One of the ways we can prepare for a greater share in global trade is to get our supply chain and logistics infrastructure ready to meet the demands of global trade. We must also take tactical advantage of the shifting supply chains in the post-Covid world. The first step we need to take in this direction is to digitize our supply chains. Information flow helps supply chains become agile and efficient. Indian EXIM (export and import) processes and Indian customs set-ups are far removed from automation. Digitization of the entire export and import process using knowledge-based, data-driven form-filling would allow for faster documentation, reduction in errors and time ... all essential for our competitiveness. This means creating an online platform for actors across the EXIM supply chain to plug into and transact, allowing for seamless data exchange between the systems of exporter/importer, container freight stations, shipping lines, airlines, cargo agents, freight agents, customs, etc. This, when coupled with a multimodal logistics infrastructure, can enhance our competitiveness drastically. That is our second step.

India uses only 6 per cent of its waterways. Our coastal shipping, too, continues to be in a nascent stage. Rules such as different risk and insurance rates attached to sea and rail modes for the same shipment and lack of end-to-end intermodal infrastructure use can increase the cost of multimodal transport. The documentation required for different modes of transportation remains patchy and inefficient and calls for standardization. Coastal logistics infrastructure ought to be substantially enhanced with robust intermodal connectivity for each of the coastal ports and the building of coastal logistics parks that can handle non-bulk cargo. The PM Gati Shakti plan recently launched by Prime Minister Narendra Modi aims to ease some of these issues.

The traditional ways of trade remain intact, but there are new ways of transacting business. The digital flows that carry data, content and information have become the new frontiers of global trade. Here too, India can be at a sizeable advantage. In his article in *Financial Express* titled 'Global Trade: Making a Start for WTO Reforms', Anwarul Hoda writes:

On January 25, 2019, at Davos, 76 WTO members (of the total 164) decided to launch talks to establish a comprehensive set of rules on the subject (e-commerce). Subsequently, the Osaka G20 Summit gave a significant push to the negotiation of an international agreement on e-commerce by launching talks on free cross-border flow of data. G20 remains divided on the issue and three members—India, Indonesia and South Africa—did not support the free data flow initiative at Osaka.[9]

The very fact that the talks at WTO and G20 featured the subject of data flow and e-commerce global frameworks is a sign that digital economy is coming of age. India is one of the world's fastest growing e-commerce market and it has the second largest mobile internet user base in the world. Given our massive data flows, we have the opportunity to be rule-framers for the ways in which the world trades, negotiates and grows in the digital economy universe. We need to take a more focused and engaged approach to these discussions whilst keeping our data security as an important consideration. We may ban apps and disallow certain companies to access our data, but we must not shy away from being rule-framers for global data flows. We must embrace the truth that this is not simply about data flows, but also about how the global order will take shape in this new age of internet, e-commerce and artificial intelligence. This is not the time to negate reality or be a bystander. Our focus and commitment will mean that 1.38 billion Indians will benefit from an equitable stake in Globalization 2.0.

Tenzing Bhutia

Tenzing Bhutia was born in 1987 in a village called Navey Basti near Gangtok, the capital of Sikkim. His parents, both farmers by occupation, had studied up to the tenth standard. Even though the elders in the family said the local village school would do for Tenzing, his father insisted on taking him to Gangtok for his education. He even took up a job as an art teacher at a local school so that Tenzing could study in the same school. As a young child, Tenzing was shy, but science fascinated him. He was inspired by the stories of Einstein, Faraday and Edison, who had pursued their dreams despite many odds. When Tenzing came to class ten, everyone coaxed him to start looking at a government job as a career, but he wasn't excited about it at all.[10]

His father insisted that he pursue engineering, and despite his best attempts to fail the AIEEE entrance exam, Tenzing passed with flying colours and found himself admitted to the National Institute of Technology (NIT) at Jalandhar in Punjab, to study chemical engineering. Tenzing remembers his time at Jalandhar as very tough. It was a different cultural setting; the food was completely different and language was hard to follow. What he disliked most was the rote-learning expected of the students there. Even though he admits the teachers there were good, he was just not interested in this type of education and so, in his third year, he quit NIT and left for Delhi.

For an entire year, Tenzing worked at call centres in Delhi. He was too ashamed to go back home, knowing how hard his parents had worked to send him to school and college. But his parents eventually called him back. Upon his return, he was again asked to apply for a government job, which he vehemently refused to do. Out of frustration at not finding a job, Tenzing resorted to all sorts of activities, even gambling. It seemed that a bright young boy was going to lose his way in life. But love happened, and the girl he was interested in refused to marry him as her family objected to her marrying a man without a stable career. This broke his heart, and to mend it Tenzing decided to do something concrete with his life.

The year was 2015. Tenzing began to read voraciously, and his life turned. As he wondered what to do with his life, he recollected an incident at the call centre in Delhi where he had worked. Everyone was talking about their favourite food, and he said his was momos. Everyone had laughed at him at that time—how could he like something that was cooked and sold in dirty food stalls on the streets? He was taken aback that a food item his family regularly ate had such a bad reputation. He realized that his colleagues had never been introduced to good-quality momos. Thinking about that incident, Tenzing came up with an idea: what if he started a momo business?

Momos are steamed dumplings brought over to India by Tibetans. Tenzing says his ancestors brought momos to Sikkim some 400 to 500 years ago. But at that point in time they were made with Yak meat or cheese. No other variety. He was unhappy with the quality of momos currently available in the marketplace. In his opinion, the eateries serving momos only made two or three varieties and their basics were all wrong. Tenzing loved momos and believed he was the best person to bring the humble food of his people to the world. Fired by this passion, at the age of thirty he co-founded Shuffle Momos in Gangtok.

Shuffle Momos is a joint venture between Tenzing and a friend of his. She used to work in the government earlier but was thoroughly bored of her job. She quit her job and invested the money she had in the venture. They started with Rs 1 lakh, after which they never looked back. Initially, their kitchen was small and they could serve only twenty-five varieties of momos, but as time progressed, they came up with hundreds of different varieties—cabbage, chicken, beef and pork momos, mushroom-corn-cheese momos, chicken cheese momos, prawn momos, mutton momos, pan-fried momos, natural desert momos, mango momos...

Shuffle Momos brought much innovation and assimilation of other flavours and ingredients to this humble dumpling. They even came up with chocolate momos! On special occasions such as Valentine's Day, they make rose-shaped pink momos, and on Indian Independence Day, they make tri-colour momos inspired by the colours of the Indian national flag.

I met Tenzing during an IEF masterclass I was conducting in partnership with Rewaj's Start-up Harbour community in Gangtok. He told me that while watching the brand campaign for Pizza Hut, he thought that if Italian food could become so commonplace in the world, then why couldn't momos become equally popular? His ambition to take his food to consumers across the world reminded me of the passion with which Alezo wanted to take Naga food everywhere. They are joined by entrepreneurs like Muheet Mehraj of Kashmir Box and Rewaj, with his NE Origin venture, who want to take their region's products to the world.

When you ask Tenzing about his future plans for Shuffle Momos, he says with excitement, 'Now that we are running a successful outlet in Gangtok's main MG Marg market and are valued at Rs 2 crore, I feel confident about taking Shuffle Momos to at least 100 locations across India. Then, we can take it across the world. Our product can be like the pizza, sold across the world with fillings and flavours that are locally inspired and assimilated to meet local taste buds.' He dreams of making his momos a global rage. He wishes that one day there would be an ad campaign for Shuffle Momos, like the one he saw for Pizza Hut.

Tenzing's mission is to change the way the world thinks about momos. He feels that even though momos were brought to Sikkim from Tibet, they are now part of the Sikkimese identity. He firmly believes that it is his duty to take something that belongs to his culture to people across the world. Tenzing wants to go global. Can he? Why not! But ideas and fresh air alone won't do for him. He will need to explore markets where his momos can sell. He will need help in understanding the rules and laws of those markets. He will need to appreciate different cultural nuances and hire local-cuisine expertise. He will need to ensure that he is able to deliver to consumers a uniquely Sikkimese experience that is assimilated with local flavours.

Tenzing is not naïve or unwilling to learn. He is probably the only momo-maker who follows the principles of the Japanese quality system of Kaizen. He read about it in a book and implemented it in his restaurant and kitchen. If he can find people who are familiar with markets in other parts of the world, who speak the languages of those countries, who can tell him where his momos will sell faster, that would be great. He is a small entrepreneur; he cannot hire the large global consulting firms who do this for their multinational clients. If Tenzing has to have a chance at becoming the owner of the next global food chain, he will need to hire expertise at an affordable cost and closer to his current place of work. Currently, that seems difficult. But what if we *did* train young people in foreign languages and skilled them in the know-how of other countries using learning modules like the GAP? What if we had a cadre of young people who are experts in global markets in addition to those who serve in the Indian Foreign Service? Wouldn't a Tenzing Bhutia then have help that is both accessible and affordable? Wouldn't he then have a chance at going multinational? If we were able to provide tools that give entrepreneurs affordable access to global value chains and supply chains through infrastructure, policy, skill-building and exposure, then wouldn't globalization become more equitable for the common Indian?

The Sadhabas of Odisha sailed to the Far East centuries ago. To think that they did so without any skills would be foolish. There must have been skills they learnt and attributes they acquired to be able to sail to distant lands for trade. The Malayalis created a sophisticated system of learning and assimilation which, even today, allows them to settle in foreign lands with ease. The role of the government is to upskill and upgrade local soft and hard power, to get its people ready to participate in global flows. While some of this is underway, it is also incumbent upon the government of the day to synergize trade and geopolitics in such a way that Globalization 2.0 is not just for large corporates and big metro dwellers, but also reaches the remote corners of the country. More importantly, our enhanced ability to comprehend India's role in shaping the world order can increase the chances of success for people like Tenzing. When our reforms at home and our contributions to the framework of global rules become catalysts for ordinary Indians like Tenzing to engage with globalization, we can succeed, and at a scale unprecedented in human history. In doing so, we can transform the very nature of globalization and how it delivers equitable benefits.

Our view of globalization must stem from our power of assimilation where we have, for centuries, understood how exchange of ideas, beliefs and trade can take place between nations. In the emerging geopolitics of the new world order, where mistrust grows at an exponential rate, we will need to carefully choose our partners with whom mutual trust, equitable benefits and openness to share are possible. This will only be feasible when we are able to once and for all bury the ghost of colonial victimhood and rise to the occasion by assimilating the systemic transformation of globalization with the values we consider sacrosanct. Our power of assimilation will be our biggest ally in this endeavour and will propel us to usher in a new age of globalization anchored in the truest spirit of *Vasudhiava Kutumbakam*—the world is one family.

11

Power of Inclusion

Palace of Fairies and Suleiman Charitra

Nestled in the rocky folds of the mighty Zabarwan mountains is a palace of fairies, a seven-terraced garden that overlooks the city of Srinagar in the valley of Kashmir. Pari Mahal, as it is popularly known, was built by the Mughal Prince Dara Shukoh in the mid-seventeenth century. Over the years, whenever stories of pain, conflict and struggle for peace weighed heavy on my chest while in Kashmir, I would get into a car and drive up the mountain to this palace of fairies. Something in the ambience here is other-worldly, and there is a whiff of magic in the air. In early spring, when the flowers are in nascent bloom and the Zabarwans still have snow on their peaks, a mist surrounds the ruins of Pari Mahal, giving it an enchanting aura, as if it were filled with mystery.

I can understand why the Mughal prince built this residence-cum-library. He was, after all, no ordinary prince. Disguised in royal paraphernalia as the heir to the Mughal throne, Dara was a lover of the arts and a seeker of knowledge, love and truth. When life in the courts of the Mughal empire became too mundane, Dara left the hustle and bustle of the plains and retreated to this serene abode. There are many theories about what the actual purpose of this palace was. But the most plausible explanation is that Dara Shukoh built it for his Sufi Master Mullah Shah Akhund Badakhshani.[1] Its many rooms for stay and rest, its terraced gardens, water tanks and even the baradari—a pavilion designed for convening—all point to the fact that Pari Mahal was a place for meditation, study and the monastic pursuits.

Dara himself was deeply interested in mysticism and comparative study of religion. Whilst the rest of his family members built lush gardens for leisure in Kashmir, he built a centre for knowledge and spiritual seeking. He was inspired by the possibility of Hindu Vedic thought and Muslim Sufi thought coming together. He encouraged scholars and saints from different sects and religions to exchange ideas and was fascinated by Hindu texts such as the Upanishads, and even translated them into Persian. Dara Shukoh visited Kashmir many times and may have authored several works when he stayed at Pari Mahal. The most notable of his works was *Majma-ul-Bahrain: The Mingling of Two Oceans*. It is a short treatise in Persian that talks about the mystical and pluralistic similarities between Sufi and Vedantic ideas.

Dara spent several years studying both Vedic Sanatani thought and Sufi Islam. In a sense, he was a paragon of religious inclusion and harmony. He went beyond religious tolerance and saw much promise in syncretic cultural and religious interaction. He befriended the seventh Sikh guru and immersed himself in learning yoga, the Vedas and the Puranas, and made sure that their translations in Persian were available to scholars in Persia. He believed in the power of inclusion for ushering in peaceful coexistence among the people.

Dara was only walking in the footsteps of those before him, who indulged in bringing different religious and cultural thoughts to the fore. He was able to do it with greater impact as he was a prince. But many artists, authors, poets, musicians, saints and even merchants did their bit to further the syncretic nature of Indian society. One among them was Kalyan Malla. Many may have not heard of this son of the soil who was born into the Karpura clan of Kshatriyas. He served in the court of Prince Lad Khan, the son of King Ahmed, the Lodi Ruler of Ayodhya in erstwhile Awadh and present-day Uttar Pradesh. The Lodi dynasty ruled the Delhi Sultanate starting from mid-fifteenth century for up to seventy years. In the early sixteenth century, almost a hundred years before Dara's authoring of the *Majma-ul-Bahrain*, the Hindu poet Kalyan Malla wrote a biblical story of Hebrew and Arabic origin. Written in Sanskrit, the story was titled *Suleiman Charitra* and was written for his Muslim Lodi prince.

Suleiman Charitra is essentially the story of David and Solomon. Malla's style was in the sringara rasa, the most evocative and elaborate of all the writing styles in Sanskrit. The first three chapters are from the tale of David and Bathsheba's love story, as originally found in the second book of Samuel in the Old Testament. The final chapter is a collection of stories from the Arabian Nights. What is amazing is how Kalyan Malla took a Judaic tale with an Arabic narrative and gave it a Sanskrit form. The meter and language of this work is steeped in classical Sanskrit. Even as someone who is well versed in Sanskrit, I could not fully grasp the work until the retired career diplomat A.N.D Haksar published a translation of it in 2015. What delighted me most was that the *Suleiman Charitra* is a fine example of how medieval Indians approached inclusion. It reaffirmed my belief that inclusion is our way and not an import we got from someone or someplace else. It is our inherent strength. Despite sectarian and communal forces acting wilfully time and again to tear the national fabric, we continue to express our *Power of Inclusion* in a myriad ways.

The Bazaars of Hyderabad

In her well-known poem *In the Bazaars of Hyderabad,* 'Nightingale of India' and freedom movement leader Sarojini Naidu describes the lively scenes of merchants, shopkeepers, women, goldsmiths, flower girls and fruit vendors in a Hyderabad bazaar. Due to its peculiar history, the city of Hyderabad has a mixed culture of local Telugu-speaking Hindus and Urdu-speaking Muslims. As a result, the bazaars of the city cater to the needs of people from different faiths and traditions. A few years ago, I accompanied my friend Aisha to the Chatta Bazaar located in the old city of Hyderabad. Seven generations of Aisha Baig's family have lived in Hyderabad. And now that she was getting married, wedding cards done in beautiful Urdu calligraphy from Chatta Bazaar were a must. We went around visiting several shops and finally selected something she liked.

Walking through the crowded lanes of the bazaar, Aisha told me stories from her childhood and how visits to the bazaars of Hyderabad with her grandmother, mother and aunts were her favourite outing. I was curious to know how many such bazaars the city had. I asked her. She frowned and said, 'If you haven't seen the eclectic bazaars of Hyderabad, then you ain't seen nothing in life!' I knew that was a bit of an exaggeration, but in deference to her love for her home town, I agreed to visit the bazaars with her over the next few days.

The next day we started with the Laad Bazaar, located adjacent to the historic monument of Charminar. It is locally known as Choodi Bazaar, after its world-famous glittering lacquer bangles. Lacquer bangle making is a traditional craft. They are made in every imaginable colour and come studded with semi-precious stones and

artificial diamonds. The narrow alleys of the bazaar are lined with
shops that sell everything from pearls, kohl (surma), perfume (attar),
clothes, bangles, mehndi (henna), and jewellery. But it is the bangles
that draw shoppers from across the world to its busy by-lanes. As
Aisha and I walked down one of the alleys I was awe-struck to see
shops displaying sparkling bangles of all sizes, designs and hues.
Women, some in sarees with a red bindi on their forehead and some
in long black burqas, were trying out the bangles and haggling with
the shopkeepers over the price. The lane seemed like a mosaic of
different cultures, aesthetics and faiths. I told Aisha this, and she
beamed with joy. She said, 'My friend, the bazaars of Hyderabad
are the most pronounced expression of the inclusive and composite
culture of our city. And you have only seen two of them. There are
many more. Many think of our city as the land of the Nizams, but
in truth Hyderabad is a confluence of ideas, faiths, cultures and
traditions.'

Aisha was right. The traditional cultural lifestyle of Hyderabadi
Muslims is called the 'Hyderabadi tehzeeb' or 'Dakhini tehzeeb' and
is a confluence of north and south Indian traditions. But in addition
to that, Hyderabad is also a fine example of a syncretic society
where communities not just co-exist but intermingle, interact and
constantly add to their common composite culture. Hyderabad has
its own magic. Whether in their cuisine, clothes, language, literature,
arts, architecture, festivals or business, Hyderabadis live out their
amalgamated culture effortlessly. It's heart-warming, to say the least.
The power of inclusion is thriving in this old city—now a modern
metropolis. Its 'tehzeeb', an Urdu word for culture, continues the
rich traditions of inclusion initiated by its elder Awadhi cousin, the
'Ganga–Jamuni tehzeeb'.

Ganga Jamuni

Centuries of inter-faith exchange and coexistence amongst Indians from varied faiths—Hindu, Muslim, Sikh, Jain, Buddhist and Christian—has led to a syncretic milieu in the Indian society. What is unique is that this confluence of thought was not just amongst Indic religions such as Hinduism, Sikhism, Buddhism and Jainism, which have had centuries to organically intersperse, but between Indic religions and those such as Islam and Christianity, which were imports. This exceptional intermingling of faith and culture came to be known as the 'Ganga–Jamuni tehzeeb'—a culture where different strands of humanity, just like the rivers Ganga and Jamuna (Yamuna), merge and create a flow of cultural immersion.

'Ganga Jamuni' is an Awadhi phrase, but the 'tehzeeb' could be seen manifested across the Gangetic plains in north India. It can be seen in the arts and crafts where Muslim weavers of Varanasi weave beautiful lotus motifs in sarees – a symbol of Hindu Goddess Laxmi. It can be heard in the soulful shehnai performances of Ustad Bismillah Khan, who often said that his music was the blessing of Baba Vishwanath—another name for Shiva. *Taazis* (a miniature of the Imam Husain's mausoleum) are handcrafted for the Muharram observance of the Shia Muslims by many Hindu artisans in Uttar Pradesh. The Ganga–Jamuni tehzeeb can be most clearly seen in the cuisine of Uttar Pradesh. The tandoori kebabs, desserts, biryanis and chaats are amalgamations of Persian, Indian, Afghan and central Asian food elements, and make for a rich repertoire of cuisine, relished with much enthusiasm by people from all walks of life. The most striking example of the Ganga–Jamuni tehzeeb and its impact on Indian culture and heritage can be seen in Lucknow, a city known as the home of the Nawabs.

In Lucknow, one comes across many mosques, monuments and imambaras. Simplistically put, imambaras are the prayer halls of

Shia Muslims. They normally have big halls for congregation and sometimes have the tombs of their priests, kings or spiritual masters in the same complex. The most fascinating of all the imambaras of Lucknow is the Bara Imambara or Asfi Imambara. It was built in 1784 with the primary objective of providing employment to people during the decade-long famine that had affected the region. Its architecture is a marvellous confluence of Mughal and Rajput styles, and has Gothic influences too.

The Ganga–Jamuni tehzeeb was not limited to the plains of Uttar Pradesh either, but travelled to the mountains of Kashmir, where it came to be known as 'Kashmiriyat'. In the deserts of Rajasthan, it took the form of royal patronage for Muslim singers like the Manganiyaars, who sang songs about the Hindu god Krishna, and in the Rajasthani miniature paintings, which carried Persian, Rajput, Jain and Mughal influences. It is visible even today in the weaving traditions of Bengal and Bihar and is thriving in the bazaars of Hyderabad.

But it was poet Kabir—Sant Kabir, as he is popularly known—who gave the Ganga–Jamuni tehzeeb its spiritual anchoring through his words and dohas. He was against organized religion and spent his life writing dohas that took the common man beyond the limitations of religious divisions. He famously wrote:

Hindu, Muslim, Sikh, Isai, Aaps me sab bhai bhai.
Arya, Jaini aur Bishnoi, Ek Prabhu ke bache soi.

(Hindus, Muslims, Sikhs, Christians are brothers.
Arya, Jain, Bishnoi are all children of one God).

This immense power of inclusion, which resulted in centuries of syncretic manifestations such as the Ganga–Jamuni tehzeeb or Kashmiriyat or Hyderabadi tehzeeb, does not mean that there have not been communal fissures in our society. It does not mean that forced conversions to other faiths have not happened. Nor does it mean that Hindus and Muslims have found it easy to co-exist.

History has the prerogative to highlight the most significant parts of a nation's narrative. Based on who wrote it in the first place, history can glorify or vilify kings, leaders and saints. But in reality, the larger population lives in a continuum between major historical dates, and often in the shadows of the so-called heroes and villains of those times. When I speak to right-wing Hindu organizations, they often cite the violent medieval Islamic invasions of India, the rape of Hindu women and the forced religious conversions in India as examples of the atrocities committed against native Hindus by Muslim invaders. Many even view the Mughal emperor Akbar—who spoke for religious inclusion—as a hypocrite.

But when I look at the writings of Gandhiji, who lived by his belief in India's power of inclusion and religious harmony, I see another perspective. In his book *Hind Swaraj*, Gandhiji wrote, 'The Hindus flourished under Moslem sovereigns and Moslems under the Hindu. Each party recognised that mutual fighting was suicidal, and that neither party would abandon its religion by force of arms. Both parties, therefore, decided to live in peace.'[2]

Bapu was not wrong. Examples of Hindu nobles and artists in the Muslim courts are plentiful, Kalyan Malla being one of them, and the famous Birbal of Akbar's court another. Hindu kings and queens had armies of both Hindus and Muslims. A fine example is the army of Rani Abbakka Chowta, the Tulava queen in north Karnataka who defeated the Portuguese in mid-sixteenth century. She was herself a Jain, but her armies and administration had Jains, Hindus and Muslims. She even collaborated with other Muslim rulers of the Deccan to defeat the Portuguese. Dara Shukoh may be more well known for his passion for religious confluence, but Ibrahim-II of the Adilshahi dynasty of Bijapur in the Deccan wrote a book in Dakhni called *Kitab-E-Navras,* containing fifty-nine poems and seventeen couplets, which was an attempt to introduce the nine rasas in Vedic literature and the Indian arts to Persian audiences. The first poem in this book was an invocation to the Hindu Goddess Saraswati:

> *Bhaka nyari nyari bhava ek, kaha turuk kaha barahaman;*
> *nouras soor juga joti ani saroguni;*
> *yusat sarasuti mata, ibrahim parasada bhayi dooni*

(Whether a Turk (Muslim) or a Brahmin speaking a different language—the emotion is the same. Oh mother Saraswati! Since you have blessed Ibrahim, his work Navras will last for long).[3]

Gandhiji went on fasts several times for the cause of fostering religious harmony and was appalled by the idea of India's Partition based on religion. He strongly believed that it was the British who had deepened communal tensions and stoked hatred by fanning sectarianism and reopening the wounds healed by time. We may or may not agree with Gandhi, but if invasions are our only grouse against our Muslim fellow citizens, then we may do well to remember that they have the same blood in their veins as we do, and that we are all children of Mother India, irrespective of our religious affiliation.

We should acknowledge that most wars waged in the name of religion were essentially the result of the expansionist ideas of a few, whose greed knew no bounds and whose hunger for power brought misery to millions. To this, history is our only witness. Therefore, to those who say that Ganga–Jamuni tehzeeb is a hoax, I say, let us look at the common people of India and see how they have come together to live with fraternal bonds, and do not dismiss our power of inclusion, which has been earned with pain, sacrifice, wisdom, hard work and experience, as a figment of imagination of a few. This power of inclusion is not the same as our power of assimilation. The latter is our ability to take something foreign and make it ours in a uniquely Indian way. Whereas the power of inclusion is our ability to be open and tolerant of ideas different from ours, and to co-exist with those who hold them. However, without inclusion, there is no assimilation.

Diversity and Inclusion

There is no doubt that India is one of the most—if not *the* most—diverse nations in the world. Diversity is inherent in the DNA of the country. In terms of religious diversity alone, as per the 2011 national census, 79.8 per cent of the Indian population were Hindu, 14.2 per cent Muslim, 2.3 per cent Christian, 1.7 per cent Sikh, 0.7 per cent Buddhist and 0.4 per cent Jain.[4] Four-thousand six-hundred communities of various ethnic blends, speaking twenty-two scheduled languages, ninety-nine non-scheduled languages and 19,500 mother tongues call India their home.[5] There are parts of north-east India where as many as 100 different dialects are spoken. Moreover, many of our scheduled languages have their own scripts, alphabet, grammar and literature. Many of our tribal languages and dialects vary greatly and use the English alphabet, as in the case of Khasi, the language spoken by the Khasi tribe of Meghalaya.

India's diversity in language, religion and race is matched by its eclectic repertoire of cuisine, couture and culture. Our music, literature, dance and crafts too are of a great diversity. Our diversity makes us truly incredible!

A Pew research survey conducted among the adult population in India between 2019 and early 2020 gave interesting insights into what Indians themselves think about this diversity.[6] The survey results show that 53 per cent of Indians believe diversity is beneficial for India, whereas 24 per cent believe it is harmful for the country.

Interestingly enough, Indians who believe that religion is very important to them are more likely to say that religious diversity is beneficial for the country (55 per cent) than those who give less importance to religion (39 per cent). It is also intriguing that the more developed south of the country has a lower percentage of people (42 per cent) who believe that religious diversity is good for the country than the north (68 per cent) and central India (53 per cent). While a majority of Hindus in India (77 per cent) believe in the idea of karma, what is intriguing is that an identical percentage of Muslims do as well. 32 per cent of Christians in India believe in the purifying power of the river Ganga, an important belief in Hinduism. In the north of the country, 12 per cent of Hindus and 10 per cent of Sikhs, along with 37 per cent of Muslims, identity with Sufism. If there was any question as to whether Ganga–Jamuni tehzeeb is a myth and is now lost in the Gangetic plains of India, it should be settled with these numbers.

What is heartening to note from the Pew survey is that 58 per cent of Indians don't believe that their own religion is the one true religion, and almost 51 per cent are of the opinion that many religions are true. This points to the open-minded attitude many Indians have towards religions other than their own. In fact, 91 per cent of Indians feel that they are free to practise their religion; 84 per cent believe that respecting other religions is an important aspect of being an Indian; and 80 per cent say that respecting other religions is a very important part of their own religious identity.

These are all encouraging signs. But it is a concern that many Indians, as per the survey, don't see they have much in common with Indians of other faiths and would have reservations about inter-faith marriage or co-habitation in their neighbourhoods. Dara Shukoh would have been disappointed, as he would have hoped for more fusion of people from different religious communities. What the Pew survey points to is that we are happy with and proud of our diversity, but we are hesitant about inclusion, perhaps more hesitant than our ancestors such as Kalyan Malla, Sant Kabir, Rani Abbakka or Mahatma Gandhi.

Diversity and inclusion are not the same. Diversity is the 'ingredient' and inclusion is the process of using this ingredient to co-create a free and fair societal construct. Indians have been fortunate to inherit diversity, but it is how we use our power of inclusion that will determine whether we benefit from our diversity or not. Our openness to different religions, race, languages, etc., can play an important role in fostering a truly inclusive society. In that sense, we are set up to succeed. But we will also have to deploy specific tools to counter the forces of exclusion. In recent years, cases of religious intolerance have increased in India. Religious hegemony is on the rise. There is significant radicalization in certain parts of the country across different faiths and sects. Therefore, while diversity may be thriving, inclusion is certainly under threat.

To counter this threat, we will need to rely on the Ganga–Jamuni tehzeeb and the Sanatani idea of:

Ayam Nijah Paro Veti Ganana Laghucetasam
Udaracaritanam Tu Vasudhaiva Kutumbakam

(The distinction 'This person is mine, and this one is not' is made only by the narrow-minded [i.e., the ignorant who are in duality]. For those of noble conduct [i.e., who know the Supreme Truth] the whole world is one family [one unit].)[7]

But given how sectarian forces are always attempting to polarize the common people for petty gains, these idealistic thoughts may not be enough. We may need to use modern-day ideas and tools to nurture inclusion at a societal scale.

Designing Inclusion

In 2019, I went for a two-week Executive Education Program at Harvard Kennedy School, the public policy school at Harvard University. The first class was taught by Iris Bohnet, famous for bringing the science of design thinking to issues of gender parity and inclusion. She spoke about the science of design and how it can create the necessary conditions for inclusion to be realized. Of course, her focus was gender inclusion, but my mind meandered towards the opportunity and challenge of religious inclusion in India. The entire concept of using design thinking for inclusion piqued my interest.

Design thinking is simplistically defined as an innovative problem-solving process anchored in a set of skills. I first came across it in 2012, when the Centre of Knowledge Societies invited me to one of their events in Delhi, called 'Design Public'. The objective of the event was to bring together entrepreneurs, innovators, academics and public administrators under one roof to discuss ideas for civic innovation in India. Clearly, the problem statement there was improvement in civic services, civic administration and civic engagement. The method applied was a framework that entailed listening to the various stakeholders and crowd-sourcing innovative ideas. I recommended to the organizers that they prototype, test and implement these ideas if they truly wanted to succeed at design-thinking civic innovation in the country. Nevertheless, it gave me a small peek into what is possible if we use design thinking to solve complex problems.

At Harvard, I paid close attention to what Iris was teaching. She spoke about a set of tools that one could deploy for designing inclusion. What stood out for me most was that many had successfully used this process, both in the public and private spheres. The increase in gender parity in public-listed company boards in the United Kingdom or the change in learning experience brought about in Peruvian school systems ... the examples were many. And at the heart of these successful examples lay one common factor—designing change.

So, we may ask: by designing inclusion, what change are we trying to bring in our society? Is it even needed? Research across sectors, different types of organizations and even nations has proved that inclusiveness of any kind allows for more creativity, innovation and productivity at the organizational level and fosters peace at the societal level. When we design a system to address religious inclusion, it paves the way for a framework that can also look at inclusion in caste, gender and economic backgrounds. Therefore, this is a change that bodes well. We do have some inherent strengths, in terms of a diverse population that is familiar with the idea of inclusion and doesn't fight it as hard as some other cultures do.

Many of us believe that we are open-minded and tolerant of differences, but we truly don't understand our anchored biases and are not fully aware of the limitations of our ability to discuss difficult issues with those we disagree with. That is why it is important that emotive issues such as religious tolerance, syncretic culture, racial discrimination, caste, divide and societal inclusion are discussed within a design framework. We may have many forums in the country that discuss some of these issues, but we are yet to design and build a system that uses our diversity and our power of inclusion to address communal tensions, caste divisions and racial discrimination. Also, at the heart of addressing issues around change is figuring out which biases are positively reinforcing our goal of inclusion and which ones are not.

At uber-chic coffee shops, seminars or book stores, there is always a lot of conversation on current affairs, politics and issues that affect the nation. Sometimes, either sipping my coffee or walking past people at these places, I catch phrases such as, 'Oh, we have become a religiously intolerant society. Did you see the clip of how that Muslim man was beaten?' What have we become?' Or 'What religious harmony? We are always fighting in this country about race and religion.' Or 'Us Hindus na, we will tolerate anything.' The comments I hear come from all types of people, but most of them are from people with at least a middle-class income and some level of education. When I hear these comments, I wonder if these people ever think about finding a solution to the problem. Do they ever wonder what kind of religious or other discrimination their own actions precipitate? The most important thing to understand here is that no one is free of biases. We have all our own special set of them based on our upbringing, social conditioning and life experiences.

My friends from north-east India always complain that even in the best of five-star hotels or in the business-class on flights, people will ask them if they are from China, Vietnam or the Philippines. Some people from the North-east have even been beaten up in our metro cities and have had derogatory words like 'chinky' hurled at them. Upon my return from the US in the early 2000s, I found it strange that even in corporate India people would use terms such as 'Madrasi' and 'Gujju', or say things like 'He is a typical Sardar'. It would leave me speechless, as these were the same people who would then talk about leadership, equality, diversity, community, and so on. Therefore, bias-check is a must for everyone.

The Indian Army is a fine example of religious inclusion, with its *Sarva Dharma* sthals, where religious shrines of different faiths occupy the same premises. This is partly possible because the Army has a code committing its members to being a unified force. In schools, children are taught that religious harmony is important and are even made to sing songs glorifying this concept. Community leaders frequently give out messages of religious tolerance. But has that helped inclusion? Perhaps, yes. Seeing or hearing is believing. Maybe we need more visible models and simple efforts at the community level to make people believe in inclusion. In design language, they are all good prototypes—to be scaled up after proving successful.

Inclusion is not just about having 'enough' diversity in an organization or institution. It is a way of life, where you want to take something that belongs to a person, family, clan or class and make it accessible for everyone. The truth of the matter is that inclusion is not possible without giving due regard to individualism. It is only when the power of the individual is given full opportunity to be actualized that we can make the power of inclusion deliver social justice. But more on that later ...

From street signboards in multiple languages to regional language media and content, Indian society has diverse strands working as one. But of late, even simple advertisements hinting at the virtues of religious synchronization are targeted unfairly. If this trend is allowed to progress, it will lead the nation into an abyss of hate. But who will arrest it? An important design principle is building the capacity for backlash. Backlash for the changes we are trying to bring about using a design framework can come from key stakeholders. The same is true when we want to design inclusion. Radicalized groups in different communities can reject the very idea of inclusion and can create a polarized environment. For example, in our politics, minority appeasement cannot be replaced by majoritarian bravado. Both are unnecessary, when most common folk in the country, as the Pew research shows, are amiable towards people from different faiths. Indians respond to diversity quite positively. But translating this preference for diversity into an everyday experience of inclusion for all the people everywhere is not as easy.

This is where design thinking is helpful. It gives us a set of tools and small steps to take before we address the problem. The most important step in this process is to empathetically listen to people with divergent views. Without empathy, inclusion is not possible. A large part of my time at the Design Public seminar in

2012 was spent in listening to people and what they thought about civic challenges and the solutions thereof. Listening with empathy takes place in an environment of trust. How can we build spaces for such conversations at the community level? Can schools and colleges help? Will corporations support? In a country that is deeply religious, leaving conversations around religion to be anchored by religious institutions alone will be like perpetuating echo-chambers. What we need is a community-level mechanism for dialogue, not debate. What we need is an attitude of problem-solving and not verbal fighting matches. Do we have institutions that can anchor such conversations? Maybe a few, but we need many more. Once we have more such spaces, then we can hope for conversations to lead to collaborations. This aspect of design thinking is critical to its success as a method—a conversation about divergent views on the problem statement and diverse ideas about the solution.

Sometimes, conflict is inevitable as religion, caste, etc., are emotive issues and are about one's identity. Do we have enough people trained to mitigate such conflicts? Mediation is a technique widely used around the world for resolving legal or corporate conflict. I got to learn about it from my close friend Radhika Shapoorjee, a successful communications professional who left her two-decade career and trained in mediation. She discussed some of the hypothesis on identity association that she was working on, and how identity association could result in conflict and how that could be resolved. Her venture, Mediation Mantras, is focused on addressing this. But how many people and organizations do we have that are trained in the skill of mediation? For a country so diverse in identities of all kinds, should we not invest in this skill set? When people are made aware of their own biases and are provided a space and a framework designed to maintain mutual trust, respect and empathy and equipped with mediating differences, they will be more willing to be open and honest about their ideas around inclusion. As chefs say—this is a slow brew. Perhaps we may not see results of any effort made in this direction in our lifetime, but should we not plant the seeds that will bear fruit for our future generations?

In 2015, when Alok and I decided to get married, we discussed how best to include our many friends, who were from different faiths, in our wedding ceremony. We were aware that as Hindus, our wedding ceremony would be conducted with Vedic rituals, but we wanted our Muslim, Zoroastrian, Jewish, Buddhist, Sikh, Jain, Christian, Naga and Khasi friends to feel equally involved. So we requested them to come prepared with a blessing for us from their respective religious or ancestral texts.

After the Vedic Hindu rites, our friend Shalaka Joshi took the microphone and introduced our friends one by one. James Abraham read a passage on love from the Holy Bible; Anjali Anit chanted a Buddhist prayer; Akshat Rathee explained the role of marriage in spiritual evolution in the Sikh faith and played a song he got recorded from the holiest of Sikh temples—the Golden Temple in Amritsar; Gary Sussman travelled all the way from Israel and read from the Song of Songs and said a prayer in Hebrew; Mehernosh Shapoorjee, dressed in traditional Parsi attire, read from the Holy Avesta; our neighbours in Mumbai sang the Jain Manglashtak; my soul sister from Kashmir, Shazia Bakshi, read out blessings from the Holy Quran; our Khasi friends from Meghalaya, Hasina Kharbhih and Aiban Swer, performed the traditional rice and betel-nut ceremony and read out blessings in Khasi; and our friends from Nagaland, Hekani Jakhalu, Theja Meru, Mmhonlumo Kikon and Abu Metha, draped the traditional Naga shawl around our shoulders, placed Naga crowns on our heads and gave us their blessings. Whenever we recall our wedding day, the richness of these traditions and faiths remind us how blessed we are to be born as Indians. On that day, we lived out our power of inclusion fully, and it made us feel happy and hopeful.

Therefore, even without massive systemic or design changes, and given that we have such immense diversity all around us, we can each create occasions to celebrate our power of inclusion. Not doing so is akin to not realizing our full potential as human beings, for not many on this planet can hope to find such a bounty of diversity right at their doorstep. And even fewer people will have the power of inclusion at their disposal.

Vaibhav Kaul

I met Vaibhav Kaul when he came to visit us at Munsyari. His parents are well known to my husband Alok. Vaibhav is a mountain geographer and is a scholar in climate change, geo-hazards and disaster risk. He has a PhD in geography from University of Sheffield and an MSc in environmental change and management from University of Oxford. He wanted to study the glaciers in the higher reaches of the mountains that surround Munsyari, so he came to visit.

We started talking about his passions and interests, and I quickly discovered that apart from mountain climbing and geographical exploration, Vaibhav also dabbled in photography, loved watercolour painting and aesthetic cartography. He was also passionate about medieval and modern South Asian music—including classical Hindustani and Carnatic, semi-classical, courtly, mystic, folk, et al. I was thoroughly impressed with this thirty-something young man who had such rich interests, which he pursued with enthusiasm.[8]

Sitting by the fire in our living room in the evening, Vaibhav began a beautiful rendition of a Sanskrit hymn. The purity of his voice and the clarity of his diction compelled me to ask him if he had studied classical Sanskrit. He replied that he had a deep interest in and had studied the Upanishads, Kashmiri Tantric Shaivism and Shaktism, and was fascinated by Indic philosophy. His passion for contemplative mysticism had led him to explore Tibetan Vajrayana Buddhist ideas and Indo-Persian Sufi Ma'rifa metaphysical traditions too. I tried to grasp what he had just said. That meant that he would know Sanskrit, Urdu and Persian. He nodded.

I was astonished that a young millennial should be so deeply entrenched in literary and artistic pursuits while also being a celebrated student of science. What made him interested in these subjects? Vaibhav told me that it started in his childhood. Growing up with three great-grandmothers, two sets of grandparents and other family elders in Ghaziabad, on the outskirts of Delhi, he had been nudged towards these passions. Vaibhav's family are Kashmiri Pandits who left the valley of Kashmir two centuries or more ago and settled in the Indo-Gangetic plains. Perhaps it was this ancestral lineage that made it easy for Vaibhav to learn Urdu and Persian. He told me that during his childhood he was exposed to pluralistic ideas of faith, language, the arts and cuisine. Even though his own family had left Kashmir Valley, perhaps to escape religious persecution, he remembers his childhood as being bereft of hate. In fact, India's composite and cosmopolitan cultural aspects were an integral part of his life. As a child, he did not think there was a world without inclusion.

Vaibhav's elders used to read to him the works of several Sufi and Bhakti poets from across the country, including those of the Kashmiri mystic poet Lal Ded, and had told him of the mysticism of the Sufi saint Nund Rishi. He smiled and said, 'The fact that he was called a rishi tells you of the syncretic nature of religious thought in Kashmir several centuries ago.' It reminded me of the 'mystical magic' I always felt when I visited the Pari Mahal in Srinagar and why Dara Shukoh would have thought Kashmir an ideal place for pondering on a possible amalgamation of Sufi and Vedantic thought. Dara would have been proud to meet this young Kashmiri man who can recite Sanskrit hymns and Persian couplets in the same breath.

I couldn't help but ask Vaibhav if he felt he was more of an
exception rather than the norm among his classmates at school. He
mused for a moment and then replied with a tinge of sadness, 'Back
then, when I was studying in boarding school, I had to hide under
the blanket in my hostel bed and read my Persian books. I felt that
if my fellow students came to know of my fascination for Persian,
Sanskrit and Urdu works, they might shun me. I was a normal young
kid and wanted to fit in and not be singled out. It was much later
when I came to terms with my own syncretic identity that I became
comfortable with sharing my interests.' Growing up in Ghaziabad,
his family's considerable status and interests meant he met many
artists, spiritual masters, authors and poets. He became interested
in Tantric texts and Sufi mysticism by the age of twelve or thirteen.

Vaibhav gleefully shared with me that in 2009 he had won the
first prize for Ghazal Sarāī (musical rendition of Urdu ghazals)
at the annual All-India Bazm-e-Adab literary festival hosted by
the University of Delhi. He gave a mystical vocal recital in the
Hindustani classical style, singing solo in Vedic Sanskrit, Avestan
and Persian, at the Music for Interfaith Harmony festival at
St Ethelwold's House in Oxfordshire in the UK in 2012. He fondly
remembered his Qawwali-style singing and dramatized recitation
of a self-written mystical Urdu ballad, titled *Mūsā aur Galahbān,* as
part of Religion of Love at the seventh Jahan-e-Khusrau World Sufi
Music Festival in Delhi. Vaibhav continues to pursue his interests—
Vedic texts, classical Sanskrit, medieval and modern Indo-Persianate
and European classical/art music and poetry. He continues to
explore registers of the Hindustani (Hindi–Urdu) language and
cultural syncretism in south Asia as a matter of study. In fact, says
his knowledge of the Jain Kalpasutra and other texts gives him the
spiritual anchoring to understand the idea of non-violence and the
importance of minimizing his environmental footprint.

At night, before going to sleep, I thought about how fortunate Vaibhav was to be able to fully explore his diverse ethnicity and lineage. How lucky he was to have an environment at home that encouraged his interest in languages and traditions. How nice it would it be if children from all walks of life across India had the opportunity to explore, understand and celebrate the multiplicity of their cultures and societies? Would it not make us a better society? I thought of our wedding day. Alok and I are richer in the wisdom of what marriage entails because we received guidance from so many different faiths and traditions. Why shouldn't everything in our lives have the benefit of this composite culture? Would it not make us better human beings?

The next morning, during breakfast, I asked Vaibhav if he thought he was a Hindu. He thought for a moment and then said, with absolute clarity, 'I am a Hindu. My Upanishads teach me the concept of "*Aham Brahmasmi* (I am Brahman)", a philosophical concept that says there is no difference between the atman (individual self or soul) and brahman (the Absolute). But that does not mean that I cannot fathom the wisdom of Sikh gurus who say "*Ek Onkar*"—there is only one God. That doesn't mean that I am incapable of understanding the ideas of Wahad-al-wujud or Wahad-ash-shuhud—the Sufi Islamic idea of the love-drenched transcendental experience of dissolution of the self into a singular all-embracing reality.' I thought for a moment about what he had said. It was indeed very profound. I then asked him, 'How do you deal with the contradictions among these different faiths and ideologies?' He was quick to respond, 'I don't try to reconcile them, I am absolutely comfortable with their contradictions and embrace them fully. For instance, in my Buddhist practices I try to reach the shunyata—nothingness—whereas in my Vedantic practice I aim to realize the cosmos within. If you ask me, love is the common thread in all these different ideas and is the cornerstone of compassion. It is this compassion that transcends divisions and allows me to negate exclusion.'

I looked at him in awe. He was so sure of his roots and so empowered with his power of inclusion that it would be almost impossible to seed the idea of 'otherness' or 'hate', based on religion, race or ethnicity in him. I prayed in my heart that all children of India might attain this clarity of self about who they are and where they come from. May they all, while being devout followers of their own faiths, fearlessly explore the various faiths they can so intimately and proximately experience just because they have the fortune to be born as Indians. Would that not make us a nation with a more enhanced collective understanding of human nature and human society? If we give space for our power of inclusion to live and prosper, then we have the possibility of becoming the light unto the world or, as Mark Twain, once remarked, the cradle of the human race for centuries to come. The choice is ours.

12

Power of Individual

Khau Galli

In the lanes between New Marine Lines railway station and the Cross Maidan ground in Mumbai, there is a street full of food vendors and hawkers. SNDT Khau Galli, as it is more popularly known locally, is one of the many street-food lanes found across Mumbai. Khau Galli literally means 'food alley'. The SNDT Khau Galli is packed with customers for most of the day. An invigorating range of Indian, Chinese and Western food is cooked and served in this narrow lane. The stalls have unique names, from 'Lenin Pav Bhaji' to 'Raju Chinese', and serve delicious mouth-watering food at breakneck speed.

Street food is an important feature of city life across India. Mumbai has more than a dozen Khau Gallis in different neighbourhoods, each serving common dishes but each also known for its own specialities. The Mohammad Ali Road Khau Galli is a gastronomic paradise for non-vegetarians, and the Ghatkopar Khau Galli is well-known for its vegetarian fare. The Mahim Khau Galli is known for its falooda, kheechda and haleem. What has always amazed me about these Khau Galli vendors is their ability to customize every plate of food they serve. You can hear customers say, 'Add more teekha (spice)', or 'No butter for me', or 'Can I have extra onions?' The degree of customization offered is mind-boggling, and I cannot imagine even the most organized of the large franchise corporations such as McDonald's or Burger King being able to do one tenth of this in their outlets. Khau Galli dishes are very affordable as well, which is why, on any given day, you can find people of all strata patronize these stalls and shops.

Ask a bhelpuri (a street snack made of puffed rice) vendor in one of the Khau Gallis about the extent to which he can customize your dish, and he will fluidly give you options such as: teekha (spicy), meetha (sweet), tez (hot), sukha (dry), gila (wet), with or without lasoon chutney (garlic paste), extra sev (a type of savoury), with or without peanuts, with or without pomegranate ... the list is very long indeed. This customization offered by a small street food vendor is the result of his customer's eclectic tastes and their expectation that food be precisely suited to their individual palates.

In Gujarati households where a large family of several generations lives together, the regular daily dal is served up in several different versions—sweet, spicy, sweet-sour, etc. This is not an exception, but rather the norm. In south Indian homes, on the other hand, it is commonplace to find filter coffee made in various different ways—strong, light, or with or without sugar—for the various members of the family. Indians love to have their goods and services customized to their liking. This need for customization stems from our need for individualization of just about everything in our lives. Perhaps that is why we have individualized even the humble bhelpuri!

Our need for individualization is not in the matter of our food alone, but in our architecture too. Every house in a village looks different. When I was studying in the United States, I would be amused to see the rows of houses in the city suburbs, all looking similar, irrespective of whether it was in Chicago or Phoenix, with little adaptations here and there. The malls would all look the same, and so would the markets. When I asked an architecture student why this was so, she explained that Americans believe that this standardization allows them to achieve quality and price performance at scale. Her answer made me realize that, in India at least, individualization of goods or services happened in far greater measure than in many places across the world. Its most unique ambassador, in fact, is the omnipresent neem tree.

The Neem

Driving across India, you will see one tree nearly everywhere: the neem. The tree might be universal, but its uses are unique to individuals. Interestingly, its botanical name is *Azadirachta indica*— literally meaning 'free tree of India'. Hidden in the story of the neem, its near-universal presence from the southern tip of the Indian peninsula to the foothills of the Himalaya and its very use by the people is also the story of India's individualism. Ask around in your friend and family networks what people use neem for, and you will be amazed at its many uses. People have customized the neem for uses as diverse as cooking, bathing, pest control or medicine.

Neem is used for natural pest management in farms. Its natural properties allow it to be an alternative to chemical pesticides, which is why in the olden days, grandmothers would keep dried neem leaves in rice bins or in clothes cupboards. In organic farming, an extract of neem is sprayed on crops as neem acts as anti-feedant, pest repellent and egg-laying deterrent.

In cooking, the uses of neem vary from family to family. Some will add it to lentil preparations like dal/rasam, and others will add it to vegetables. In Bengal, it is cooked with eggplant and eaten with rice at the end of a meal to help digestion. In south India, a chutney made of neem leaves is served with dosa or idli. Neem tea is made in many parts of India and is considered to have immunity-enhancing properties. It has been established that neem leaves help improve metabolism and can naturally detoxify the body. They have high anti-inflammatory, antifungal and antibacterial properties and are rich in minerals and vitamins. Additionally, they also contain fatty acids and antioxidants. Neem is indeed a superfood and is used uniquely by every family, community and region in India.

The bark extract of neem is used in toothpastes, and there are neem-based shampoos and soaps too. There are also beauty treatments that use neem for detoxification. In fact, the neem's unique uses in traditional Indian medicine and in Ayurveda are huge. Medicine is made from its bark, leaves or seeds, and sometimes even from its flowers and fruits. Its leaves are used in the treatment of leprosy, eye infections, intestinal worms, digestive issues, ulcers, heart disease, fever, diabetes and liver problems. Its bark is used in the treatment of malaria, its flower used in medicinal preparations for reducing bile and its fruit in the treatment of urinary tract issues. Neem twigs are used to treat asthma and neem seeds are used for birth control. There are neem applications for skin diseases.

It amazes and delights me that one tree can be used in so many ways. In a way, the neem and its myriad uses across India reinforce the fact that our ability to individualize or personalize goods and services has been around for ages. It thrives even today.

Merawala Cream

The desire for individual customization or personalization of common resources or goods has been observed in the Indian consumer behaviour as well. In January 2011, Amit Syngle, then vice-president of sales and marketing at Asian Paints, said in an interview to *The Economic Times*, 'It all started with the "Mera wala" campaign. The tagline became so popular that people would go into stores and ask for "mera wala blue" or "mera wala green." It became a generic term and showed the involvement of people with the campaign.'[1] He was speaking about a campaign that the paint giant Asian Paints undertook in the 1990s. 'Mere wala' literally means mine. Until then, advertising and marketing campaigns for paints had been along generic lines, but the 'mera wala' campaign changed that. It tapped into the Indian need for individualization and created a market shift. Customers went to the stores and asked for their own favourite green, blue, cream or other colour of their choice. The company was trying to market the diverse colour palette its paints had, and customers loved it.

In fact, the early 2000s saw a wide range of Indian companies move towards personalization and individualization. The expansion of Asian Paints, for instance, into interior decoration products had a campaign that said, '*Har ghar kuch kehta hai*', meaning 'every house has something to say'. The trend towards individualization of personal care products was first ushered in by the FMCG company Cavin Kare for their shampoos. In 1983, the company came up with a Re-1 sachet of its Chik shampoo.[2] This initiative was followed by companies like Unilever launching face wash, skin care and shampoo products in sachets in India. Other brands followed suit, and today even a premier brand like L'Oréal has launched a hair colour product in sachets. In fact, sachets constitute almost 70 per cent of shampoo sales in India now. This raises the question of why sachets work in India.

Firstly, the sachet is an individualized product, as far as its size goes, and is designed for single-person use. Most of those who buy it would use it only once, some twice. This allows a family to buy affordable products that each of its members likes. One can see mother and daughter sometimes buy different brands of shampoos in sachets in many households. It gives greater flexibility in indulging individual preferences in the family at a value-for-money price point. The success of such products sold in sachets or small, individualized packing has been so massive in India that many companies have now taken the campaign to other markets across the world. Meanwhile, ideation in terms of selling other products in individualized, small packs continues in India, with Unilever also experimenting with water purification powder sachets.[3]

In India's humble street food, in its uses of the neem tree, and in its one-rupee shampoo sachets and advertising campaigns like Asian Paints' 'mera wala' campaign—one can see that the Indian ability to take something common and make it personal to create an individualized experience of it is omnipresent. A survey conducted in 2017 by Adobe Digital Insight for India Advertising Report found that 75 per cent of Indian consumers prefer to receive personalized advertisements. The report also said a similar survey conducted in South Korea and Australia had far fewer people wanting personalized ads. Attesting to the survey results, Mickey Mericle, vice president of marketing and customer insights at Adobe noted: 'Personalised experiences are key to winning customer confidence, and brands in India are strongly positioned to ride on this trend by leveraging the digital wave sweeping across the country.'[4] Arvind R.P., director of marketing and communications for India at the retail food giant McDonald's, makes this observation about the strong Indian predilection for individualization: 'Today's consumer wants personalization. They want brands to engage with them. And brands that win in the consumer experience space will win this battle.'[5]

Perhaps it is our desire for individualization that makes us embrace the idea of 'one man, one vote' with enthusiasm. The reason the Indian election process is so incredibly robust, whether it is the village, city, state or national elections, is because it taps into and empowers that individualistic nature of every Indian by giving it due regard and expression. Even government policies and programmes that take into account the need of the Indian people to exercise their own 'power of individual', as I call it, do better than those that focus on group benefits. Take, for example, AADHAR, the unique ID project that aimed to give proof of identity to every Indian. Or the Jan Dhan Yojana, which brought access to the banking system for individuals across the country. They have done well because, in essence, they have benefited and empowered the individual.

This makes me wonder why this individualistic approach should be limited to a few government programmes alone. If we can have the individual at the centre of hundreds of policies at the Union and state levels, we will create a framework for success in public sector-led development. But are we prepared to shun group identities and give more regard to the individual instead? Indians deeply associate with their social identities—of family, clan, caste, tribe, village, religion, etc. These identities are all extremely important and make up a citizen's overall identity. Indians are socially mindful and are afraid to lose their group identities. Social acceptance is rated very high in the evaluation of an individual's success. Therefore, is there merit in even exploring the idea of individual-centric development?

Individual Rights and Group Rights

Let us take the very organization of some of our government policies and programmes, or of our ministries. They continue to focus on groups and not the individual. The tribal affairs ministry is mandated to look into the affairs of the tribes of India as recognized in the Fifth Schedule of our Constitution. In clubbing India's tribal citizens into one large group without room for individualization of the programmes meant for them, we fail to recognize the customs and needs of individual tribes, and their individual socio-economic development opportunities. For example, we have grouped the Ao tribe of Nagaland, known for their early embrace of Western education, with the Gonds of Chhattisgarh, who continue to struggle even today for primary education. Why? Because we presumed that they all need one type of education scholarship. Instead, we can focus on creating a wider framework where tribes, through their tribal/hill councils, have a choice in how they avail of the education funds marked for them and are able to customize them for local and individual application. It is possible to create a common framework for a large population, despite the differences among the groups that make that population. What we need to ensure is that individuality is respected. Only then will inclusion be assured.

Take, for example, gender parity issues or affirmative-action initiatives in Indian companies. Sometimes, even with the best of intentions, many of them fail. Those that fail do so because in wanting to include women or socially disadvantaged groups, they create specific programmes that only focus on those groups, creating exclusion instead of inclusion. In fact, I have personally witnessed the futility of initiatives targeting specific groups or communities in the private sector. In 2010, the prime minister of India constituted a group of public and private sector leaders to address the issues faced by the Kashmiri youth. One of the recommendations of the group was a programme called UDAAN. It was set up as a collaboration between the National Skills Development Corporation and the corporate sector. Under UDAAN, post-graduate or graduate students from Kashmir were to be given skills training and then placement in companies. The Kashmiri youth were enthused by it and many came forward to enrol in the programme. Several modules were launched and I got involved in the recruitment, design and deployment of the first batch under the aegis of the Confederation of Indian Industry. I could see, during the training phase of the programme, that the Kashmiri students were enthralled by the exposure and skills they were being given. But the challenge came after the programme, when we started placing the students in corporations across the country. Despite many students getting the opportunity to work in some of the best companies in India and the sincerity of the companies themselves in providing equal opportunity to the Kashmiri youth, a large number of students would call up and say they were not happy at their jobs. When I interacted with these students, they explained that it was not the nature of the job or the company that was their problem, it was their constant identification as 'special-opportunity candidates' that made them feel unworthy and, in fact, harmed their sense of self. They felt their colleagues did not see them as equals. Many of these students eventually returned to the Valley to work in companies operating there. I learnt an important lesson in why initiatives aimed at specific groups struggle to succeed, despite the best intentions of all concerned. It was amply clear that such initiatives tend to precipitate inequality and exclusion.

Even public sector programmes such as reservations, despite some clear benefits, have created doubts as to whether merit is of any importance. This doesn't help the cause at all. So, should India do away with reservations? How will we then assure our socially backward communities that their overall development will not suffer?

People resort to group rights when they are not assured of individual rights. But group identities that create exclusion can sow social discord and harm social equity and fraternity. The bigger question is: have the reservations or special treatment helped these communities advance as much as they should have? Have gender-based reservations helped? It is heartening to see that a gender lens is being used in India's fiscal budget allocation, but we cannot say for sure that this will reduce gender inequality. This makes us question group-based development seeded in group rights, as to whether it works at all.

At the heart of a liberal democratic system is the idea of liberty, labour, enterprise and well-being of the individual. But, over the years, in many pluralistic democracies across the world and in India as well, we have noticed the politicization of ethnic and religious group identities leading to extreme polarization in the political system. This leads to more importance being given to groups than to individuals in government development programmes. In India, caste has played a distinct role in determining the vote share of candidates in any election. In fact, those who don't understand the caste maths in the Indian electoral system may never fully comprehend the Indian voter mindset.

Historically, liberal democracies have operated on the hypothesis that protecting individual rights should lead to protection of everyone's rights, including those of the disadvantaged or the minorities. This hypothesis stems from the philosophy that human beings possess rational and moral agency. Therefore, the idea of human rights is anchored in the idea that human rights are protected when societies nurture individual rights. It is also observed, and India is no exception here, that when individual rights and liberties are respected and nurtured, societies tend to do well collectively, and human rights are further enhanced. But what if societies are constructed to ensure that only some individuals get to pursue their individual rights and others don't? Alluding to this, B.R. Ambedkar, the chairman of India's Constitution Drafting Committee said in the Constituent Assembly:

On the 26th of January 1950, we are going to enter into a life of contradictions. In politics we will have equality and in social and economic life we will have inequality. In politics we will be recognizing the principle of one man one vote and one vote one value. In our social and economic life, we shall, by reason of our social and economic structure, continue to deny the principle of one man one value. How long shall we continue to live this life of contradictions? How long shall we continue to deny equality in our social and economic life? If we continue to deny it for long, we will do so only by putting our political democracy in peril. We must remove this contradiction at the earliest possible moment or else those who suffer from inequality will blow up the structure of political democracy which this Assembly has so laboriously built up.[6]

Ambedkar was alluding to the fact that we have not yet created social equity amongst individuals and therefore cannot rely on individual rights to secure human rights. He was a proponent of equitable representation and voiced his support for reservation for Dalits and Scheduled Castes for a certain number of years, as he believed that this representation would set backward communities on a par with other communities. However, he was certainly not in favour of reservations for perpetuity. As a woman, I feel that he may not be totally wrong. Today, both India's grassroots panchayats and boards of public listed companies are legally mandated to include women—the proportion of representation they must be given varies. Could women have managed a seat at the table without these systemic changes? Yes, but it may have taken longer for sure. Mandated representation allows for a larger number of women to participate in local and corporate governance. But should a woman unqualified to be a panchayat official or board member be allowed to serve in those institutions? I think not. If reservations discount merit, then they may create more damage. Should students who appear for competitive exams be differentiated in terms of cut-off marks based on their caste? Does this not make the goal of equality null and void? Does it not negate individual rights? No wonder that when reservations were first introduced in the late 1980s by the then prime minister V.P. Singh, they resulted in violence and polarization on campuses across India. Even today, general category students continue to begrudge students who have obtained entry through reservations. In this case, did our policy for reservations create equality, inclusion, and therefore social unity, or was it counter-productive? Did group rights secure individual rights at all?

In 2011, I came across an organization called National Confederation of Dalit and Adivasi Organisations (NACDAOR)—a federation of Dalit, Scheduled Caste and Scheduled Tribe organizations from across the country. Their vision is to 'build a Prabuddha Samaj (Enlightened Society) based on the principles of dignity, justice, equality, freedom and fraternity', amongst other noble goals that focus on fighting discrimination of any and every kind. In my discussions with them, I understood that the social stigma faced by Dalits continues in some ways, even till date. Untouchability remains deeply entrenched in rural Indian society, irrespective of religion or ethnicity. This made me wonder whether our seventy-plus years of reservations had worked. I realized that the reason an organization such as NACDAOR is still functional and approached by those from disadvantaged groups is because the social inequality that the group-rights mechanisms such as reservations were meant to address has not been addressed fully. Come to think of it, representation for women in panchayats or corporate boards has also not directly resulted in more equal social status for women. But they have helped in inspiring younger women to pursue an education, as they know they will get opportunities for bettering their lives from doing so. I asked NACDAOR members if they thought reservations had created incentives among the youth in their communities to pursue education or livelihood skills. They answered in the affirmative, adding that earlier 'our young thought that they could only do certain jobs as they were born in a certain caste, but now they feel they can do any job they are qualified for'.

Their answer made me wonder whether group rights were a necessity for those from the margins of society to be able to avail of their individual rights. If there are no individual rights, then how does the *Power of Individual* be of any help? The relationship between individual rights and group rights is complex, and this debate has affected most societies around the world. At the heart of it, I feel that group rights and individual rights are about social equity and individual liberty, respectively. There is bound to be tension between equity and liberty, therefore we have to be nuanced in how we view them.

Blanket equity ensured by group rights, but one that threatens individual liberty, may not yield much, but absence of equality may not bode well for a liberal, pluralistic, democratic society, as Ambedkar pointed out. We have to understand where to apply group-centred development and where to focus on individual development. The 'power of individual' cannot be given its due at the expense of the common good. When we think of our need for individualization, our preference for personalization and our 'power of individual', we have to ensure that they are not ideas whose underlying objective is selfish aggrandization of wealth, power and fame. On the contrary, they need to be rooted in the possibility that individual human development is the cornerstone of societal advancement. Without the individual advancing, inclusion is not possible. And without inclusion there is no room for assimilation. If the individual is nurtured, then our civilizational powers of enterprise, nature, heritage, creativity, knowledge, food, beauty and wellness will flourish and help us in nation building or else they will lie dormant. For, every Indian is the torchbearer of these superpowers; and without individual Indians unleashing these powers in their own lives, our collective ability to call these superpowers to action will not be expressed fully.

Fortunately for us, Gandhiji, in his ideas of Sarvodaya, and Pandit Deen Dayal Upadhyaya in his thoughts on Antyodaya, have dived deep into the relationship between the individual and the group/society. There are many ideas that these two leaders articulated. I do not think I agree with everything they have said, but I feel that as far as the relationship between the individual and the commons (group) is concerned, both offer us some food for thought.

Antyodaya and Sarvodaya

The genesis of 'Antyodaya'—integral humanism—rests in the belief of its chief architect Pandit Deen Dayal Upadhyaya that India needed its own model of economic and social development where the human being was the core focus. In 1965, his philosophy was adopted by the Jan Sangh party, which eventually became the present-day Bhartiya Janta Party (BJP). Many may say that Deen Dayal Upadhyaya borrowed generously from the Gandhian thoughts of Sarvodaya and Swadeshi, but I see no harm in a latter-day public figure using Gandhi's ideas to develop his own. Going by his own writings and views, Gandhi would have been fine with it. He may have tested the new philosophy and would have challenged it if he felt it was based on wrong principles, but he would not have questioned the right of any human being to use what he had proposed in order to take it ahead further.

Antyodaya looks at both socialism/Marxism and capitalism from an objective point of view. It takes a middle path from these systems and even acknowledges and criticizes them when warranted. It rejects capitalist systems, in which individualism is supreme, but it also rejects communism, in which individualism is subjugated. Literally, 'Antyodaya' means 'rise of the last person'. Pandit Deen Dayal Upadhyaya was in disagreement with the blind import of Western industrialization and its tools and policies for India's development. He was not dismissive of Western science and scientific methods, though. Indeed, his ideas were inspired by the philosophy of Sarvodaya that Gandhi articulated for India.

In 1908, Gandhi wrote a paraphrased translation in Gujarati of *Unto, This Last*, an essay on political economy written by John

Ruskin. He called it 'Sarvodaya'—meaning 'welfare for all'. He was inspired by Ruskin's thought that the good of the individual is contained in good of all. But soon, Gandhi gave this idea his own embellishment, based on India's context and his own ideas of human development. His idea of Sarvodaya embraced dignity of labour, equitable distribution of wealth, communal self-sufficiency and individual freedom.

At the core of Sarvodaya was a network of self-sufficient village communities. Gandhi envisioned a community that went beyond relations of blood and beyond distinctions based on caste, religion, creed, race, language, etc. Sarvodaya was envisioned as a movement that would bring individual enterprise and initiative to work for the collective good. But at the same time, it would lead to a society where individual development has the fullest potential. It sought equality and justice in socio-economic aspects but encouraged individual growth. It professed a system incentivizing the individual to rise for the commons (group).

The concept of Sarvodaya lays great importance on moral and spiritual values; Antyodaya does the same, but differently. If Sarvodaya seeks to establish the role of the individual in the welfare of all and aims to forge the causality between individual and social development, then Antyodaya gives methods for synthesis of the individual and the collective. Both bridge the spiritual, social, economic and political worlds for the nation's future path in their own unique ways.

Perhaps what they are pointing to is that the 'power of individual' is important to exercise and actualize, but for this to be done only for one's own personal welfare may not serve the purpose of democracy. Both Sarvodaya and Antyodaya have faith in the individual's capacity to shape society and both provide tools and framework for the same. They may vary in their details and we may not agree with all their principles, but what is important to understand is that they don't see individual rights and group rights as opposing forces. They see them as interdependent forces. They stress that the binary systems of the West, which make one choose between individual-centric capitalism and group-centric socialism or Marxism, are rendered useless in the Indian context. Once the individual is considered an integral part of the whole, then development of the individual and the group are tied to one boat. But in our current politics and governance, this linkage between the individual and the group is often missing. There is undue focus on the group, and the individual is negated even. Then the question arises: where are those systems and frameworks that link individual and societal (group) development in India? Gandhi identified one such framework and called it 'Swaraj'.

Swaraj

I first heard the term 'Swaraj' when I started visiting Mani Bhawan in Mumbai for school competitions. My school would send out participants for middle-school and high-school competitions organized by Mani Bhawan on the subject of Gandhi, his writings and other literature on him. There would be elocution, debates and poetry reading competitions. I thoroughly enjoyed participating in them. Mani Bhawan was the home of a merchant family where Gandhiji stayed during his visits to Bombay. Apart from restoring the house and converting it into a museum, the Gandhian organizations that run it continue to host programmes and discussions on Gandhi, his life and his work.

While researching Gandhi's views on societal development, I learnt about his ideas on Swaraj. For him, Swaraj meant the sum total of the swaraj (self-rule) of individuals who constitute the commons. He articulated his vision further when he wrote:

Independence must begin at the bottom. Thus, every village will be a republic or panchayat having full powers. It follows, therefore, that every village has to be self-sustained and capable of managing its affairs even to the extent of defending itself against the whole world. It will be trained and prepared to perish in the attempt to defend itself against any onslaught from without. Thus, ultimately, it is the individual who is the unit. This does not exclude dependence on and willing help from neighbours or from the world. It will be free and voluntary play of mutual forces. Such a society is necessarily highly cultured in which every man and woman knows what he or she wants and what is more, knows that no one should want anything that others cannot have with equal labour. In this structure composed of innumerable villages, there will be ever-widening, never-ascending circles. Life will not be a pyramid with the apex sustained by the bottom. But it will be an oceanic circle whose centre will be the individual always ready to perish for the village, the latter ready to perish for the circle of villages, till at last the whole becomes one life composed of individuals, never aggressive in their arrogance, but ever humble, sharing the majesty of the oceanic circle of which they are integral units.[7]

Swaraj for Gandhiji was intricately tied to Sarvodaya. He envisioned Swaraj as a system in which the individual would be nourished by the oceanic circle rather than being marginalized by it. He saw it as a system where citizens called upon their 'power of individual' for the collective good. His ideal of a decentralized village government is the reason for panchayats at the village level and their institutionalization as the governing bodies of villages in India. But the sad truth is that the seventy-third and seventy-fourth amendments to our Constitution, which empower village panchayats and urban local bodies, respectively, have remained not fully realized, despite sincere efforts by successive governments. This is because we have created local governance through these amendments and institutions, but we have still not engaged the individual. In essence, the individual who was to be the centre of the oceanic circle is missing.

India has 788 members of Parliament, 4,121 members of state Legislative Assemblies, 426 members of state Legislative Councils, thousands of elected officials of the 3,723 urban local bodies and over a million elected officials of the 630 Zilla Panchayats, 6,614 Block Panchayats, and 2,53,163 Gram Panchayats. If we don't include those working full time in the government, both at the state and Union levels, then we can deduce that just over 2 million citizens have the privilege and responsibility of building a nation of 1.38 billion. How absurd is that! We need to create mechanisms in our local, state and Union governance and programmes for a role for the individual citizen that goes beyond just voting in elections. Individuals have the time and skills that can be drawn for development at all levels. There is no framework for this today in our governance bodies and institutions.

If we want the Indian democracy to truly deliver the vision and ideals enshrined in our Constitution, then we need to create an avenue for the citizen to get engaged in nation building. Without this, there will be no Swaraj, no Antyodaya and no Sarvodaya. If we create the Indian sandbox of development and put the individual at the centre of it, we will automatically create an intuitive adaptability and agility in our developmental agenda. We must also ensure that the individual at the centre of our developmental framework is not just a taker from the oceanic circle but a major contributor to it. The advent of social networks and other technologies makes this easier than ever before to accomplish. The sweet spot of our democracy lies in using this kind of thinking to engage the country's millions in the India growth story. So, we need to ask, how can we construct a society fostered by our 'power of individual', where individual aspirations are in harmony with the collective good, and where individual rights also deliver equity for the collective to which this individual belongs.

Gandhi and Deen Dayal Upadhyaya would agree on one thing here—that if we want endow the individual with the ability and power to act for the larger group, then individual capacities in terms of skills and education are imperative. But, more importantly, moral and spiritual anchoring must be brought about. We need to have a mission for the nation that is enshrined in the belief that every Indian has a unique and irreplaceable role to play in making India a beacon of light for the world. Whether in politics, business or everyday life, we need to commit to not leaving any Indian behind in our quest for national development. Individual Swaraj committed to collective Swaraj will lead us to Antyodaya, and that will eventually allow us to actualize Sarvodaya.

Mark Laitflang Stone

Early December is when Shillong, the capital of Meghalaya, starts preparing for the annual Christmas festivities. The first two weeks of the month are when everyone can be seen scampering about, finishing as much work as possible before the festivities start. In 2014, after visiting Nagaland for the Hornbill Festival, I headed to Shillong to complete some work I had with the Meghalaya Institute of Entrepreneurship.

One evening, when I had sat down to supper next to the fireplace, I was introduced to Mark Laitflang Stone. He was impeccably dressed in a three-piece suit, was medium-built and had a beard. But the most striking thing about him were his twinkling eyes and his humble demeanour. He said he was an entrepreneur who worked with young adults and would love to tell me what his company, Avenues, was doing. My schedule for the next few days was packed, and so was his, so the only time we could meet was after a service on the following Sunday at his church.

We met at the Cathedral of Mary Help for Christians just after sunset—which, by the way, was at 4:15 p.m. As the service at the chapel at the lower level was coming to an end, Mark and I started walking up to the grounds of the main Cathedral. I asked him, 'So Mark, how did you decide to become an entrepreneur?' I had no idea that this seemingly innocent and ice-breaking question I use every time I meet an entrepreneur would bring tears to his eyes. We walked up the remaining stairs in deafening silence. As we stood in the cathedral grounds overlooking the courtyard below, he said to me, 'Bhairavi, I always come here to pray and I feel when my heart is pure, my prayers are answered. So, may I pray for you?' How could I refuse? I nodded. After he finished praying, he asked me if I would like to pray for him. I was dumbfounded and asked him, 'Is there anything you want?' He said, 'I just don't want to disappoint my family. My children, my wife and my parents. So, can you pray that I find strength to continue my journey as an entrepreneur and my work with young adults despite the challenges I am facing right now?'

I paused a moment to ascertain whether this was simply a charming act on his part or an authentic confession. I have had many entrepreneurs tell me about their ventures, their challenges and their opportunities, but this guy was definitely different. I looked at him with empathy, and a big smile and something in my heart told me that this young man was not lying. It was apparent from his emotional state at that moment that he brought to his venture not just his dreams but his faith too. That swelled my heart. I told him that of course I would pray for him. Later that evening, Mark had to go home to take care of his children, so we decided to meet the next day over coffee for me to understand what he did at Avenues.

Over many cups of coffee, I came to understand the exceptional journey this young man had made so far.[8] No wonder he was so fearful of not meeting his own expectations of himself! Mark was born into a Khasi family. His parents, Vincent Stone and Cecilia Laitflang, came from a humble background. He grew up in Shillong. Even though he was in the educational capital of the North-east,

Mark wanted to pursue better-quality education elsewhere. And, against his parents' advice, he travelled to Kolkata to pursue his education. He was only sixteen. To make ends meet while in Kolkata, he decided to sell flowers. He had loved flowers from his childhood, and that made this an easy choice. He loved computers too. He assembled them and even started a software development company. He thought he would be the next Bill Gates, but soon he had to close his venture. For an entire year, he sold pool and snooker tables to earn a living and did graphic designing to earn cash. He hosted events and played in a band that disbanded soon after. He did all of this before he turned nineteen, by which time he had abandoned his formal education.

But Mark is a dreamer, so he kept going and never looked back. His eureka moment came when a friend sought help in cracking a job interview. He was all nerves, but Mark gently guided him and motivated him. He guided him on everything from the length of his shirt sleeves to the use of appropriate language and manners. In a week's time, this friend had the job! At that point, Mark knew that he had a special gift—the gift of inspiring people to believe in their own individual power.

A year later, a friend called him and said there was an opportunity to train call-centre employees in Shillong. Avenues took birth from this phone call. Avenues is a social enterprise that teaches young people to use their own power of transformation. Through well-designed and curated training workshops, Avenues imparts skills in communication, presentation and self-actualization to young people. I was curious and wanted to see Mark's work first-hand. The next day, we went to the Avenues training centre, which was located on a busy street in Shillong. The office was a bright white and orange. One could see teenagers and young adults in different rooms being taught by relatively young faculty, many of them women. Mark insisted that I interact with the students, but I wasn't prepared for that. He said to me, 'Bhairavi, you just need to tell them to dream. You are a dreamer, I am a dreamer—we have both gotten somewhere with our dreams—can you tell them to believe in their dreams? That's all I ask of you.'

After an hour-long emotionally and intellectually fulfilling interaction, I walked away from the Avenues office feeling that what Mark and his team were doing was truly magical. They undertook many training programmes imparting specific skills, but the core of their venture was to make young people feel that they could fly to the moon. They were in the business of making the youth of Shillong realize their own power.

Mark told me that when he started Avenues he had no money. All he had was the art of communication he had learnt from his mother and the grit he had inherited from his father. His talent and his belief in himself more than made up for his lack of formal education. He was confident in his own strength as an individual and as a human being. He said, 'Bhairavi, I took everything I knew that had made me succeed and put it into a workshop pedagogy.'

Avenues has now impacted more than 1,00,000 lives and trains a wide variety of people—young adults, illiterate adults, unemployed adults, newly employed youth, teachers, government officers, corporate teams, politicians and even little school children. Mark is committed to bringing unconventional education techniques to empower the youth of the north-east with resilience, hope and self-assuredness. He himself is a sought-after speaker at college and school campuses across the region. His motivational lectures have so far touched 25,000 young people in Meghalaya, Manipur and Nagaland. He has built a team of young coaches and is looking at scaling up the various programmes offered by Avenues.

During a workshop in Switzerland a few years ago, someone told Mark that he was an ardent humanist. Mark says his only passion is to help as many individuals as possible achieve their dreams. He told me that children and young adults passing out from the rural and semi-urban school and college institutions in the North-east lack confidence and purpose. They lack clarity and need guidance. He worked with the ministry of tribal affairs to tackle this problem by creating special modules for tribal youth in the rural and semi-urban areas. The programme teaches these youth not to be ashamed of their ethnicity but to use it as a strength to build their future. Mark brought his individual power to action and addressed a group-based development issue. Not just that, he also empowered the individuals in the group to recognize and actualize their own 'power of individual'.

Mark believes that our youth are the biggest wealth India possesses today, and he says that if we can imagine a way for every young person to fulfil his or her destiny, then we can transform the nation. He is motivated by the idea that the bridge between you and your highest self is what you are inspired by. He says passionately, 'When you are inspired to be greater than you are and believe in a certain value system that echoes passion, that is where success comes from.'

Over the years, Mark has become a close friend, and I often tell him that I believe he is in the business of unleashing the 'power of individual'. What I find heart-warming about my friend is that he remains immensely grateful for the learnings he has had. He is a committed family man who continues to serve society. He loves his family and thanks his wife Aishisha for being his rock through the years. His son Badonbor, whose name means 'having immense strength' in Khasi, and his daughter Maisha, whose middle name is 'Faith', often joined him in the Instagram live stories he did during the pandemic to engage the youth across the region and keep them motivated and positive. Mark lives his life with as much authenticity as possible and draws his strength from his oceanic circle of family, friends, colleagues, and the society at large.

Whenever he is at crossroads about the future of Avenues, it is never about whether what he is doing makes any sense or not. He is purposeful in his endeavour. He has called upon his 'power of individual' for the greater good of the society and therefore feels no tug of war between his own advancement (liberty) and those of others (equality). His own dreams are tied intricately with others realizing theirs. I have always wished that more and more young people in our country would be able to follow their heart and use their individual power for societal growth as Mark is able to.

Gandhiji would be proud of this son of India. Mark not only believed in his own higher self and dreamt of becoming his higher self but also worked hard with commitment, passion and honesty in becoming that higher self. He did that while enabling and nurturing thousands in his own town, state and region to do the same. Through personal and individual Swaraj, he created the necessary conditions for Antyodaya for many families. Today, he continues to toil for Sarvodaya to be realized for his community. That is the kind of individualization that India needs—where individuals call upon their own superpowers to empower the collective. We need more Indians like Mark who enrich the oceanic circle while fulfilling their own individual destinies with their intrinsic power of self-actualization. That is when we will row the raft of the republic in sync with the flow of our civilization. Doing so will not just unleash the individual potential of millions of Indians but will also pave the way for a new framework for democracy—a framework seeded with Indian values but one the world can embrace too. A framework where pursuits of liberty and equality are not contradictory and where individual rights and group rights nurture each other for the advancement of society.

13

Power of Community

YMA

Rolling lush green hills, gushing waterfalls and clouds that walk into your balcony ... Mizoram is truly enthralling. Tucked away in India's north-east, this state is unique in more ways than one. On my first visit there, I woke up to a valley full of clouds floating effortlessly amidst the urban hubbub of the state capital Aizwal. I had gone there to meet the leaders of the Young Mizo Association (YMA), a community organization with over 800 branches and more than 4,25,000 Mizos as its members.

When I first heard about the YMA, I was quite impressed. The YMA was established as a non-political community organization in 1935 in Aizwal. The organization was started to ensure that the traditional tribal ways of the people did not get subsumed by the arrival of Christianity and Indian home rule. Back then, the tribal system of Zawlbuk was disappearing from the region, and the community's conventional social systems, ways of life and the training of young men was nearing its end. The YMA was founded in this context at the time. Its intention was to help the tribal community systems and organs to continue, but within a modern institution. Over the decades, it has now come to represent the Mizo society and its power of community in more ways than one.

Any Mizo above the age of fourteen can become a member of the YMA. Its three main objectives are: *Hun awl hman that* (good use of leisure); *Zofate hmasawnna ngaihtuah* (development of the Mizo society); *Kristian nun dan tha ngaihsan* (revere Christian ethics).[1] Mizos usually join the organization at the branch level in their local community. Many renew their membership annually by paying a fee of Rs 5. The YMA mandates commitment to ten principles: self-discipline and righteousness; good management of family; just and truthfulness; tolerance; politeness; chivalry and usefulness, social commitment; respect for religion; preservation of culture; and abstinence from liquor and drugs. Gandhi would have surely approved of this moral and spiritual anchoring in a local community!

The YMA has several sub-committees that look into the areas of sports, cleanliness, youth training, disaster management, environment and music, to name a few. Whenever I have visited Mizoram, I have often heard a programme or a cleanliness drive being announced by loudspeaker, inviting the YMA members of the area to join it. The YMA is a voluntary organization, yet people turn up for its community activities with great enthusiasm. It also supports bereaved families and helps with funeral arrangements. This is a very unique feature of the organization, as is its active crusade against alcoholism and drug addiction. It goes without saying, then, that the impact of YMA on the ethos and working of the Mizo society is huge. With almost 40 per cent of Mizos connected to the YMA, its influence on politics is obvious, even though its aims and objectives remain steadfastly non-political.

In essence, the YMA is the cornerstone of Mizo society and thrives on the power of community it represents for the Mizo people. Over the years, my interactions with Mizos who are actively involved with the YMA have left me inspired. I have been enthused by the manner in which they prepare their community to meet the challenges of the present day, even as they explore opportunities for the future—all this while they stay committed to keeping the traditions of their past alive. A Swaraj framework, indeed.

One can say that YMA is unique in the ways in which it ties the Mizo society together. There is no doubt that YMA is a shining example of what self-motivated communities committed to societal welfare can do, but I do not think it is an exception in this respect. Community organization comes naturally to Indians. From civil society outfits, neighbourhood groups, spiritual and religious sects and groups, voluntary organizations like The Ugly Indian from Bengaluru—there is a wide variety of community mobilization one can see across the country. Even when they have moved abroad, Indians tend to organize quickly. The number of Indian associations in universities and cities in several countries is a good reminder of that. Interestingly, from Tilak and Bose to Gandhi, every one of our Independence struggle leaders called upon this power of community for the cause of India's freedom. Therefore, we may surmise that the *Power of Community* is deeply seeded in our tenets as a civilization. The Khalsa of the Sikhs and the Sanghas of the Buddhists are fine example of it. So are the Satras of Assam and the dargahs of sufi saints like Hazrat Nizamuddin. In fact, the ruins of the Harappan city of Dholavira are a glorious testimony to the faith ancient Indians had in power of community living and how they wielded this power for their life and livelihood.

Dholavira

At the peak of summer, the earth in the Rann of Kutch in India's
western state of Gujarat is so hot that you can literally heat water on
it. In the winters, however, temperatures can drop to the single digits
post sunset. This acute polarity of summer and winter temperatures
gives these 27,454 sq. km. of salt marshes a unique natural ecosystem.

Humans came to live in the Rann of Kutch as early as 3,500
BC. The most notable footprints of our existence in the region can
be found in the excavated Harappan site of Dholavira. It is one of
the few well-preserved urban settlements of the Indus civilization.
But while its antiquity is impressive, it is the evidence of a vibrant
community life, along with the tools and infrastructure to achieve
that kind of life, that actually makes Dholavira an outstanding
example of the Indus period.

In 2014, Ejji, Mahesh, Venkat and I took the road through the
Rann of Kutch to reach Dholavira. It was late April and the heat had
cracked open the surface of the earth. For miles on end, there was
no vegetation to be seen. A double-lane road lined with salt pans
led us to the Gujarat Tourism accommodation facility at Dholavira.
Given the soaring temperatures during the day, we decided to visit
the excavation site early next morning. Dholavira is known locally
as Kotada, which literally means 'large fort'. Its occupants traded
with other civilizations of the age from Mesopotamia and Egypt.
A city of the past, it could very well be a city of the present, given
the manner in which it was planned. The site gets its name from
the nearby village and is the fifth largest Harappan site amongst the
1,000-plus that have now been discovered.

The next day, we arose along with the sun. At 7 a.m. we entered
the excavation site. As the rays of the early morning sun lifted the
veil of the night, a portal to another time appeared in front of our
eyes. What I saw left me awestruck. In an area spread out over acres,
the ruins of a once-great city lay before us, complete with fortified

walls, citadel, burial grounds, water reservoirs, drainage networks, step-well, homes and more. Our guide explained to us that the city had been pre-planned with three distinct areas: the citadel, the middle town and the lower town.

The remarkable advancement of the people who lived in Dholavira in the areas of urban planning, water management and trade is visible even today. The channels for water, sewage and underground water-harvesting reservoirs—all give us a peek into the engineering achievements of these early Indians and their ideas about what constituted community living.

We wandered around a bit, admiring the construction techniques and use of materials, but also the thoughtful planning of this ancient city. Even in the ruins, one can see the remnants of separate residential areas based on the occupation of the residents, distinct community areas such as wells, burial grounds and stadiums. In fact, it was the stadium that completely bowled me over. Our guide explained that there was a signboard in the Harappan script (now in the museum next to the site) placed at the entrance of this stadium, which could very well be one of the oldest signboards in the world. We stepped into the stadium area and Venkat and I exchanged a glance. 'Wow!' we exclaimed in unison.

It was a large area of over 1,60,000 sq. ft. We were informed that the stadium is the larger of the two that existed in the city of Dholavira. During its day, it could possibly host as many as 10,000 spectators. As we looked around the remains of the stands that had survived more than 5,000 years, we were struck by the nuance of community living this ancient city had. We realized that Dholavira was designed so that its citizens could live together, work together and even enjoy sports and entertainment together. The museum next to the site is home to rich artefacts, such as remnants of seals, pots, cookware, tools and jewellery. To me, the Dholavira site is a reminder of the power of community and strong familial networks that continue to form the basis of Indian society even today.

Driving from Dholavira to Porbandar later that day, I couldn't help but think about how, thousands of years ago, ancient Indians had figured out the ethos of communal living. How, whilst giving due regard to personal space, there was so much planned for the community at large. It made me think of how people gathered in Kolkata during the Durga pooja festival and how, from its tea houses to its open maidans, Kolkata continues to embody the spirit and power of community even today. Even though they are two cities separated by time and distance, both Dholavira and Kolkata celebrate the power of community. They are joined by cities and villages across India who put a strong emphasis on community, creating the basis for fraternal bonds between the people of different faiths, ethnicity and beliefs who live in them.

Fraternity and Collective Purpose

The Greek philosopher Aristotle wrote:

> Man is by nature a social animal; an individual who is unsocial naturally and not accidentally is either beneath our notice or more than human. Society is something that precedes the individual. Anyone who either cannot lead the common life or is so self-sufficient as not to need to, and therefore does not partake of society, is either a beast or a god.[2]

For the earliest humans, the rationale for forming communities was survival and the ability to hunt together. By the time the civilization of the Indus came about, the needs of communities were more sophisticated. The people of Dholavira, for instance, needed consistent water supply, health and sanitation, and emotional nourishment through sports and the arts. They designed their city to meet those needs. For the YMA in Mizoram today, the community's need is to ensure that their old ways continue in the new reality, without their losing their traditional sense of belonging.

Communities, therefore, have always been both formed and sustained in order to serve individual needs through collective means.

Since 2007, the growth of digital platforms through social media and other online forums has been exponential. This only accentuates the idea that humans crave to be part of a community. The needs of today's humans from their communities are centred on peaceful co-existence, quality of life, common interests and collective action, to name a few. The power of community is not unique to Indians in any way, but the idea of social interdependence is deeply ingrained in our society. To be left out from their community is one of the greatest fears many Indians have. Even at the family level, social interdependence is emotionally intense. It is commonplace for an Indian to look for kin from the same village, clan, caste or family wherever they go.

B.R. Ambedkar, who led the Constitution-drafting process for our republic, was acutely aware of the boon and bane of the power of community in Indian society. That is why he laid the foundations for fraternity in our Constitution, along with the principles of liberty and equality. Expounding on the need for fraternity, he said:

> We must make our political democracy a social democracy as well. Political democracy cannot last unless there lies at the base of it social democracy. What does social democracy mean? It means a way of life which recognises liberty, equality and fraternity as the principles of life. These principles of liberty, equality and fraternity are not to be treated as separate items in a trinity. They form a union of trinity in the sense that to divorce one from the other is to defeat the very purpose of democracy.[3]

At its core, the philosophy of Swaraj alludes to this very principle of social democracy, which weaves equality, liberty and fraternity into a common fabric.

In a country as diverse as India, it would be foolish to think that language and religion will unite the nation. Our Constitution was drafted with this foresight. The principle of fraternity enshrined in our Constitution is the basis of many laws, rights and duties that give our civilizational power of community a modern-day outlet. Unfortunately, in the past few decades the organs for enhancing fraternity, such as policies and programmes that give minorities the same access to social goods as the majority, have become nothing but protectionist policies to seek votes based on divisive politics. This has been met with a majoritarian backlash in equal measure. Yet, both circumstances are detrimental to our desired outcome: fraternity. The very idea of fraternity is the foundation for many institutions and policies that are designed to propagate and protect peaceful co-existence in our society. The question is: have we used our power of community to build new organs for achieving greater fraternity? Have we used it to ease the tensions between individual liberty and social equality? Have we called upon our power of community for a collective purpose for the nation? And what should this collective purpose be?

This collective purpose must mean something. It must have goals and actionable agenda for Indians from all walks of life—a la moonshot. It should nudge us to bring our individual superpowers for the betterment of the commons—a la Pahale India. It should be a vision for our future so that we can converge for a shared future. Looking back, it can be seen that Gandhi had mastered the art of building collective purpose through individual action. The Salt Satyagraha, Prabhat Pheris, Non-cooperation, Non-violence and Quit India movements are all great examples of how meaningful goals, in this case home-rule and Independence, were moulded into a collective purpose and inspired large-scale individual action.

Over the past seventy-five years post-Independence, Indian governments of different political hues have tried to emulate this in some measure. Pandit Nehru led the foundation of the modern Indian state and society and gave huge impetus to scientific and higher learning. Lal Bahadur Shastri gave the clarion call of '*Jai Jawan Jai Kisan*', and Indira Gandhi led the Green Revolution mission. Rajiv Gandhi's call for computerization and phone connectivity laid the basis for India's IT industry, and P.V. Narasimha Rao's economic liberalization and reforms saved the nation from economic mayhem. Atal Bihari Vajpayee's Sarva Shiksha Abhiyan created the foundation of 'education for all', and his road-connectivity missions transformed how Indians travelled. Manmohan Singh's AADHAR and Skills missions created tools of empowerment on a mass scale and, in more recent times, Narendra Modi's Swachch Bharat mission seeks to improve sanitation and cleanliness. These are all examples of leadership working through collective purpose for the collective good. All of these programmes have had their share of success in enhancing individual well-being and creating social equity, and therefore in augmenting conditions for fraternity in the country. This gives us the confidence that we can set a shared vision for our present and future and actualize it with collective action. Of course, it will not be easy, but then, no moonshots are.

The India of the twenty-first century is a behemoth moving at lightning speed. The raft of the republic is going through some severe-grade rapids because the world is changing at an accelerated pace. There is a risk, today, of the raft overturning and some people falling off. Now, more than ever, we need to have a collective purpose that ties Indians from all walks of life together. Now, more than ever, we need fraternity at work. I think back to the time when we were river rafting, manoeuvring through the difficult rapids in the Ganga. It was our agility, our collective purpose and our interdependence that led us to safe shores. In the same way, we need to deepen our power of community so that we can work together for our collective purpose and ensure that the raft of the republic does not capsize and we move forward as ONE. The question arises: who will lead this action towards a collective purpose, and with what tools, and how and when.

Who

In February 2014, India unveiled a National Youth Policy which articulated a vision for the youth of India: 'To empower youth of the country to achieve their full potential, and through them enable India to find its rightful place in the community of nations.' The policy defined 'youth' as persons in the age group of fifteen to twenty-nine.[4] The earlier draft policy in 2003 had identified 'youth' as persons in the age group of fifteen to thirty-five.

Today, more than 65 per cent of Indians are below the age of thirty-five. That is a staggering figure of approximately 900 million. If this vast community can be engaged and activated for a collective purpose, it would be the largest manifestation of the power of community seen anywhere in the world. Our young are more than ready for this. When we came together to start Young Indians (Yi), we were trying to give shape to this very idea. Twenty years later, Yi has grown and scaled its action significantly, and is forging ahead to achieve its mission of becoming the voice of young Indians globally. Just like Yi, though, today there are many youth organizations, fellowships and programmes that use creative ideas to engage the young in community and nation development.

As the largest democracy in the world, we are blessed with the demographic dividend of the largest population of youth in the world. It is our strength and it is what attracts investors, companies and entrepreneurs to our country. There are more than 400 youth organizations in the country. Technology and mobile phones have broken geographical, racial, class and gender walls. Today's young are born digital and are borderless and limitless in their thinking. The assimilation of India's heritage with new global trends comes easily to them. They socialize much more than their earlier generations and collaborate naturally with people they don't even know. Not afraid to express their individuality, they are well informed and committed change-makers. Most importantly, they are inspired to work for their future. Despite these advantages, India does not have a focused policy for engaging these young citizens in articulating and actualizing a collective purpose for our republic.

Currently, the ministry of youth affairs and sports is responsible for the policy and long-term vision for issues that concern the youth of India. But the youth of India need a community-level framework that reflects their needs and shared aspirations. What will a community platform for our youth look like? How will it be different from the current National Service Scheme (NSS) and the Nehru Yuva Kendra Sangathan (NYKS)—programmes run by the ministry of youth affairs and sports? Indeed, how we can engage our young in shaping our collective purpose for the nation remains one of our major challenges today.

Before we think of involving our young in a collective purpose for the nation, we must spend more time in understanding what they think about the current and future course of the nation. A survey conducted in 2019[5] by Youth Ki Awaaz, a user-generated Indian youth media platform, throws some light on what our young are thinking today. It seems 82.15 per cent of our young are happy that India is a democracy and 84.79 per cent believe that elections can make a huge difference; but only 56.7 per cent of those are willing to join active politics, even though 73.1 per cent of them like to follow political news. This begs the question that if India's youth feel that democracy and elections works and also follow political news, why do they shy away from participating in active politics? We must think about how best to engage and empower our youth to shape both the social and political aspects of our democracy. This will mean that we must dive deeper into understanding the socio-political ideas of our youth.

Listening to our young, then, must become one of our foremost priorities as a nation. A few years ago, I was in Jalgaon in central Maharashtra to interact with a large gathering of over 400 young people on entrepreneurship. A few of them stayed back for more and I was delighted. The conversation veered towards what the young feel their role is in nation-building. A young girl said, 'Our leaders do not care about us or what we think.' When I asked why she felt so, her friend explained, 'They only think of us as a market or a vote bank. It feels so exploitative. We don't know who is really interested in us.' It came as a surprise to me, frankly. I had always thought that our young were happy being cajoled by companies to buy something and persuaded by political outfits to vote for them. But, over the course of my travels, I have found that whenever I ask this question (and I make it a point to always do so), I get the same answer. Contrary to what I have always believed, our young feel 'used', not 'engaged' or 'empowered'. One young man in Kota, Rajasthan, once told me, 'We are a good commodity to sell to make India look attractive.' The fact that they thought of themselves as a commodity and not a community troubled me deeply.

If we want to engage our young in deepening social and political democracy, we will need to address this feeling of exploitation. We will also need to listen, and to listen with open minds and hearts to what they have to say. Many young people I interact with are worried about inequality. Quite a few are fearful of discrimination based on gender, caste or religion. They have concern for their environment and they struggle with issues that range from malnourishment and obesity to mental health. Jobs are not their only mojo to live. They crave a sense of belonging and want to contribute meaningfully and collaborate constructively with others in society. What they need is a space where trust and respect are guaranteed, where openness is assured and where thinking differently is encouraged. What should such a space look like? How can we use technology to facilitate such conversations? What should be the role of public and private leaders and institutions in creating such a space?

What, How and When

In partnership with the Government of India, the United Nations released the first State of Youth Volunteering in India report in 2017. The report highlights that Indian youth are willing volunteers; it shares several case studies but is unable to give accurate statistics on the number of young people volunteering in India. During my time at India@75, one of our tasks was to build a national volunteering framework. In 2011, when the team at India@75 began this exercise, there was no such initiative in the country. In January 2014, India@75 eventually launched a national volunteering week during which more than 116 million Indians were engaged in one way or the other. As part of the CII national council on India@75, I had the privilege to work with the India@75 team on ideating and executing this first-of-its-kind national volunteering week. We reached out to people across the country, but it was the young who drove this initiative to success. This further sealed my belief that our young are more than ready to play their part in the nation's welfare.

Across India, we have young people who are both socially aware and willing to contribute to society. Yet, as we have seen, they are also averse to political participation and harbour a deep feeling that they are being exploited by the state and the markets. This is a risk to our social and political democracy. We must address this with urgency.

In November 2010, US President Barack Obama visited India. During his tour, he was scheduled to interact with young people in Mumbai. At Yi, we were privileged to be involved with this through our college network Yi Bridge, now known as Yuva. The interaction was to be held at St Xavier's College in Mumbai, with around 300 students from different colleges participating. The excitement among the students was palpable in the air, and I thought about how consistently President Obama chose to engage with young people everywhere he went. Over the years, I researched how the former US President engaged with the young beyond just public interactions. What I discovered made me respect him even more.

In 2011, the Obama administration launched an initiative called '100 Youth Roundtables'. The idea behind it was to listen to what young people were thinking about the challenges and opportunities prevalent in American society. The initiative was announced by President Obama himself when he dropped in on a youth round-table in Cleveland, Ohio. The programme had clear guidelines and was open to all young Americans everywhere. It was the simplicity of the idea that caught my attention. A website was dedicated to the initiative. Young Americans were invited to host a round-table in their community. If they wanted someone from the administration to join the event, they could write an email and someone would be sent. For some reason, if an administration official didn't or couldn't make it for the round-table, the youngsters were asked to send in their feedback. After this, the administration would personally contact the participants. A Youth Round Table Toolkit was developed and made available on the website. The kit contained the detailed framework for the round-tables, templates and instructions. It had guidance on how to hold a round-table, templates for sign-up sheets and feedback, and a section for FAQs. While being very clear about the process, the initiative gave complete freedom to the youth to discuss what they deemed appropriate. There was only one request made to them that the issues be identified along with solutions.

As executive director of India@75, I found this fascinating and imagined what would happen if such a process was undertaken in our country. Our opportunity came when the Planning Commission launched a consultative process for the Twelfth Five-Year Plan. Deputy Chairman Montek Singh Ahluwalia and member Arun Maira encouraged us to reach out to young people and seek their thoughts on India's Twelfth Five-Year Plan. We used both online and offline tools to garner feedback and gather ideas. I was overwhelmed with the kind of responses we got and the enthusiasm I saw in our young towards societal development. I secretly wished more and more governments at the local, state and Union levels would do this. The key is to not make this a one-off exercise but to institutionalize it so that a consistent and iterative feedback loop can be created between the young and the government of the day.

The Modi government launched the MyGov platform in 2014 with the aim of fostering citizen engagement with the government. It now has 23.3 million registered users[6] and several tools such as discussion groups and document-sharing. The platform works with various government departments to co-opt Indians in designing a logo or writing a software code or for any other requirement of the departments' respective government programmes. One can see that the technology already exists for citizen engagement; what we need to do now is to design it to engage our youth to come up with ideas for actionable agenda for the future of our country. Platforms such as MyGov need many more of us on it. It currently engages only 1.6 per cent of our population. Therefore, we need to think of how such a platform can be further used. During the India@75 volunteering week, we learnt that people want to be connected to a collective national purpose, but seek local action. I wonder if a platform such as MyGov can increase its reach if it partnered with state and local governments.

The seventy-third and seventy-fourth amendments to our Constitution provide an institutional framework for rural and urban citizens to participate in their local government. This pathbreaking framework allows for the deepening of democracy and engagement of the local community in local issues in order to provide solutions. What would happen if these local bodies could put their requirements for, say, an app or local infrastructure such as school computers, or a training module for college students, on a platform like MyGov? How would it be if young people could volunteer and come forward to help with these requirements?

Code for America is a non-partisan, apolitical organization founded in 2009 to bridge the gap between public and private sector use of technology and design.[7] Volunteers were initially recruited to work for local city governments, but now the organization has over eighty brigades of volunteers working with governments at the local, state and federal levels. There have bene several laudable efforts by organizations such as iSpirt[8] in the Indian context, but what we need is a platform that has the potential to link millions in India for local and collective action.

We can also contemplate going a step further and think of an institutional framework where the young get to participate in local, state and Union government projects. This participation doesn't have to be limited to giving views and discussing ideas, but we can create mechanisms for the young to be actively involved in governance and nation building. They can do this pro-bono or even as a job. When I was advising the Meghalaya Institute of Entrepreneurship of the government of Meghalaya, we set an ambitious goal of deploying entrepreneurship facilitation centres in every block. To run these centres, we needed young people at the block level to conduct trainings, visit villages and also understand the needs of the local communities. The MIE eventually hired more than 300 young people on contractual jobs to carry out its mission of propagating entrepreneurship at the grassroots level in the state. Its director Baphin K. Sohliya created and deployed the mechanism for co-opting the young for the mission. Through the years, whenever I have interacted with these young cadres of change-makers, I have been delighted to hear that it was not the salary but the purpose of the mission for the betterment of their state that drew them to work with MIE.

Over the years, the Panchayati Raj and urban local bodies have suffered from the political agenda of caste-based, religion-based and gender-based divisions. This has driven many young citizens away from these institutions. We need to ensure that we do not repeat these mistakes. We must ensure that a platform for youth engagement deepens fraternity among the people through liberty of thought and equality of participation; that it remains focused on the nation and is devoid of political point-scoring. The willingness to do this may need a commitment to the nation that goes beyond party politics. It may need a long-term view of the republic that supersedes the short-term compulsions of politics. Most importantly, it needs courage and conviction.

Then we may ask, what if the political leadership of the day doesn't have these intentions? I often wonder what Gandhi would do under such circumstances. My educated guess is that he would tell the people not to wait for the government to take the leadership in these matters. Gandhi's political mentor, Gopal Krishna Gokhale, created the 'Servants of India' movement in 1905 inviting Indians from different walks of life and training them for service of the underprivileged, rural and tribal people. Gandhi was a firm believer in the ability of young people to lead the nation. In his own publication *Young India*, he wrote extensively on how the youth could get involved in issues of social development. It is easier for the young to converge today if they wish to do so, purely because so many of them are on social and digital platforms. Six hundred and fifty-eight million Indians now use the internet—a large percentage of them youth. As of April 2022, India had 467 million social media users.[9] These are massive numbers, twice the population of entire nations even. Therefore, we have the tools to connect, convene and collaborate on a large scale. Then, why must we wait?

The one lesson that we all took home from the rafting trip on the Ganga was that it is we, the people of India, who have to take up the oars and make the raft of the republic move forward. This cannot be outsourced. We cannot reap the benefits of a system we are not willing to work on. It will not last, and sooner or later there will be a chasm in our society. Our fraternity, liberty and equality will be at risk. In communities across India, we can see amazing examples of how people have been able to take the leadership in working for a collective purpose. There is a reason why Gandhi thought Indians would be able to usher in Swaraj on a mass scale.

Johar Football Club

When we first moved to Munsyari, our quaint hamlet in Uttarakhand of 8,000 people, we were considered outsiders. We didn't come from the same caste or ethnicity as the locals. We kind of expected this, as this is the norm in small, rural communities across the country. Our opportunity to become part of the community came when we were invited to the inaugural football match of the local football club in June 2019.

Munsyari has had a football club since 1956, called Johar Football Club, named after the Johar valley in which it is located. Before even telephones, internet and social media reached this small town, people here had figured out how to organize themselves for sports. When we first visited this cluster of villages, we were fascinated to see the children here playing a variety of sports in the only large playground the area has. Munsyari has a vibrant sports culture, and there are teams for different age groups in each village. Kids practise sports through the year for the annual tournament, and players come from across the country to participate and compete in them. There would be teams playing football, cricket and softball on the playground. What thrilled me was that there were girls' teams too, and these girls played in full sports gear. Recently, one of the girls also won the state championship in boxing. It was a reminder to us that Indians know how to form communities and nourish them for shared aspirations.

In 2019, Alok was invited as one of the chief guests to the opening tournament of the annual sports meet organized by the Johar Club. The first match was played between two girls' teams, and the crowd cheered with every goal. After the opening match, we were invited by the organizing committee to join their discussions in the club premises. Alok and I were simply amazed at the commitment and passion that the committee in this small settlement displayed for sports. It reminded me of Dholavira. I imagined that such conversations would have happened in that ancient city and people would have gathered for a sports event in the large stadium, cheering the players from the spectator stands. Maybe their games were different, but their idea of community seemed to have been the same as here, in Munsyari. That day at the Johar Club meeting, a sense of collective purpose was on full display, and people had gathered despite their caste and other social differences. We offered our help to get coaches from other places to train the teams. There was deep appreciation from the committee members, since access to professional coaches was a big challenge for them. It seemed suddenly that our willingness to contribute to this shared goal of the community had diminished our 'outsider' tag. We were now part of the community, involved in a collective purpose, and that was all that mattered to the people in the room.

Once back home, Alok and I wondered why it was that people so adept at deploying their power of community for sports were not calling that same power into action to address their social challenges in employment, education, healthcare etc. Why was it easier for them to convene for sports but not for cleanliness? We spoke to a few young people and discovered that there was willingness to convene but they just didn't know if they could do it for cleanliness the way they could for sports. We wondered why this was so. Perhaps these aspects of social development were outsourced to the government of the day and, as a community, they had simply abandoned their own involvement in these matters. The power of community was alive, but unlike in the case of the YMA, it was not the anchor for the social well-being of the community.

Communities across India have this inherent power that they can deploy for the collective good. I tend to be biased towards youth as they are our future and our largest demographic group. But many senior citizen groups, women's groups and community organizations do impressive work in their local neighbourhoods. Some do it independently, and others do it through resident welfare associations, mohalla committees, housing societies, condominiums or panchayats. The power of community is at work at various levels in our society already. I saw it at work through the successive waves of the Covid-19 pandemic. From arranging oxygen, medicines, hospital beds and funerals to even supplying food, vegetables, and household supplies, residents across the country banded together without any invitation or official mandate to do so.

In 2014, I spent three months at a stretch in Kashmir working on disaster response in the aftermath of the devastating floods that savaged the Valley in early September that year. A community of young volunteers came together and formed a group called 'SOS for Kashmir'. They worked with the local masjid committees to reach aid to people and also reached out to organizations across India and even outside to seek support for the people who were suffering. This further strengthened my belief that our young can band together for a shared purpose. The more we do to augment their power of community, the more we will do to deepen the sense of fraternity in the country. It is important for us to do this because it will strengthen social and political democracy and ensure a more sustainable future for the republic.

As India celebrates the seventy-fifth year of its Independence, we ought to reflect on how we have called upon our power of community after Independence. Did we call upon it to exclude people based on religion and caste, or did we use it to deepen the bonds of fraternity in society at large? Did our power of community empower Indians from all walks of life to enjoy equal opportunities for livelihood, education and healthcare, or did it precipitate preferential treatment? Did we deepen equality or not? Was our power of community used to give a safe space for individuals to voice their ideas without fear, or did we use it to overpower dissent? Did we use our power of community to deepen liberty or not?

Our political equality of 'one man, one vote' has not translated into social and economic equality in the past seven-and-a-half decades. This continues to remain our major challenge. Equality is a basis for fruitful fraternity. No fraternity is possible when members of a community feel left out or underserved. The residents of Dholavira understood this over 5,000 years ago and planned their city and life to ensure equal access to a scarce resource such as water by building a series of reservoirs for people living in the walled citadel, fortified middle town and the lower town. The YMA is a fine modern-day example of how communities can help to deepen equality, both in terms of rights and duties, in a modern society. Can our young collaborate to address some of these challenges through enterprise, innovation, knowledge and technology? Can they be empowered to pursue a Pahale India scenario?

In his last speech to the Constituent Assembly, Ambedkar gave us sound advice. He said:

If we wish to preserve the Constitution in which we have sought to enshrine the principle of the Government of the people, for the people and by the people, let us resolve not to be tardy in the recognition of the evils that lie across our path and which induce people to prefer Government for the people to Government by the people, nor to be weak in our initiative to remove them. That is the only way to serve the country. I know of no better.[10]

The triumvirate of liberty, equality and fraternity is a unique feature of our Constitution and is a tribute to the power of community deeply seeded in Indian society. The Indian way is the collective way. But it is only possible to enjoy this commune when the power of community deepens social democracy through equality and enhances political democracy through individual liberty. Our challenge will be to build new models and seed a system of constant innovation for organs and institutions that can enhance our power of community. We may begin with the youth, but can we then make such institutions accessible to all Indians? Only once we find a way of doing so will we find a method of truly actualizing our Constitution fully. And only then will the raft of the republic, despite the rapids and turns along the way, will flow purposefully, safety and steadily in the flow of the river of civilization.

14

Call to Action

Rishikesh Again

In May 2017, I found myself at a camp on the banks of the Ganga again, upstream from Rishikesh. But this was a different kind of camp. There were seventy-five children, aged twelve to eighteen, from schools across India, at the camp and my role was to moderate a few seminar sessions for them. Ananta Aspen Centre, an institution committed to values-based leadership and The Shri Ram School, one of India's finest private schools, had joined hands to offer a two-week residential programme for students. The programme's goal was to build values-based leadership skills in young adults and nudge them to take ideas to action.

One evening, post dinner, while casually discussing with a few students their ideas on what gaps they see in our country and how would they like to address those, I fondly remembered the discussion Sudha, Mahesh and I had many years ago during our Yi retreat. The serendipity of it hit me hard. I suddenly became quiet and went back to my room. It was almost thirteen years since all of us from Yi had engaged in a similar conversation by the Ganga on how we could engage India's young in the act and process of nation building.

I tried to reflect on these thirteen years. So much had changed in my life. I was no longer a young entrepreneur running a small venture but was part of my family's large business. I was now married and had a partner to share my life with. I had left business and engaged in public policy work for some time. All my experiences spanning more than a decade played in my mind, like a movie. I tried to think which one of these experiences was my favourite. I smiled to myself as I realized what my answer was. Some of my most cherished experiences over the years had happened while I was on the road, travelling, meeting Indians from different walks of life and learning from them about our India.

The next morning, I went for a walk. It took me to the Ganga. She was flowing purposefully with the same gusto as before. My heart swelled with joy upon being with her again. I admitted to myself that the ebb and flow of civilization continued—and always would. On the opposite bank I saw a few young people trying to get their raft into the river. I recollected that night when the Ganga opened my eyes about the relationship between our civilization, which was more than 10,000 years old, and our republic, which was just over seven decades young. I thought of all the questions I had then:

'What does it mean to be an Indian?'
'What are the bonds that tie us Indians together despite our diverse identities and moorings?'
'Despite these differences, how can we work as ONE?'

As the rays of the early morning sun danced on the waves of the Ganga, I reflected on these questions again. Had I found the answers to these questions? I strongly felt that over the years, through my travels, work and my interactions with Indians from every nook and corner of the country, I had indeed been able answer these questions to a large degree. At that moment, a wave from the Ganga brushed against my legs. I realized that had I not immersed myself in the story of India and got to know its people intimately, I would not have been able to answer some of these questions. I had been privileged to do this over the last few years. Not everyone gets that kind of opportunity. Perhaps, I thought, it would be good if I shared my learnings with other people.

As ONE

When I started writing this book almost three years ago, I realized that I was expounding the idea that India had some kind of magical superpowers. For a moment I thought I would be laughed at. What superpowers, some may point out. We cannot even fix our roads! I have always believed that the real superpower of India lies in its people—We the People. We have immense strength, resilience and perseverance. It is we who possess the superpowers that have been discussed in this book. The flow of civilization is eternal, like the Ganga, but the raft of the republic is steered by India's citizens. We are not short of talent or ideas; what we need is collective commitment to call them to action.

I am not shy to admit that I am madly in love with India and the very idea of India. My endeavour while writing this book has been to remain in a state of reverence and love towards India and Indians. During this time, my mental model has been biased towards optimistic, future-oriented and sometimes crazy ideas. But I would rather be authentic and say what I really think than make a show of sobriety. Through it all, however, I have tried to see the gaps and opportunities for each of the superpowers with some objectivity and a decent degree of realism.

My aim was for the reader to explore India's superpowers. I am hoping that you will identify with some of these superpowers and call them to action in your own life. I am also dreaming of a day when many of us will be able to use our individual superpowers to augment India's collective power. I hope we will find occasions to nudge each other into bringing our individual powers to action for the common good of the nation.

A few years back I was pointed to a book, *As One – Individual Action Collective Power*.[1] It was a collection of case studies written by Mehrdad Baghai and James Quigley. It explored various models and archetypes of organizations, movements and teams that worked and moved forward as ONE. The book contains a set of questions for the reader to answer about his or her own organization in the form of a decision tree. Based on that, the book suggests which archetype might suit the reader's endeavour best. I thought about India and tried to answer the questions in the book in the context of our nation. Based on my answers, it seemed what suited our context was The Producer and Creative Team archetype. Explaining the Producer and Creative Team archetype, the authors shared several principles that go into making this type of team, organization or, in our case, nation, succeed.

The first was: 'The producers articulate an overall objective or idea; the creative team, made up of the right people with the right chemistry, brings it to life.' I thought of the ideas of Swaraj, Antyodaya and Sarvodaya that our leaders had articulated. We have never had a dearth of ideas in India. But the challenge had always been getting the right people together to take those ideas to action. The book gave several examples, from Disney to Pixar, as success stories, but what stood out for me most was the quality of leadership the principle alluded to. I thought about our national *moonshot* of

Swaraj and realized that the kind of leaders (or producers, in the context of this archetype) we need are people who have a great deal of purpose. Otherwise, even with the best of creators we will have the scenario of *Atakta Bharat* materialize, where we fail to converge and collaborate.

The second principle was: 'The members are recruited not only because they excel at what they do but also because they complement the rest of the team.' I thought about our power of inclusion and how we have the opportunity to call it to action to create the right chemistry for our success as a nation. Our inherent diversity is our greatest strength as it phenomenally increases our ability to bring complementary skills to any national goal or agenda. Our power of inclusion is also our conduit to our power of assimilation.

Our power of assimilation can help us co-create a global order of mutual trust, respect and equity by collaborating with other nations. Our ability to assimilate others' ideas with our own can be hugely beneficial here. We have the ability to collaborate with other nations and bring our own strengths to work towards the welfare of humanity at large. This is exactly what we have done with our Covid-19 vaccine development efforts, where we have complemented our ability to produce vaccines on a mass scale with those of other nations who could develop the vaccine first. We also brought our own research and development to the fore and developed our own home-grown vaccines too. We played our part in augmenting vaccine equity in the world by shipping vaccines to developing and poor nations across the world. The Vaccine Maitri programme, though it was criticized on the home front, gave us a glimpse of the power of assimilation India brings to the global community. Given this, we do not have to worry about whether we matter in the global order or not, instead we only have to focus on *how* we matter.

The third principle literally spoke to my heart. It stated: 'The creative team is given complete freedom to express ideas.' I felt this was so important in our context. Even though most Indians enjoy significant liberty of thought and action, our social conditioning comes in the way of our expressing our minds and innovating. The power of creativity we have can only be actualized if we make the negative social conditioning around creative economy careers null and void. Without a vibrant creative economy, our ability to make the best of the fourth industrial revolution will be blunted. That will further limit our prospects of being leaders of the knowledge economy globally. Our power of knowledge cannot be limited to only certain streams but needs to be all-encompassing to include the creative and humanistic pursuits too.

The fourth principle was quite clear in the matter of how success was looked at in such a team setting: 'Success is measured by the ability to innovate as well as by the ability to match the overall objective.' I thought about this for a long time. Our power of enterprise is measured today by the success of our unicorns and start-ups, but are we measuring it against our constitutional values of equality and fraternity? If we could measure the success of our enterprises to see if they matched the principles of Antyodaya or Sarvodaya, then perhaps we could marry purpose with profit and actualize the *Pahale India* scenario. We could then bring our individual enterprise to play to address our challenges in health and wellness, agriculture, nutrition, education, etc.

'Dissent is used to push the creative boundaries of the team'— this was the fifth principle. I felt that the years of strongman/woman politics, either at the Union or state level, had created a '*Salaam Saab*' (Salute, O Master) social system among our people. We expect one man or woman to solve all our problems, even though we know that this is a pipe dream. We have also used this situation to morally disengage ourselves completely from our duty towards social and national well-being. So much so that we are not even interested in cleaning the road in front of our homes, unlike the villagers of Mawlynnong.

We vote for our leaders, expecting them to solve all our problems and make a show of complete agreement with their ideas—some of which may be flawed—simply to recuse ourselves from our responsibility for our collective well-being as a nation. We discourage dissent because it threatens to break our collective amnesia about our role as citizens. In ceding our individual power to a few, we have compromised our agency for change. We are happy to have the freedoms a democratic polity accords us, but are unwilling to pick up the oars and steer the raft of the republic forward. This is why India continues to lag behind in actualizing Sarvodaya.

It reminds me of the time when we were all rafting on the Ganga in 2004. After some time, we had started enjoying the adventure because we had learnt a few tricks. But just as the guides started steering us towards more difficult rapids, we objected. We did not want to push our boundaries. It was only when we were told that we could not reach our destination without tackling those difficult rapids that we relented. I often feel that when it comes to realizing our power of food for the betterment of our annadaatas—our farmers—and bringing our science of the diverse plate and farm back in vogue, we are unwilling to push our boundaries. We are unwilling to rethink our food ecosystem because we are scared of tackling new challenges. The same is true of our relationship with our natural world. We are okay to suffer air pollution because we don't want to push our boundaries. We do not want to aim for moonshots when it comes to making our development journey in partnership with nature. Nature-based solutions are moonshots that we badly need, if we want to ensure that our large population does not face unmanageable climate-change risks. But we are reluctant to move forward.

The sixth principle, I thought, was the critical success factor for this archetype. It said: 'The creative team collaborates closely: discussions will be intense, communications continuous.' Indians have a phenomenal ability to build a community wherever they are. Even when we leave our shores and go abroad to study or work, we focus on building a community with our kith and kin. It is time we brought this power to use when it comes to improving the wellness of our people. There is no reason we cannot follow in the footsteps of the Nuka system of the Alaska natives. We have only to understand the importance of collaboration for such a system to succeed. The same would be true for restoring our monuments and improving our museums. They belong to the community in whose region they are located and they augment the collective power of heritage of that community. We have to shun our inhibitions in this regard and follow in the footsteps of Lawrence Koj from Ziro. We need to work together with experts, governments and local communities to pass on the intergenerational equity of our civilizational heritage to our future generations.

The idea of continuous communication is also essential; that is why we need to create platforms where we can listen to Indians from all walks of life, especially our young, who are going to lead the republic in the future. My school had a motto: 'Youth shall Re-shape the World.' It had an image of the planet being worked upon by young girls and boys in school uniforms, standing on a ladder with tools in their hands. It is an image I have carried close to my heart always. It reminds me that those who ran my school envisaged that the children they educated would be involved members of their community and shape the future of their societies. It was clear that they expected us to be responsible citizens who acted individually or collectively for the greater good of the nation and the world. That was their understanding of what it means to be an Indian. And that has been mine too.

To Be an Indian

As I wrote this book, I thought about how I had experienced these superpowers in my own life. I felt that if I could not hold a mirror to myself in this aspect, then I should not write this book at all. I didn't randomly select these twelve superpowers, and they are not the only superpowers of India. But these were the ones I thought were relevant for our path forward as a nation, currently and also the ones I was actualizing in my own life. To me, being an Indian means calling upon these superpowers, not just for my own personal growth but also for the progress of the nation. To me, being an Indian means bringing your individual power to play for the collective good.

Therefore, I have taken the liberty of sharing with you how I am actualizing some of these superpowers in my own way. I am hoping that you too shall find it in your heart to actualize one or a few of these in your own life.

I have only shared how I have chosen to engage with the superpowers I have discussed in this book so that you can also dabble in yours. By no means am I trying to make a show-and-tell case of it. On the contrary, I choose to share these examples with you so that you may know that even though the superpowers are of civilizational scale, you can still experience them, claim them and actualize them in your own unique way.

Power of Enterprise

I grew up around entrepreneurs. I saw my father and his two partners from Blue Dart, Khushroo Dubash and Clyde Cooper, work tirelessly to chase their dreams. My father grew up in a Mumbai chawl (a tenement with common toilets) for the first ten years of his life, where he would wait in a queue to use the common toilet. Clyde and Khushroo too didn't have much family backing. The three just about managed to gather the Rs 30,000 they needed (Rs 10,000 each) to start the company. I have seen them toil night and day to make their dream come true. They took to heart the idea of investing in people and believed that with good people they would be able to give good service, and good service would earn them good profits. They enjoyed their crazy journey, and at the age of fifty, they exited from the listed entity with a valuation of several hundred crores of rupees. The wealth they created—not just in terms of money but also in terms of knowledge, reputation and success—belonged to the 3,500-plus people who worked for the company at that time.

Therefore, I have seen what the power of enterprise can do when called to action. I too chose to become an entrepreneur because I believed in it so much. But during our road journey across India in 2014, I realized that there were many Indians who wished to take the path of entrepreneurship or who had taken it, but needed guidance and support. This was the genesis of the IEF Entrepreneurship Foundation. We set up the foundation to bring entrepreneurship and business skills to entrepreneurs in tier-3 and tier-4 towns in India, as they were the most underserved. I also realized that if a small business in a small town did well, then it would create local jobs and help mitigate the migration challenge in our big cities. We continue to train entrepreneurs across India, and as you have read in the book, many of the entrepreneurs went on to help others take the path in their own community. The torch was passed on.

Power of Nature

I have to admit that it was my visit to the Changthang in Ladakh that made me truly aware of the power nature has on us humans. I came back from that visit with a deep reverence for our natural world and respect for the people who recognized its awesome powers. When we moved to Munsyari a few years ago, I realized that even though the local people worshipped nature, they did not have the scientific tools and skills to nurture it. I concluded that if we have to protect the oak, horse-chestnut and rhododendron forests in our backyard, we will need to give the local communities economic incentives to do so. Fortunately, Alok was embarking on his regenerative, nature-based agriculture venture, and I decided to get involved.

Then, in 2020, through the Forum of Young Global Leaders at the World Economic Forum, I came to know of the trillion trees campaign. The initiative focuses on growing and protecting a trillion trees on the planet by 2030. They had an American chapter, an initiative in the Amazon, another one in Africa and one in China, but none in India. I felt compelled to work with the team at WEF and few YGL colleagues to help co-create a multi-stakeholder platform for India. The work I do with Alok and with the trillion trees campaign allows me to express my reverence for nature and gives me immense hope and satisfaction.

Power of Heritage

In 2013, I visited my ancestral village of Sihor in Saurashtra, Gujarat, after nearly three decades. I had gone there to meet the people who work with our family's foundations for social development in the area. While on the visit, I came to know that there was an ancient step-well in the village. I promptly went to see it. But I was heartbroken upon seeing it. The entire heritage structure was in shambles and trees were growing out of its ancient walls. There was litter everywhere and the water in the step-well was filthy.

I came back to Mumbai and asked my father if we could get involved in its restoration. We made some inquiries but were told that the local government department would look into it. But nothing happened for years. I am still pursuing this idea to see if we can bring this beautiful step-well back to life. This is my way of living out my power of heritage. Although it is a work in progress, I am hoping we will eventually succeed.

Power of Creativity

Do you have a creative hobby you pursued but have left it for lack of time? I did. I loved playing the piano when I was at Miami University, but after my graduation I abandoned it. Work and business took over and I hardly got the time to think of playing the piano. Then, one day, my friend Srinivas Krishnan called. He said a special show of Global Rhythms was going to be held. This was an initiative he started when we were all at Miami in the 1990s. Global Rhythms was designed to bring different traditions of global music together. Srini insisted that I come back to the campus that fall to see the show. I couldn't resist.

When I arrived, 650 artists had convened from different corners of the world and were all collaborating to create a new kind of musical experience. The show was a magical production, and having all those artistes on the stage was, in the words of the maestro A.R. Rahman, like having a musical Noah's Ark. At dinner that night, Srini told me that he always thought I was happiest when I was surrounded by artists, and that was why he had called me over.

Years later, when Srini decided to spend more time in India, we spoke of recreating the magic of Global Rhythms for Indian students. We felt that this time we wanted to work with school children instead of young adults in colleges. With the help of a few like-minded people and with Srini's commitment, the LEAP Foundation was started. This foundation is focused on using the creative arts—music, dance, theatre, painting and so on—to improve leadership and learning capabilities among school children. We began in Chennai, and Srini is now dedicating half of his time to the foundation as its creative director.

Even if we cannot foster creativity in our community, I feel we can always begin by pursuing our own power of creativity. I am inspired in this by my dear friend Shalaka Joshi, who truly pursues her creative powers while juggling her professional commitments as the Gender Lead for South Asia at the International Finance Corporation (IFC). Shalaka will snatch an evening out to watch a play or attend a music concert even while travelling for work. She gives her creativity vast room for expression. She will manage to take a dancing class in the middle of the week and play the piano at her home in Mumbai whenever she desires. Inspired by her, when we moved to Munsyari I got myself a piano. When I play it, I transcend to another plane; something other-worldly takes over my sense of being. It allows me to expand my personal boundaries to a great extent. My next goal is to go back to dance!

Power of Knowledge

My friend Gitanjali M. Swamy is an intellectual powerhouse. Apart from having a BTech from IIT Kanpur, she also has a PhD in computer science from University of California, Berkley, an MBA from Harvard Business School and a degree in law. A few years back, she told me to look at a presentation she had made. It spoke of things like deep learning, connected devices and advanced applications of computer science that could be used to improve a massive government programme. I was left awestruck. The ideas she had put down in the note were way beyond my comprehension then. I asked her what to do about it, and she was kind enough to suggest a couple of books and articles for me to upgrade my knowledge of 4IR technologies. But she insisted that only when I personally experienced the power of 4IR technologies such as artificial intelligence and internet of things would I realize where humanity was headed. She recommended a scheduling assistant programme called X.ai, a tool that would help me schedule my appointments and would also communicate on my behalf with the people I had to schedule meetings or conference calls with.

Taking her advice, I signed up on the platform. There were a few basic questions I had to answer in a form, and then the algorithm took over. It knew my working hours and holidays and my preferences for certain types of meetings—such as company reviews—to be scheduled on specific days. At one point I did feel a bit afraid so see the kind of access to my personal information a programme was getting, but despite that I decided to take this experiment to its logical conclusion.

The programme gave me options for names I could choose to call it by and communicated with everyone as my assistant. Andrew was a programme, but it had all the knowledge my office assistant had. It had good skills and more efficiency at its disposal because it was never on holiday or asleep at night. In about a month, Andrew knew my colleagues, my family and my personal preferences. There was suddenly much more efficiency in my life and I eventually started referring to Andrew as 'he' and not 'it'. When I told Gitanjali about it, she laughed. She said that a tool like X.ai is just the tip of the iceberg of what is to come.

I thought of all the assistants in offices across India and felt uncomfortable knowing that they were completely unaware that a computer code was going to take their jobs away within the next decade. I understood that although I considered myself tech-smart, I would need to upgrade my knowledge and skills to fully comprehend how 4IR tech was going to transform my world. Since then, I have taken several classes online and offline to understand these technologies and have called upon my power of knowledge to prepare myself for this imminent future awaiting humanity.

Power of Food

This is a power many of us rejoice in daily. But of late I have started thinking more about my eating habits, ensuring that I focus on the diversity of my plate. We eat a different grain and millet daily in our home now, and when in the mountains, we eat what we grow on our small farm.

It has been a marvellous learning experience to be able to see my husband Alok, a career marketing professional, bring his skills to use for marketing the produce grown by small farmers across the Himalaya. I consider myself fortunate that I am a farmer's wife. Seeing our small farmers grow their income in the past few years has helped me understand the issues in India's food system more clearly. I intend to bring my power of food to use even more, by taking the produce grown through regenerative farming practices by our farmers, from seeds of vast genetic variety, to people across the world. These are early days, but I am confident that we can make this happen.

Power of Beauty

Our little hamlet Munsyari is endowed with breathtaking natural beauty, but it has no garbage collection and processing services available. When we take long walks through the forest, Alok and I often notice trash left behind by tourists and clothes and plastic dumped in the village streams. In fact, the public square just outside the local government block office is even infamously referred to as 'Gobar Chowk', gobar meaning cow dung.

We have been having conversations with our community to arrest this problem. We feel a few young people could be incentivized to set up a garbage collection and processing venture. But, as Alok points out, unless we inspire the locals to beautify their villages, we will struggle to convince them to pay for garbage collection. We intend to call upon the obsession with beauty the local people have here for the cause of civic cleanliness. This is not an easy project, but based on a few local conversations we have had, we will be able to pull the community together to beautify Gobar Chowk and use that as a stepping stone to talk about the larger need for garbage collection and processing.

Power of Wellness

Once I was back from the hospital and recovering from Covid, my father spoke to me at length on the phone about my health. He pointed out to me that I was the only one who had got infected in my household and one of the very few who had suffered the disease with the severity that I did in our village. I was not old and had no comorbidities, then why did I land up in an ICU? And not to mention that I had already had one dose of the vaccine. He felt that the life I was leading was not healthy. He pointed out the different lifestyle risks I could face as I approached my fifties if I continued to live the way I did. He said that for me to catch Covid and suffer from it so badly, my immunity was already compromised due to my imbalanced lifestyle.

In the months that followed, I have taken help from both allopathy and Ayurveda to regain my strength and re-energize my body. I have to admit the Ayurveda protocols were immensely helpful here. But so were yoga and brisk walking. I have understood that my power of wellness is for me to claim and nurture. Not doing so could keep me at a disadvantage when it came to fully experiencing my life. I continue to pester the local block officers to allow me to develop a Nuka-like project in our community. I am generally acknowledged, but then nothing happens. This continues to be my struggle, but I am deeply committed to making this a reality.

Power of Assimilation

From the very first time I visited China, I have felt the need to learn Mandarin. I even got myself a teacher in 2005 so that I could learn it. But life got busy and I never got to it. When we moved to Munsyari a few years ago, I felt the urge to go back to learning Mandarin. Perhaps because we are only 50 km from the India–China border and the community we live in continues to bear the economic consequences of the 1962 War between the two countries. Perhaps I have more time now.

I have been learning Mandarin for the past three years now, but I have also acquainted myself with a lot of contemporary writing on China available in English. A big resource for me in this journey is Mahesh, who has spent years travelling in hinterland China and understanding the Chinese people and culture.

I have also taken help from friends who write on foreign policy to understand what books or articles I should read to upgrade my knowledge of China. I am no global affairs expert and don't intend to be, but if there is anything I took away from my experience at Clawson Hall, it was that we live in a highly interdependent global society, and that understanding global linkages is going to help me personally and professionally.

Power of Inclusion

Every time I meet my friend Sheyna Baig, a celebrated artist, I feel that she represents what India's power of inclusion should look like. Her father is a Muslim and her mother a Hindu. Sheyna is at ease with both those identities. She celebrates Eid and Diwali with equal fervour and has been a keen student of Vedanta for many years. When we were planning to have a painting done for our home in Munsyari, I spoke to her. I told her that I wanted a large-sized painting of Goddess Tripura Sundari. I showed her a picture of what I was looking to get done. Sheyna immersed herself completely in creating the painting. There would be days when she would not even eat or sleep properly because she was painting the devi.

She told me that when she was painting the Sri Yantra, she was nervous that she might make a mistake, but she felt the goddess spoke to her mind and her hands just worked in a divine commune. For me, Sheyna will always remain one of the finest examples of our power of inclusion.

Alok and I read and discuss ideas from different faiths and masters of different theologies regularly. It was Alok who got me the translation of the *Suleiman Charitra* by A.N.D Haksar. Given India's immense diversity, I sometimes feel that all you have to do to exercise your power of inclusion is to pick up a book or attend a talk on, or visit a shrine of, another religion.

Power of Individual and Power of Community

For Alok and me, living out our power of individual is important. But we also firmly believe that the individual is not separate from the community. While we both follow our individual vocations and passions, we make it a point to engage with our local community. Whether it is an event at the local sports club or training farmers in the area, or working with young people to find a solution to the garbage problem in the village, engaging with local schools, or attempting to make our local health centre more resourceful, Alok and I believe that individual actions with collective purpose are the need of the hour. We believe that our 'power of individual' rests in the collective power of the community that we live in, and we do our best to augment both.

Onwards and Upwards

During my Aspen leadership seminars, one of our moderators would always say, when the sessions ended, 'Onwards and Upwards'. What he meant was that with our new understanding (post a session) of who we are and where we belong and where we ought to go, the only thing left to do is to move onwards and upwards. It is like the raft of our republic in the Ganga—once we are in the flow of the civilization, the only thing left to do is to pick up our oars and get to work.

I hope that you too find your moments of epiphany and create opportunities for yourself to actualize your superpowers. I dream of an India where individual action has resulted in collective power and every Indian is able to enjoy their own personal Swaraj. I wish that our dreams for a better India do not leave any Indian behind. That will be the true dawn of Antyodaya. I pray that through our relentless efforts, we are able to co-create the conditions for Sarvodaya to materialize. There is no assurance it will, but as the Bhagwad Gita says:

कर्मण्येवाधिकारस्ते मा फलेषु कदाचन

(*Karmanye Vadhikaraste Ma Phaleshou Kada Chana*: 'You have a right to perform your prescribed duty, but you are not entitled to the fruits of action.')[2]

Onwards and Upwards!

Units and Measures

INR/Rs = Indian Rupee

Rs 1 lakh = Rs 1,00,000

Rs 1 crore = Rs 10 million

ft = feet

km = kilometre

mm = millimetre

m/mtrs = metres

0 degree Centigrade = 32 degrees Fahrenheit

1 kilometre = 0.6214 miles

1 foot = 0.305 mtrs

Acknowledgements

Ejji K. Umamahesh, for being a friend, guide and mentor and forever willing to explore the nuances of our country and our world with open, honest and eye-opening discussions.

Mahesh Sriram, my dearest friend and co-traveller, for being my guide and a beacon of knowledge for me through the years. His passion for India as a civilization and a nation has left incredible imprints on my mind.

Venkatesan Nagarajan, for his consistent captures on camera of our Highway to Swades drive and the many interviews we conducted. They served me well as eclectic research material for this book.

Rewaj Chettri, Tabish Habib, Mukti Datta, Krishna Devaraya, Lawrence Koj, Aditya Patwardhan, Alezo Kense, Aman Preet Singh, Thomas Zachariahs, Tenzing Bhutia, Vaibhav Kaul and Mark Laitflang Stone, for taking time out to be part of this book by sharing their personal journeys and for inspiring me with their superpowers.

A.R. Rahman, music composer, for coming up with the title of our journey in 2014—Highway to Swades—from which the title of this book is inspired.

Shekhar Kapur, filmmaker, for believing in my ability to write and manifest my personal power of creativity.

Arun Maira, former member, Planning Commission of India, for always giving me a listening ear and encouraging a young woman to reimagine India's future.

Ram Mohan Mishra, former secretary, Government of India, for nudging me to believe in India and its immense potential.

Baphin Sohliya, former director, Meghalaya Institute of Entrepreneurship, for co-opting me into the mission of propagating entrepreneurship and development.

Young Indians (Yi), for giving me the opportunity to meet people from across the country and serve my country through collaborative leadership.

Confederation of Indian Industry (CII), for encouraging a young woman entrepreneur to think and act beyond business.

Tarun Das, founding director general of CII, for believing in the power of youth and giving a young woman the opportunity to serve.

G.V. Sanjay Reddy, founding national chairman of Young Indians, for his exceptional leadership of Yi in its early days.

Vijay Kumar Dhar, for sharing with me his incredible vision for Kashmir and Kashmiri people, and including me in his family.

Nazir Bakshi, for giving me his invaluable insights on Kashmiri society and politics and for making me feel at home in the Valley.

Waseem Tramboo, for sharing his remarkable knowledge and ideas about Kashmir and its business community and being a fantastic brother.

Rahul Bajaj, for kindly supporting our work for Kashmiri youth.

Jamsheyd Godrej, for supporting our work for Kashmiri youth and welcoming them with open arms in Mumbai.

Hekani Jakhalu and members of the North East Leaders Connect (erstwhile Young Leaders Connect), for opening their hearts and minds and allowing me to learn about north-east India.

India@75 Foundation, for giving me the opportunity to dream, ideate and execute solutions for India at an enormous scale.

C.K. Prahalad, for his path-breaking ideas for India and for believing in the power of youth to transform India.

Chandrajit Banerjee, director-general of CII, for incubating and supporting the India@75 foundation and giving me the opportunity to serve for the mission.

K.V. Kamath, former chairman, ICICI, for believing in the power of youth to shape the journey of India@75 and encouraging us through the initial days of the visioning exercise.

Adi Godrej, first chairman of India@75 Foundation, for encouraging all of us to do more for the nation with humility and excellence.

Rajan Navani, national chairman of CII's India@75 Council, for being a generous partner in our long journey of India@75.

Arun Chaube, chief operating officer, India@75, for being a wonderful colleague and educating me about the workings of the government.

Forum for Young Global Leaders and **World Economic Forum**, for giving me a platform to comprehend and actualize India's role in meeting global challenges.

Nicole Schwab, co-head, nature-based solutions, World Economic Forum, for educating me, guiding me to learn and do more for our planet's natural world.

Ananta Aspen Centre and Ananta Centre, for exposing me to the world of values-based leadership.

Kiran Pasricha, for encouraging me to learn more about India's foreign policy.

My co-fellows from my Ananta Aspen Fellowship, for being my talisman through the years.

BMW Responsible Leaders Cohort, for giving me the opportunity to learn about impact-driven philanthropy.

Family Business Network, for introducing me to the idea of intergenerational equity.

Notes

In Gratitude

1. Swades a conjunction of two words—Swa means 'mine/my' and des is colloquial for 'desh', meaning 'country', Swades means 'own country'.
2. Throughout the book I will use the word Himalaya instead of Himalayas. The original Sanskrit Himalaya means the abode of snow and needs no plural. There has been much debate on this matter but I choose to stick with the original Sanskrit.

1: The River of Dreams

1. 'River of Dreams Lyrics', Lyrics.com, STANDS4 LLC, 2022, accessed on 2 January 2022. Source: https://www.lyrics.com/lyric/593783/Billy+Joel.

2: Power of Enterprise

1. Interview with Rewaj Chettri, 2020.

2. WEF Scenario India World 2025 Report, The World Economic Forum, 2010. Source: http://www3.weforum.org/docs/WEF_Scenario_IndiaWorld2025_Report_2010.pdf

3. Arun Maira, 'India: Many Million Fireflies Now', *RSA Journal*, August 2007, pp. 28–31.

4. Source: https://www.financialexpress.com/industry/amul-becomes-first-indian-dairy-company-to-be-in-rabobanks-global-top-20-list-nestle-leads/2069079/

5. Klaus Schwab, *Stakeholder Capitalism: A Global Economy that Works for Progress, People and Planet.*

6. Source: https://news.mit.edu/2021/mit-harvard-transfer-edx-2u-0629

7. Source: https://theprint.in/tech/modi-govt-is-looking-for-zoom-google-meet-equivalents-for-offices-schools-medical-clinics/439502/

8. Source: https://timesofindia.indiatimes.com/business/india-business/pm-modi-launches-app-innovation-challenge-urges-tech-community-to-build-aatmanirbhar-app-ecosystem/articleshow/76785047.cms

9. Source: https://www.wipo.int/edocs/pubdocs/en/wipo_pub_gii_2021.pdf

10. Source: https://thegedi.org/global-entrepreneurship-and-development-index/

11. Interview with Tabish Habib, 2020.

3: Power of Nature

1. Source: http://snowleopardindia.org/conflict-mitigation.php

2. Source: https://megbiodiversity.nic.in/sacred-groves; http://www.megforest.gov.in/forest_sacredgroves.html

3. Source: https://tnbb.tn.gov.in/sacred-groves.php

4. Source: http://www3.weforum.org/docs/WEF_More_Sustainable _World.pdf

5. Source: https://www.hindustantimes.com/environment/ india-added-at-least-800-species-of-plants-animals-in-2020-101632207311999.html

6. Source: http://www.bsienvis.nic.in/Database/Biodiversity-Hotspots-in-India_20500.aspx

7. Source: https://www.business-standard.com/article/news-ani/ ganga-gets-a-new-breath-of-life-in-kanpur-119062400389_1. html

8. Source: https://www.thethirdpole.net/about/; https://www. scientificamerican.com/article/worlds-third-pole-is-melting-away/

9. Source: https://ipbes.net/news/Media-Release-Global-Assessment

10. Source: https://www.wwf.org.uk/sites/default/files/2018-10/ LPR2018_Full%20Report.pdf

11. Source: https://www.campaignfornature.org

12. Source: https://portals.iucn.org/library/sites/library/files/ resrecfiles/WCC_2016_RES_069_EN.pdf

13. Source: https://www.iucn.org/theme/nature-based-solutions/ about

14. Lawrence Busch, *Standards: Recipes for Reality*, MIT Press, 2011.

15. Interview with Mukti Datta, August 2020.

16. Source: https://www.indiatoday.in/magazine/crime/story/ 19891115-uttar-pradesh-minister-z.r.-ansari-accused-of-rape-bid-816748-1989-11-15

4: Power of Heritage

1. Interview with Krishna Devaraya, April 2014, September 2020.

2. Source: https://www.india-seminar.com/2004/542/542%20abha%20narain%20lambah.htm

3. Source: https://indianexpress.com/article/cities/mumbai/mumbai-150-yr-old-heritage-in-concrete-jungle/

4. Source: https://unakoti.nic.in/tourist-place/unakoti-heritage-site/

5. Source: https://unakoti.nic.in/history/

6. Source: https://www.indiatoday.in/magazine/heritage/story/20071119-heritage-fall-of-the-citadel-734518-2007-11-08

7. Source: https://www.deccanherald.com/content/196553/jaislamers-living-fort-crumbling.html

8. Source: https://www.indiaculture.nic.in/legal-mandate

9. Source: https://indiankanoon.org/doc/9107/

10. https://www.business-standard.com/article/current-affairs/indias-disappearing-monuments-114022000943_1.html

11. Source: https://www.thehindu.com/news/national/list-of-monuments-under-asi-likely-to-be-reviewed/article30957860.ece

12. Source: https://lamo.org.in/index.html

13. Source: https://www.reachladakh.com/news/in-conversation-with-reach-ladakh/in-conversation-with-dr-monisha-ahmed-executive-director-lamo

14. Source: https://indianmuseumkolkata.org/about-us; https://www.lifeberrys.com/holidays/9-of-the-oldest-museum-in-the-world-168883.html

15. Source: https://vikaspedia.in/education/childrens-corner/national-portal-for-museums

16. Source: https://economictimes.indiatimes.com/magazines/panache/museums-turnaround-makes-history/articleshow/34419772.cms?from=mdr

17. Source: https://pib.gov.in/PressReleaseIframePage.aspx?PRID=1788923

18. Source: https://www.magzter.com/stories/Art/Fortune-India/
    Piramal-Museum-of-Art-Rise-Of-The-Private-Museum

19. Source: https://www.theheritagelab.in

20. Source: https://rereeti.org

21. Source: https://www.indiaculture.nic.in/national-list-intangible-
    cultural-heritage-ich

22. Source: https://timesofindia.indiatimes.com/city/mumbai/new-
    definition-for-museums-will-give-them-boldness-to-argue/
    articleshow/71463206.cms

23. Source: https://www.livehistoryindia.com

24. Interview with Lawrence Koj, April 2014.

5: Power of Creativity

1. Source: https://johnhowkins.com

2. Source: https://unctad.org/system/files/official-document/ditcted
   2018d3_en.pdf

3. Source: https://unctad.org/topic/trade-analysis/creative-economy-
   programme

4. Source: https://www3.weforum.org/docs/WEF_Future_of_Jobs_
   2018.pdf

5. Source: https://unctad.org/topic/trade-analysis/creative-economy-
   programme/2021-year-of-the-creative-economy

6. Source: https://www.wto.org/english/docs_e/legal_e/27-trips_04
   b_e.htm

7. Source: https://ipindia.gov.in/gi.htm

8. Source: https://www.wipo.int/edocs/pubdocs/en/wipo_pub_941_
   2017-chapter6.pdf

9. Source: https://www.ibef.org/blogs/india-s-handicraft-crafts-a-
   sector-gaining-momentum

10. Source: https://www.ifpi.org/wp-content/uploads/2020
    /07/091018_Music-Consumer-Insight-Report-2018.pdf

11. Source: https://www.livemint.com/opinion/online-views/just-
    how-big-is-india-s-creative-economy-11593446149540.html

12. Source: https://www.ted.com/speakers/kai_fu_lee

13. Source: https://www.theguardian.com/books/2019/mar/12/the-
    creativity-code-marcus-du-sautoy-review

14. Source: http://artsites.ucsc.edu/faculty/cope/Emily-howell.htm

15. Source: https://techseen.com/2017/04/11/artificial-intelligence-
    ai-music/

16. Source: https://www.digitaltrends.com/cool-tech/japanese-ai-
    writes-novel-passes-first-round-nationanl-literary-prize/

17. Source: Interview with Aditya Patwardhan, 2020.

6: Power of Knowledge

1. Source: https://www.indiatoday.in/education-today/featurephilia/
    story/personalized-technology-platform-is-changing-k12-
    education-in-india-divd-1651523-2020-03-02

2. Source: https://www.statista.com/statistics/1175285/india-
    number-of-enrolled-students-by-school-type/

3. Source: https://www.drishtiias.com/daily-updates/daily-news-
    analysis/pisa-program-for-international-student-assessment-oecd

4. Source: https://web.worldbank.org/archive/website01503/
    WEB/0__CO-10.HTM

5. Source: https://archivepmo.nic.in/drmanmohansingh/speech-
    details.php?nodeid=908

6. Source: https://www.cable.co.uk/mobiles/worldwide-data-pricing/

7. Source: https://www.business-standard.com/article/education/we-
    re-working-to-make-india-a-knowledge-economy-pm-narendra-
    modi-120090700340_1.html

8. Source: https://www.orfonline.org/research/indias-innovation-ecosystem-mapping-the-trends/

9. Source: https://www.livemint.com/education/news/three-indian-universities-in-top-200-in-qs-world-rankings-iisc-ranks-1st-for-research-11623238368230.html

10. Source: https://www.merriam-webster.com/words-at-play/moonshot-words-were-watching

11. Source: https://www.aspeninstitute.org/about/heritage/

12. Source: https://www.jfklibrary.org/visit-museum/exhibits/past-exhibits/moon-shot-jfk-and-space-exploration

13. Source: https://www.weforum.org/agenda/2016/01/the-fourth-industrial-revolution-what-it-means-and-how-to-respond/

14. Source: https://analyticsindiamag.com/github-analysis-shows-india-as-an-emerging-ai-superpower/

15. Source: Safi Bahcall, *Loonshots*, Macmillan US, 2019.

16. Source: https://www.isro.gov.in/about-isro/genesis

17. Source: https://www.isro.gov.in/about-isro/dr-vikram-ambalal-sarabhai-1963-1971

18. R. Aravamudan and Gita Aravamudan, *ISRO: A Personal History*, HarperCollins, February 2017.

19. Source: https://www.isro.gov.in/about-isro/isros-timeline-1960s-to-today

20. Source: https://www.isro.gov.in/about-isro/isro-centres

21. Source: https://www.goodreads.com/quotes/212612-dream-dream-dream-dreams-transform-into-thoughts-and-thoughts-result

7: Power of Food

1. Interview with Alezo Kense, 2020.

2. Source: https://www.arcjournals.org/pdfs/ijhsse/v4-i7/4.pdf

3.　Source: https://grain.org/es/article/entries/514-reviving-diversity-in-india-s-agriculture

4.　Source: https://www.deccanherald.com/opinion/in-perspective/crop-diversity-key-to-reducing-hunger-malnutrition-in-india-1104519.html

5.　Source: https://www.statista.com/statistics/269924/countries-most-affected-by-hunger-in-the-world-according-to-world-hunger-index/

6.　Source: https://www.globalhungerindex.org/india.html

7.　Source: https://www.indiafoodbanking.org/hunger

8.　Source: https://indianexpress.com/article/opinion/columns/starvation-deaths-in-india-global-hunder-index-unicef-poverty-national-health-mission-5276194/

9.　Source: https://pib.gov.in/PressReleasePage.aspx?PRID=1601902

10.　Source: https://worldpopulationreview.com/country-rankings/arable-land-by-country

11.　Source: https://www.fao.org/3/y5609e/y5609e02.htm

12.　Source: https://www.firstpost.com/tech/news-analysis/nagaland-to-revive-traditional-rice-varieties-in-wake-of-climate-change-4257221.html

13.　Source: https://vikaspedia.in/agriculture/crop-production/weather-information/agro-climatic-zones-in-india

14.　Source: https://www.ifad.org/en/web/latest/-/blog/why-small-farms-are-key-to-the-future-of-food-and-how-we-can-support-them

15.　Source: https://agricoop.nic.in/sites/default/files/Web%20copy%20of%20AR%20%28Eng%29_7.pdf

16.　Source: https://wri-india.org/news/time-think-sustainable-food-and-land-use-system-india-mitigate-climate-risks-and-support

17. Interview with Aman Preet Singh, 2018, 2021.

8: Power of Beauty

1. Source: https://agarathi.com/word/கோலம்
2. Source: https://timesofindia.indiatimes.com/life-style/beauty/solah-shringar-the-science-behind-it/articleshow/54520592.cms
3. Source: https://www.mkgandhi.org/articles/gandhian-thoughts-about-cleanliness.html
4. Albert Bandura, *Moral Disengagement: How People Do Harm and Live with Themselves,* Worth Publishers, December 2015.
5. Source: https://www.theuglyindian.com/intro3.html
6. Source: https://www.news18.com/news/india/in-mann-ki-baat-pm-modi-lauds-us-returned-engineer-for-transforming-delhi-with-street-art-2248983.html
7. Richard Thaler and Cass Sunstein, *Nudge: Improving Decisions About Health, Wealth and Happiness,* Penguin Books, February 2009.
8. Source: https://www.bi.team/press-releases/nesta-acquires-behavioural-insights-team-to-help-tackle-societys-biggest-social-challenges/
9. Source: https://www.bi.team/publications/east-four-simple-ways-to-apply-behavioural-insights/
10. Source: https://www.bbc.com/news/world-asia-india-29502603
11. Source: http://www.publishingindia.com/GetBrochure.aspx?query=UERGQnJvY2h1cmVzfC85NC5wZGZ8Lzk0LnBkZg==
12. Source: https://swachhindia.ndtv.com/swachh-survekshan-2021-results-top-highlights-of-the-annual-cleanliness-survey-64882/
13. Source: https://www.ndtv.com/india-news/asias-cleanest-village-is-in-meghalaya-702737

9: Power of Wellness

1. Source: https://www.bionity.com/en/encyclopedia/The_Citadel_ %28novel%29.html

2. Source: https://www.ima-india.org/ima/free-way-page.php? pid=18

3. Deepak Chopra, *Perfect Health: The Complete Mind and Body Guide*, RHUK, 2001.

4. Source: https://smithsonianapa.org/bookdragon/how-to-know- god-the-souls-journey-into-the-mystery-of-mysteries-by- deepak-chopra-author-interview/

5. Source: https://www.business-standard.com/article/current-affairs /india-worse-than-bhutan-bangladesh-in-healthcare-ranks- 145th-globally-118052400135_1.html

6. Source: https://economictimes.indiatimes.com/industry/ healthcare/biotech/healthcare/around-65-hospital-beds- cater-to-50-population-of-country-niti-aayog-report/ articleshow/89437029.cms?from=mdr

7. Source: https://www.indiaspend.com/budget-2018-indias- healthcare-crisis-is-holding-back-national-potential-29517

8. Source: https://thelogicalindian.com/mentalhealth/mental-health -indians-30811

9. Source: https://www.indiatoday.in/education-today/ latest-studies/story/98-million-indians-diabetes-2030- prevention-1394158-2018-11-22

10. Source: https://www.ncbi.nlm.nih.gov/pmc/articles/PMC3752 290/

11. Source: http://vol10.cases.som.yale.edu/sites/default/files/cases/ Design%20at%20Mayo/WW%20Mayo%20Speech.pdf

10. Power of Assimilation

1. Source: https://wits.worldbank.org/CountryProfile/en/Country/IND/Year/1988/Summarytext

2. Source: https://www.macrotrends.net/countries/IND/india/trade-gdp-ratio

3. Angus Maddison, *Contours of the World Economy, 1–2030 AD*, OUP Oxford, 2007.

4. Source: https://www.worldhistory.org/Periplus_of_the_Erythraean_Sea/

5. Thomas Freidman, *Thank You for Being Late: Succeeding in the Age of Acceleration, Farrar*, Straus and Giroux, 2016.

6. Syed Akberuddin; Source: https://indianexpress.com/article/opinion/columns/antonio-guterres-united-nations-coronavirus-pandemic-syed-akbaruddin-6485727/

7. Source: https://www.britannica.com/biography/Ram-Singh; http://www.namdhari-world.com/ram_singh_kuka_by_gkvenkateshamurthy.html

8. Source: https://www.livemint.com/news/india/india-must-remain-vocal-for-global-11594822682912.html

9. Source: https://www.financialexpress.com/opinion/making-a-start-for-wto-reforms/1638829/

10. Interview with Tenzing Bhutia, 2021.

11: Power of Inclusion

1. G.M.D. Sufi, *Kashir: Being a History of Kashmir From the Earliest Times to Our Own*, 1948.

2. Source: https://www.mkgandhi.org/hindswaraj/chap10_hindumahomedans.htm

3. Source: https://en-academic.com/dic.nsf/enwiki/1113662

4.   Source: https://pib.gov.in/newsite/printrelease.aspx?relid=126326

5.   Source: https://indianexpress.com/article/india/more-than-19500-mother-tongues-spoken-in-india-census-5241056/

6.   Source: https://www.pewforum.org/2021/06/29/religion-in-india-tolerance-and-segregation/

7.   Maha Upanishad, Chapter VI.

8.   Interview with Vaibhav Kaul, 2020.

12: Power of Individual

1.   Source: https://m.economictimes.com/asian-paints-journey-is-in-the-spotlight/articleshow/7262599.cms

2.   Source: https://www.livemint.com/Companies/LIANw0QeehKTyU9DJvt6eP/Instant-recall-CavinKare-style.html

3.   Source: https://www.thehindubusinessline.com/companies/Unilever-test-markets-water-purifying-sachets-in-India/article20457689.ece

4.   Source: https://www.warc.com/newsandopinion/news/indians-strongly-prefer-personalised-ads/38622

5.   Source: https://www.thehindubusinessline.com/brandhub/mym/todays-consumer-wants-personalisation-they-want-brands-to-engage-with-them/article30355629.ece

6.   Source: https://www.livemint.com/Home-Page/JHyUYYjoMzBFWSKuptd8LK/BR-Ambedkara-man-of-many-parts.html

7.   *Harijan*, 28 July 1946, p. 236. Source: https://www.mkgandhi.org/voiceoftruth/villagepanchayats.htm; https://www.mkgandhi.org/voiceoftruth/decentralization.htm

8.   Interview with Mark Stone 2014, 2017, 2021.

13: Power of Community

1.   Source: https://centralyma.org

2.   Aristotle, *Politics*; Source: https://www.goodreads.com/quotes /183896-man-is-by-nature-a-social-animal-an-individual-who

3.   Source: https://www.livemint.com/Home-Page/JHyUYYjoMz BFWSKuptd8LK/BR-Ambedkara-man-of-many-parts.html

4.   Source: https://pib.gov.in/newsite/PrintRelease.aspx?relid=102398

5.   Source: https://www.youthkiawaaz.com/2019/03/youth-ki-awaaz-survey-reveals-interesting-things-on-what-young-india-wants-this-election/

6.   Source: https://www.mygov.in

7.   Source: https://codeforamerica.org/

8.   Source: https://ispirt.in

9.   Source: https://www.theglobalstatistics.com/india-social-media-statistics/

10. Source: https://www.barandbench.com/columns/dr-ambedkar-1949-constituent-assembly-speech

14: Call to Action

1.   Mehrdad Baghai and James Quigley, *As One – Individual Action Collective Power*, Portfolio, 2011.

2.   Source: https://www.speakingtree.in/allslides/karmanye-vadhikaraste-ma-phaleshu-kada-chana/180646

Index

doshas, types of, 223; established on wellness principle, 223–224; Ministry of AYUSH (Ayurveda, Yoga and Naturopathy, Unani, Siddha and Homeopathy), 226; *Sushruta Samhita,* 224

Azad, Maulana, 148

B.A.K. Swadhyaya Bhavan, 5

Baghai, Mehrdad and Quigley, James: *As One - Individual Action Collective Power,* 349–354

Bahcall, Safi: *Loonshots - How to Nurture Crazy Ideas that Win Wars, Cure Diseases and Transform Industries,* 157, 159

Baig, Sheyna, 363–364

Banaras Hindu University, 263

Bandura, Albert: *Moral Disengagement: How People Do Harm and Live with Themselves,* 206

Bangladesh, 14, 62, 66

Barma, Pradyot Bikram Manikya Deb, 90

Basant Panchami festival, 141–143

Bay of Bengal, 66

bazaars of Hyderabad, 281–282

beauty in India, 201–203, 361–362

Behavioural Insight Team (BIT), United Kingdom, 212; Easy, Attractive, Social and Timely (EAST) framework, 209, 211, 215, 217

behavioural insights, 208

Bharatiya Janata Party (BJP)-led National Democratic Alliance (NDA), 2, 314

Bhutia, Tenzing: and founded Shuffle Momos in Gangtok, 272–277

BITS Pilani, Rajasthan, 144

block chain, 154, 158

Blue Dart, 355–356

Bohnet, Iris, 290

Bollyworld, 32–34

Busch, Lawrence: *Standards: Recipes for Reality,* 75

Campaign for Nature by Wyss Campaign for Nature and National Geographic, 72

Chand, Prem, 124

Chaturvedi, Atul, 11

Chennamkary village in Kerala, 251–254

Chettri, Rewaj, 21–27, 30, 35, 42, 50

Chhattisgarh, 18

China: building of roadmap to economic prosperity and development, 270

Himalaya, 61–62, 69–70

Howkins, John, 122

hunger and malnourishment in
  India, 173–174

IBM, 42

IEF Entrepreneurship
  Foundation, 48, 186, 356

inclusion process: and empathy,
  293; defined, 289; designing
  of, 290–296; religious, 292

Incredible India campaign
  (2005), 211

India@75, 337–339

Indian Institute of Remote
  Sensing, Dehradun, 162

Indian Institute of Science,
  Bengaluru, 143

Indian Institute of Space
  Science and Technology,
  Thiruvananthapuram, 162

Indian Medical Council
  (Professional Conduct,
  Etiquette and Ethics)
  Regulation 2002, 221

Indian National Congress
  (INC)-led United Progressive
  Alliance (UPA), 2

Indian Ocean, 66

Indian Space and Research
  Organisation (ISRO), 160,
  163; active incubators of, 162;
  Chandrayan-2, failed landing
  of, 159; difficulties in early

years of, 160; established
  in 1962, 160; first rocket
  flight launched in 1963, 160;
  Mangalyaan-1 mission, 162

individualization, 302–303,
  305–307

Indore city, awarded cleanest city
  in Swachh Survekshan 2021,
  212–215, 218

INOVAR programme of Brazil,
  40–41

Intangible Cultural Heritage
  (ICH), 105

intergenerational equity, concept
  of, 94

Intergovernmental Science-Policy
  Platform on Biodiversity and
  Ecosystem Services (IPBES),
  72

International Council of
  Museums (ICOM), 109

International Fund for
  Agriculture Development
  (IFAD), 177

International Union for
  Conservation of Nature
  (IUCN), 73–74

internet of things (IoT), 123,
  154–155, 158

IT industry/sector in India,
  148–149, 156

Iyer, Sudha, 3–5, 8–10

Jaisalmer, collapse of sewage
  system drains in, 93–94

with young people in
Mumbai, 337–338
Organisation for Economic
Co-operation and
Development (OECD):
analysis of Microsoft-owned
code-sharing platform
GitHub, 155; Program
for International Student
Assessment (PISA) by, 145
OTT platforms, 130

Paepcke, Walter, 151
Pahale India (India First), 32–37,
41, 44, 50, 332, 345, 352
Pakistan, 14, 61, 66
Pal, Bipin Chandra, 267
Palitana Jain temples, Gujarat,
116
Panchatantra tales, 65
Pangtey, Sher Singh, 103–105,
110
Pari Mahal or Zabarwan
mountains (palace of fairies),
278–281, 297
Partition of Bengal, 267
patent system India vs world, 150
Patwardhan, Aditya (films,
documentary and dramas)
by, 73; *A Touch of Aurora (Um
toque da Aurora)*, 135; *And the
Dream that Mattered*, 135;
*Eastern Shores of the Western
World*, 136; *I.C.E Cream*,

135; *Nomad River*, 135; *Red
House by the Crossroads* film,
133–136; *Transference*, 135
PEI Organic Foods, 186
phone timers, 247
Porbandar, 330
Prahalad, C.K., 147; *Fortune at
the Bottom of the Pyramid*, 17
Print, 265

quality education system, need
for, 145–146
quantum computing, 154

Rai, Lala Lajpat, 266
Rajadhyaksha, Niranjan, 269
Rajula-Malushahi, 105
rangolis in India: aipan in
Uttarakhand, 201; alpana in
West Bengal, 201; chaook
in Chhattisgarh, 201; jhoti
chita in Odisha, 201; muggu
in Andhra Pradesh and
Telangana, 201
Rao, P.V. Narasimha, 333
rasas, 197
religious: harmony, 292;
hegemony, 289
religious diversity of India,
287–289
researchers in India vs world,
149–150
Right to Education Act 2012,
144

About the Author

Bhairavi Jani is a successful logistics and supply-chain entrepreneur, a social-development enthusiast, a nature conservationist and a committed philanthropist. Bhairavi has been listed among 'India's 25 Power Women' by *India Today*, and has been featured in *Stree Shakti* by CNBC Awaaz and *Young Turks* by CNBC TV18. She was recognized as a 'Supply Chain Maven' by *Business Today*.

She is the World Economic Forum's Young Global Leader and was the national chairperson of Young Indians, the youth wing of Confederation of Indian Industry (2010–11).

Bhairavi is an avid traveller, a trained classical dancer and is passionate about the arts. Her own experiences of growing up in Mumbai, studying and working in the United States, running logistics ventures pan-India, working for developmental programmes and now living in a rural settlement in the Himalaya, give her the unique ability to observe India's journey as a young republic and an old civilization through multiple lenses.